# To Thailand With Love

## A Travel Guide for the Connoisseur

# TABLE OF CONTENTS

# Introduction

Imagine that on the eve of your upcoming trip to Thailand, you are invited to a party. At this party are dozens of guests, all of whom live in or have traveled extensively through the country. Among this eclectic and well-versed group of connoisseurs are contributors to acclaimed travel guides, popular newspaper writers, veteran gourmets, and pioneering adventurers. As the evening passes, they tell you tales from their lives in these exotic places. They whisper the names of their favorite shops and restaurants; they divulge the secret hideaways where they sneak off to for an afternoon or a weekend to unwind. Some make you laugh out loud, and others seduce you with their poetry. Some are intent on educating, while others just want to entertain. Their recommendations are as unique as their personalities, but they are united in one thing ... their love of Thailand. If you can envision being welcomed at such a party, then you can envision the experience that *To Thailand With Love* aspires to give you.

Kim Fay
Series Editor, To Asia With Love

Ever since I first visited Thailand in November of 1993, I have had special feelings for this country. Like a rubber stamp dipped in indelible ink, the kingdom has left a permanent impression on my soul. Though the guys at immigration don't exactly stand up and cheer every time I seek permission to reenter Thailand, I get the warm, fuzzy sensations of homecoming the moment I step off the aerobridge into Suvarnabhumi Airport. It's as if the country is handing me back my very own place in its grand scheme of things, a place it hasn't reassigned to any other tourist, knowing I'll be back to reclaim it. Again and again and again.

I do not pretend that my relationship with Thailand is exclusive, however, because plenty of other people I know respond to the country in exactly the same way. They feel spiritually expanded by Thailand. They feel empowered and free—free to be whoever they want to be because the Thais don't waste time judging *farangs*. They're just glad to see tourists enjoy their country so much, like little children let loose in Wonderland.

As editor of *To Thailand With Love*, I was in a quandary as to how to do a book on the unique wonders of a place that is already so well-known as a tourist wonderland. It has been since the 1980s, when Bangkok started metamorphosing from a sleepy city to its present avatar, and Western tourists started coming here in droves to experience the Exotic East without spending too much money. There is such a glut of information on Thailand in guidebooks, websites, and periodicals that there's very little wow-factor left for a travel "connoisseur" anymore—sure, there's a lot to be enjoyed, but how much is there still to be curious about?

*To Thailand With Love* hopes to remedy that. This isn't the sort of publication that tries to offer exhaustive information on the country. (If you were hoping for an ordinary guidebook, my advice is that you rush out and buy a Lonely Planet.) The idea behind *To Thailand With Love* is to leave the top layer of tourism alone and see what's lurking underneath. Find hidden facets of Thailand—mostly hidden, let's say—and extend your travel options beyond the well-established tourist trail.

Within the pages of this book, you will meet a group of seasoned explorers who have taken on the responsibility of showing you a very different Thailand from the one you may already know and love. Their essays take you to places you never knew existed, show you sights that don't feature in your guidebooks, and feed you dishes that you never thought to taste. Their recommendations may not make the Top 10 list of things to see and do in Thailand, but they certainly don't lack the potential to take you by surprise ... and impress you with the variety of experiences still waiting to be discovered and enjoyed here.

*To Thailand With Love* has more than one hundred essays that you can use as a resource when drawing up a travel itinerary. Divided into nine chapters, they contain unusual tips and recommendations for almost any sort of holiday you have in mind. If you're into extreme adventures, for instance, there is enough information to send you off on one hair-raising expedition after another. If you're fascinated by the gentleness of the Thai people and wonder why they smile so much, there are essays that give you an inside track into their psyche. If your real goal is shopping, you can depend on our authors to lead you by the hand to some really marvelous purchases. Instead of presenting travel information in a hard-fact format, the essays read like stories about intensely personal experiences, so they do double duty as great armchair reading material as well.

*To Thailand With Love*'s mission is to make connoisseurs out of first-time tourists and inspire frequent visitors to renew their love affair with the country. Our authors tell spellbinding stories of their forays into lesser-known aspects of this jewel of Southeast Asia, and gladly share their secret discoveries, so you can follow in their footsteps. They put you in intimate touch with the unique people, culture, and traditions of the land and introduce you to a Thailand that is luminescent with fresh travel possibilities.

Nabanita Dutt
Editor, *To Thailand With Love*

# How This Book Works

*A good traveler has no fixed plans, and is not intent on arriving.*
~Lao Tzu

*To Thailand With Love* is a unique guidebook with chapters organized by theme as opposed to destination. This is because it focuses foremost on the sharing of personal experiences, allowing each place to serve as the colorful canvas on which our writers overlay vivid, individual impressions. Within each themed chapter you will find the recommendations grouped by region, and then by towns or areas within each region.

Chapters begin in the capital city of Bangkok and flow out to Central Thailand and such popular destinations as Ayutthaya and Pattaya. From here the essays travel to Northern and Northeast Thailand, encompassing Chiang Mai, Chiang Rai, and hill tribe villages. Finally, each chapter ends in Southern Thailand, known mainly for its tropical islands. There are also general essays in some chapters that include experiences that can be had in more than one part of the country. For attractions or experiences by destination, a complete index of cities can be found at the end of this book.

Each recommendation consists of two parts: a personal essay and a fact file. Together, they are intended to inspire and inform. The essay tells a story while the fact file gives addresses and other serviceable information. Because each contribution can stand alone, the book does not need to be read in order. As with an old-fashioned miscellany, you may open to any page and start reading. Thus every encounter with the book is turned into its own distinctive armchair journey.

Keep in mind that *To Thailand With Love* is selective and does not include all of the practical information you will need for daily travel. Instead, reading it is like having a conversation with a friend who just returned from a trip. You should supplement that friend's stories with a comprehensive guidebook, such as Lonely Planet or Rough Guide.

Confucius said, "A journey of a thousand miles begins with a single step." We hope that this guide helps you put your best foot forward.

## Key Terms & Important Information

CURRENCY: Prices in this book are noted either in U.S. dollars or Thai baht. Current exchange rates can be found at www. XE.COM/UCC/.

HONORIFICS: If you learn key Thai phrases, be sure to end them with the polite particle "Ka" if you're female and "Krup" if you're male. To omit these particles is boorish and disrespectful to the Thai ear—it's impossible to say them too often. They also serve as terms of agreement in a pinch: "Do you want—? Ka."

PRONUNCIATION: Romanized Thai is based upon British pronunciation. The "r" found in words like "*larb*" (a common dish) or "Porn" (a common nickname) is not pronounced. It indicates a broad vowel, for example, "a" as in "ah" and "o" as in "on."

TEMPLE ETIQUETTE: Although Thai people are very forgiving of travelers in their midst, when you visit a temple, please be respectful and don't wear shorts, tank tops, or tube tops.

TRAVEL PREPARED: Always carry a roll of toilet paper in your handbag or backpack—remove the inner cardboard core and squash it as flat as possible.

USEFUL PHRASES: The most useful phrase in Thailand—other than *aroy mak* (very delicious), *sawatdee* (hello) and *kop khun* (thank you) followed by the ubiquitous *ka* or *krup*, is *khor tawt* (excuse me). The next most useful is: *Hong nam yu tee nai?* (Where is the toilet?)

# MOVEABLE FEASTS

*A tasting menu of exotic flavors*

A few years ago, I went to Hua Hin to stay at a very famous "fat farm." I was not overweight—not then anyway, and not so much now—but I wanted to try the new, healthy food fad called "spa cuisine" at this world-class spa.

The experience proved disappointing on many counts. It cost too much, and the "villa" I was given had a lopsided design plan, with an enormous bathroom and a bedroom so tiny I had to sleep hugging my suitcases. But the very worst thing was the much-vaunted spa cuisine that had brought me here. I'm sure the chef was doing a grand job of feeding people who wanted to eat a six-course gourmet meal and still lose weight, but after two days of eating zucchini and carrots that had been blanched, poached, and seared before being presented on fine Wedgwood china with a drizzling of shaved white truffles, I was roasting in an epicurean sort of hell.

Every waking moment was filled with my longing for real, down-to-earth, extraordinarily aromatic Thai food. Finally, when a dish of gloriously yellow *mussaman* curry started visiting me nightly in my dreams, I decided to run away. I couldn't sneak out the main entrance without being seen, so I headed down the beach, still wearing a pair of those white fabric slippers the hotels provide to pad around the room in. They tore open in the sand, but I couldn't stop. I ran and ran until I reached Hua Hin town. Not caring that people were staring at my bare feet, I ducked into the first street-side restaurant I could find, ordered half the menu, and really ate that day.

Between spoonfuls of *mussaman* curry—the beast had to be exorcised!—I realized how fanatic Thai food lovers like me really are when it comes to their meals in this country. Our 45-baht portions of heavenly stir fries, soups, and curries are something we travel halfway around the world for sometimes, and no spa cuisine chef has the right to mess with our privilege to eat off the streets.

Yes, I'm an undying fan of Thailand's sidewalk food. And food courts, and wonderful Thai chain restaurants like S&P and Greyhound Café. I have never been to a country where there is less reason to spend a lot of money on food than Thailand.

The contributors to this chapter must also feel the same way, because most of their essays have come off the streets as well. They share experiences of some fabulous local foods and anonymous little sidewalk restaurants they have stumbled upon during their travels. Timothy Talen Bull, one of our authors, calls them "Four Cat Restaurants." Usually small shacks with rusty tin roofs and—by Bull's estimation, at least—an average of four stray cats loitering inside. They don't look like much, but these are the places where locals and well-informed foodies go to eat the best food available in Thailand.

For tips on how to dine in Thailand, David Kovanen describes curious tabletop items you have to learn to use at these sidewalk restaurants—such as toilet paper. Hugh Leong tells us about one-dish Thai lunches that are the quick, comprehensive meal choice for most locals at midday. Danielle Koffler draws a cozy picture of friends devoting a sizable portion of their evening to a marathon meal, as is the proper tradition when eating at a *moo kata* barbecue. And Oliver Fennell and Timothy Talen Bull dig into the underbelly of Thailand's food culture to bring up an astonishing selection of offal delicacies, bugs, worms, crocodiles, and even *yam ngu hao krob*, a salad with diced cobra.

Each essay goes beyond the ritual of eating and offers a glimpse of Thai life that is both authentic and ordinary. Over the past decade or so, the country—especially Bangkok—has become a fine-dining capital with superb, upscale restaurants opening everywhere. (My favorite among them: Sirocco at the lebua at State Tower hotel on Silom Road. This place does great steaks, and the rooftop view has got to be one of the most spectacular in the world.) Their large advertising budgets make them easy for any tourist to find, so this chapter leads you in the opposite direction: to places unhindered by Michelin stars, to foods that have not been "fusioned" by enterprising chefs or watered down for Westerners. Places like Nicholas Towers' favorite hole-in-the-wall soup restaurant, which has hundreds of Thai customers crowding the pavement outside every night, waiting for a table, but only two kinds of soup: standard and special.

## BANGKOK

### Nicholas Towers recommends a Bangkok hole-in-the-wall

After living in Bangkok's Khao San backpackers' district for several months now, it has become clear to me that not all Thai food is created equal. Why else would locals who work in Khao San Road pointedly ignore the countless food stalls and small restaurants located here during lunch? My guess is that the Khao San eateries tinker with flavors and food quantities to suit Western customers to such an extent that they have lost their local Thai clientele in the process.

Faced with this compelling evidence of the hybrid nature of Thai food sold on Khao San Road, I have stopped eating here as well.

Instead, my search for authenticity has led me to a nearby hole-in-the-wall restaurant on Phra Athit Road, where the *kuay jap yuan* soup is such a specialty that waiting queues of Thai customers literally block the pavement in front of it during lunch and dinner.

*Kuay jap yuan* is a noodle soup of Vietnamese origin, consisting of mushrooms, pork, and quail eggs. The broth is rich and slightly peppery, and you can change the direction of the dish by adding sugar, chili, or the ubiquitous fish sauce. The noodles used to make *kuay jap yuan* have a flour coating that dissolves in the soup as it cooks, giving the broth a smooth, silky texture. The other key ingredient is *moo yor*, a spongy white pork sausage that the people of northern Thailand have appropriated from Vietnam and made an important ingredient in their own Isaan cuisine.

During peak hours, the crowds may look daunting, but waiting time for a table here is only ten to fifteen minutes; it's hard to linger over a bowl of soup, no matter

**BANGKOK**

how delicious, so the turnover is quick. The all-Thai menu isn't hard to deconstruct either: just two basic soup choices, *tamada* (standard) or *pee-set* (special).

There's nothing like a fortifying bowl of mouthwatering *kuay jap yuan* soup at the end of a tiring workday, and I come here quite often for dinner before I head home. Geoffrey, the guy in charge, has taken a shine to me, and if he is around, my order gets bumped up to the front of the queue. Solicitously, he asks after my love life each time, and I don't mind this typical Thai curiosity to know if a pretty local girl is bringing cheer into my expat *farang* existence. The rest of the staff treat me like a regular as well, and no matter how busy they are, they always stop to say hello or give me a friendly wave from across the room.

As I tuck into my *kuay jap yuan*, I often look out the door and feel bad for all the tourists I see stepping off the pavement to avoid colliding with the crowd waiting outside the restaurant. They cast an uncomprehending glance at the Thai signage, and then wander back to Khao San Road to eat more *pad thai*. If it wasn't behavior bordering on intrusive, I'd chase after them and say: "Hey, come back! You don't know what a delicious food opportunity you've just walked away from!"

### Finding kuay jap yuan

From the end of Khao San Road (where the police station is) turn right and walk to the four-way junction. From there, turn left and head toward

Fort Phra Sumen. A gas station will come up on your right. The *kuay jap yuan* restaurant is opposite this gas station. Because of the crowds, it's easy to locate during lunch and dinner hours.

### Sweet treats

You can finish off your meal with freshly baked teacakes at the Baan Phra Athit coffee shop.

102/1 Phra Athit Road

### Little pigs

The Vietnamese *moo yor* (ground pork) sausage is wrapped in banana leaves and steamed before being sliced up and served in Isaan-style dishes. Try this sausage in a piquant *yum moo yor* salad with chilies, pickled garlic, cilantro, onions, lettuce, and a generous squeeze of lime.

### Oliver Fennell explores Bangkok's Middle Eastern quarter

My girlfriend refused the testicles. As someone raised in rural Thailand, Waew had no qualms eating rats, frogs, lizards, all manner of insects, and just about any other kind of offal. But this was going too far.

I, on the other hand, like to take my cues from the locals and eat as they do. Only, the "locals" in this particular neighborhood of Bangkok were not Thai. We were in the city's Middle Eastern and African area, where Arabic signage dominated, kebab spits outnumbered noodle stalls, men talked shop in *dishdashes* or *dashikis* and women window-shopped from behind veils. Vices ranged from sweet-smelling hookah pipes to sweet-talking hookers, and the food, as Waew had found out, was quite unlike the usual Bangkok fare.

The Thai capital, which is as cosmopolitan as most cities of its size, has a number of foreign communities—there is a Chinatown, a Little India, Japanese and Korean neighborhoods, and various Western enclaves. But none of these evoke a sense of being *somewhere else* quite as much as the Arab and African quarter.

The three parallel roads (Sukhumvit Soi 3, Soi 3/1, and Soi 5) in the Nana District, can easily transport you to Arabia. Gaudy restaurants dripping with silver decorations catch the eye at the same time as their touts attempt to catch your attention, invariably with the opening gambit of "My friend!" Moody-looking old men sit outside kebab shops, sucking on pipes and regarding the passing world with disdain. An endless stream of vendors does its best to hawk tacky toys. Clouds of fruity vapor emanate from *shishas* and blend in the air that is already heavy with the strong scent of Arabic *oud* perfume and mouthwatering aromas of grilling meat.

After dark, the neighborhood takes on more of an African vibe as Bang-kok's relatively small black community comes out to party, shooting the breeze over glasses of stout, dancing to hip-hop and R&B in the clubs, or playing endless tournaments in the pool halls.

For me, a good night out here starts at Sabai Sabai, a chilled-out open-air bar playing reggae and African music. From there, I move on to the Bamboo Bar, a popular hangout for Middle Easterners who can drink. There are seven pool tables, nightly live music, and a free buffet every Friday. Usually, I round up my night at Da Beat nightclub, which claims to be the "Best R&B and hip-hop club in town." Some more upmarket places in Bangkok might dispute that, but it's certainly the most authentic, right down to the sign requesting "no weapons." Don't be put off—it's a friendly crowd, really!

So far as food goes, it's been said that Nana boasts the best Middle Eastern cuisine outside of the Middle East. Indeed, a visiting friend once proclaimed a kebab from here as "the best I've ever had" after visiting the Nefertiti Kebab House. The beef and chicken kebabs at Nefertiti are a steal at just 60 baht each. The name of the place is written in Arabic and Thai only (don't worry, the staff speak English), so look for the open-air joint with the yellow sign and image of the Egyptian queen.

Most restaurants in the area serve dishes from all over the region, but some are country-specific. For example: Egyptian, Omani, Lebanese, or Moroccan. The best examples of these include the unimaginatively

---

**BANGKOK**

named Egyptian Restaurant, offering an impressive selection of piquant North African fare, and Tagine de Marrakesh, which is authentically Moroccan from the decor to the tableware to the food and drink. Try the *tagine*—it's so good, the restaurant is named after it—and wash it down with refreshing Moroccan herbal tea.

And if you find yourself craving lamb, a rarity in Thailand, this Middle Eastern and African neighborhood is absolutely the place to go. You can have it curried or grilled, in stews or as kebabs and steaks, and categorized by body parts. Yes, that includes the testicle-based dishes, too, in case you have the *cojones* to try what even my lizard-and-bug-eating girlfriend won't.

### Getting there

Bangkok's Arab and African neighborhood is a short walk from the Nana Skytrain station (Exit 1). If you're taking a taxi, the most convenient place to get out would be the Grace Hotel, which is situated at the corner of Sukhumvit Soi 3 and Soi 3/1.

### Tips on exploring

The Middle Eastern Quarter in North Nana hasn't had a facelift in years. The sois look shabby, somewhat mysterious and exotic, but it is advisable that you don't try to photograph anything here. The residents can get unpleasant if they feel you're trying to catch them on film. However, if you mind your own business, go exploring, shopping, and eating like an ordinary tourist, it should be quite safe. You may want to stay away at night though, when the rough crowd comes out to party or to pick a fight.

## Where to dine on Arabian and African food in Bangkok

### Bamboo Bar
Opposite the Grace Hotel
Sukhumvit, Soi 3
(02) 253-2462
www.bamboopub.com

### Da Beat
Around the corner from Sabai Sabai. Look for a blue sign and orange walls at the entrance. Take the elevator to the third floor.

Sukhumvit, Soi 3/1

### Egyptian Restaurant
Opposite the Zenith Hotel
16/6-7 Sukhumvit, Soi 3

### Nefertiti Kebab House
On the corner of Sukhumvit, Soi 3 and Soi 3/1
(02) 655-3043

### Sabai Sabai
Opposite the King Mansion
Sukhumvit, Soi 3/1

### Tagine de Marrakesh
Next to the Grace Hotel
12 Sukhumvit, Soi 3
(02) 253-0651

## Deborah Annan orders condoms à la carte in Bangkok

I could have sworn that Tess just said we're going to a restaurant called "Cabbages & Condoms."

An eatery named after the rubber contraceptive? Can't be. She must have said Fabulous Sarongs. Or Canopies and Condos. Or something like that.

"What's the name again? Did you just say condoms?"

"You heard me right. I said Condoms. Cabbages & Condoms," replied Tess. "The restaurant raises money for birth control and AIDS awareness. It's like the Planned Parenthood of Thailand."

Wow. But wasn't the name too ... progressive? Maybe it could work in New York or even San Francisco, but here in Thailand?

I was dying with curiosity when our van pulled up in front of an old Thai house in Bangkok's Sukhumvit area that had been converted into the Cabbages & Condoms restaurant. A large wooden sign in front displayed the name in bold yellow lettering without a trace of shyness.

We followed a short pathway that led into the building, which had a large courtyard dining area, a bar, and a gift shop. Wherever I looked, condoms dominated the decor. The carpet was adorned with condom designs.

Someone had made cute bouquets of condoms that looked like bunches of black-eyed Susans and arranged them in vases. The walls were covered with cartoon posters, showing the male member in different kinds of cover-up. There was The Economist, who recycled his used condom by stitching together and applying a Band-Aid over every wear and tear; there was The Flasher, who liked to keep the top three buttons on his condom open at all times; and there was The Fool, who stupidly wore a condom with holes at both ends.

Condom brands from different countries met in a sort of international congress along the wooden staircase leading up to the second floor: Rooster Extra Strong from South Africa, Black Jerk from Sweden, Glow-in-the-Dark from Canada, and Trojan from Australia.

The gift shop, naturally, was also stocked with all sorts of condom merchandize that diners could take back home as souvenirs of their visit. A coffee mug with a condom quip—"No Glove No Love"—or a T-shirt maybe, emblazoned with the legend: "Cabbages and Condoms—our food is guaranteed not to cause pregnancy." Yes, I could well see my twenty-something daughters having fun with that one.

When we sat down to eat, I wasn't a bit surprised that the dishes—a collection of regional items from all over Thailand—had clever condom names. With a straight face, I asked the waiter to bring me a Spicy Condom Salad, wondering if the food would also turn out to be "rubbery" here. Much to my relief, it was an extremely delicious fried noodle preparation, flavored with fresh herbs. If the noodles were shaped like condoms, well, I could deal with that.

Tess relished her order too, and we thought the restaurant deserved a five-star rating. After lunch, we lingered at the table enjoying a postmeal conversation, not minding the mannequins posted near our table wearing elaborate condom costumes. The waiter took our plates away and brought us some after-dinner mints. Tess, who was in the middle of telling a funny story, ripped the plastic wrapping off one and was about to pop it into her mouth when she stopped abruptly. It wasn't an after-dinner mint at all, but a bright blue condom. She showed me the unfolded condom lying limply in her hand. Thank God she had gone first, sparing me the embarrassment of opening a condom at lunch. We laughed so much at Tess's mistake, we were almost crying.

When it was time to leave, I found myself thinking of the man who was behind this bizarre restaurant: Mechai Viravaidya, the Condom King of Thailand. For almost forty years, Mechai has been working to promote family planning and prevent the spread of AIDS by desensationalizing the condom—and making it as cheap and plentiful as cabbages. He believed that if gimmicks could sell soap and toothpaste, they could sell condoms as well.

In one of his notable publicity stunts, Mechai had Christmas cards printed with the message, "We wish you much happiness and a subdued fertility in the New Year," and sent

them off to every head of state around the world. Even the Pope apparently received one. Mechai paid farmers to paint condom ads on the sides of their water buffaloes. When some devout Thais wanted their condoms blessed by a monk, Mechai got the head monk of Bangkok's Siam Square monastery to sprinkle holy water on them amidst a blaze of press publicity. He dispatched pretty Thai girls to hand out condoms to traffic policemen in the city, and the next day, their pictures appeared in a major newspaper under the headline "Cops and Rubbers."

And what of the condom-themed restaurant where I had just eaten a marvelous lunch? I have to say that I thought it was a wildly original idea. Not only is the concept great and the gimmicks funny, the food is excellent as well.

As I climbed into our van parked outside the restaurant, I giggled at the thought that I was carrying my little "after-dinner mint" souvenir in my purse. If my daughters came across it, I might have a little trouble explaining why I had it and where it came from. And I wondered: would they even believe me if I told them?

*Cabbages & Condoms*

This restaurant also has branches in tourist cities such as Pattaya, Chiang Rai, and Nakhon Ratchasima. More information can be found at the website.

10 Sukhumvit, Soi 12
Bangkok
(02) 229-4610
www.cabbagesandcondoms.com

## GREATER BANGKOK

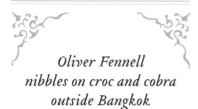

*Oliver Fennell*
*nibbles on croc and cobra*
*outside Bangkok*

While it's not unheard of for people to snack on rats, lizards, or even dogs in Thailand's deeply rural areas, this can also hold true for Bangkok. Sure, the variety of meats on a typical restaurant menu here are not out of the ordinary—beef, pork, chicken, prawns, and so on—even if the recipes may seem unusual to a Western visitor sometimes. But there are other culinary curios to be found in the city, if you have the appetite for something more unusual than *pad thai* or *tom yum* soup, and the inclination to track them down.

To sample as many curio foods as possible in one visit, I headed for Jareung Restaurant in Bangkok's neighboring province of Pathum Thani. This place specializes in "jungle food"— a particularly fiery (even by Thai standards!) style of cooking derived from the way people living near the rainforest prepared whatever wild animal they could hunt that day.

For obvious reasons, a commercial enterprise such as Jareung relies not on hunting but farmed produce, and the list of animals I could eat sounded more like the inventory of a zoo rather than the contents of a restaurant freezer: crocodile, wild boar, ostrich, frog, rabbit, deer, eel, goat, a range of lesser-known fish and birds, and Jareung's showpiece: cobra.

Though the thirty-year-old restaurant does not show up on a Google search, it has repeatedly been featured in newspaper articles and TV spots, usually with a Thai celebrity posing with a python (no longer on the menu) or cobra before eating it. Numerous photos of such moments hang on its walls, and its logo proudly boasts a rearing cobra.

Since I was only there in a party of two, we couldn't possibly try everything, so I had to prioritize. Naturally, cobra was number one on the list. Unfortunately for me, I chose a dish called *ngu hao pad phet* (spicy fried cobra) that was so overwhelmingly flavored with other ingredients, I could hardly discern the finely minced snake meat in it. The dish was nice enough, but being unable to tell what cobra tasted like rendered the exercise pointless. Therefore I would recommend that you try something less spicy, such as the *yam ngu hao krob* (crispy cobra salad).

My choice of crocodile turned out to be a simpler one. *Jarakeh tod gratiem prik thai* (crocodile fried with garlic and pepper) was delicious, with strips of deep-fried crocodile meat served with a salad and a dipping sauce. The meat was chewy but soft and not dissimilar to pork, both in taste and appearance.

BANGKOK

I was also impressed with my frog dish. *Gop gaeng ohm* (frog in north-eastern-style curry) was a zesty herbal broth in which the frog came roughly chopped. As the bones and skin were not removed, the morsels did at times look rather off-putting, but don't let the appearance disturb you. The meat is soft, succulent, and truly wonderful. It's a cliché to say a strange meat tastes like chicken, but in this case it's the most accurate description. If it wasn't for the mottled green skin, you wouldn't know the difference.

Finally, and to take a break from all the reptiles, I sampled eel. I've never understood the squeamishness many people have about eel; it is, after all, just a fish, even if it doesn't look like one. Again, I had the *pad phet* (spicy fried) option, although it was not quite the same as the cobra dish. The eel meat was presented in chunks, rather than minced, and it was not as spicy, so the flavor of the fish was not lost.

Should you wish to try jungle flavors but are not quite adventurous enough to sample the wild meats, there are also chicken, beef, prawn, and standard fish options.

Getting to Jareung could prove tricky for those unfamiliar with greater Bangkok. Since there are no train stations nearby, I would suggest that you take a taxi. For reference, it's near a giant mall called Future Park Rangsit—which every taxi driver should know—on Phahon Yothin Road, a major artery heading north out of the city. If you use the tollways, the journey should take no more than an hour from downtown. If you get lost

and can't speak Thai, ask your driver to call the restaurant for directions.

## Jareung Restaurant (Rahn Aharn Pa Jareung)
At the time of writing, average dishes cost between 95 and 175 baht.

39/14 Moo 3
Phahon Yothin Klong 1
Klong Luang, Phathum Thani Province
(02) 516-9274

## A few words on meat
There is no English-language menu at Jareung, so the following Thai word list will come in handy:

Cobra: *ngu hao*
Crocodile: *jarakeh*
Deer: *gwang*
Eel: *plalai*
Frog: *gop*
Ostrich: *nok grajok*
Rabbit: *gratai*
Wild boar: *mu pa*

## More exotic food tips from Oliver

### Live shrimp
See those vendors pushing fish tanks on their bicycles or carts? No, they're not peddling pets—the live shrimp inside are destined for the stomach, not a fishbowl. And they're not treated to the common courtesy of being killed first either. Instead, they're doused with lime juice, which complements their flavor as

well as paralyzes them. The live shrimp are then mixed with a salad and away you go. But do both yourself and the crustaceans a favor and eat quickly, before the lime starts to wear off and your meal starts to fight back. The best place to go for live shrimp is Petchaburi Road. Take Exit 3 from the Ratchathewi Skytrain station and turn left at the first junction to find a row of Isaan restaurants and street food vendors.

## Brain masala

For a sit-down meal of this unusual offal, go to any of the Himali Cha Cha chain restaurants. The bowl of finely chopped sheep brain curry looks inoffensive and has a taste and texture similar to oats.

www.himalichacha.com

## Sheep testicles

Nasir al-Masri restaurant does a comprehensive menu of grilled sheep's testicles dishes. This delicacy looks like chicken nuggets, tastes a bit like liver, and has a texture similar to that of Thai fish balls.

4/6 Sukhumvit,
Soi 3/1
(02) 253-5582

## Crocodile steak

The following restaurants offer a variety of crocodile dishes, as well as freeze-dried packets of croc meat to take home.

## Trader Vic's

Anantara Bangkok Riverside
Resort & Spa
257 Charoen Nakhon Road
Thon Buri,
Bangkok
(02) 476-0022

## Samut Prakan Crocodile Farm

Thai Ban Road
Samut Prakan Province
(02) 387-0020

## Sri Racha Tiger Zoo

343 Moo 3
Nong Kham, Sri Racha
Chonburi Province
03 829-6556
www.tigerzoo.com

## KANCHANABURI

## Jennifer Hughes is befriended at a bar in Kanchanaburi

A bright sun shining through the thin, makeshift curtain woke me and my boyfriend, David, with thoughts of a big, delicious breakfast already planted in our heads. Within moments of waking, we hurried out to the streets of Kanchanaburi, looking for a place to eat.

Instead of taking our usual one hour at least to decide on a restaurant, we headed directly to one we had seen the previous day that advertised tofu, a food we had yet to try in Thailand. But when we reached it, the sign outside read "Closed." Disappointed, we made a U-turn and started trudging back toward our starting point.

"Where you go?" a Thai woman in a faded tank top and cotton shorts shouted at us from across the street.

Somewhat annoyed by the constant inquiries from store owners, I responded without slowing my pace. "We're looking for a place to eat."

My curt reply didn't seem to faze the woman, who immediately reached for a menu and insisted that we eat in her establishment, the Valentine Bar. I was hungry, and she was friendly, so we accepted her offer.

"Our *pad thai* is very good," Mrs. Pholudom said in thickly accented English.

"*Goo ai dee oh pat thai dow hoo?*" David asked for *pad thai* with tofu in comically pronounced Thai. I ordered fried rice, in English, and then looked around the small, single room. I noticed there wasn't a kitchen. As if on cue, Mrs. Pholudom rushed off to put in the order with her cell phone that was plugged into one of the bright red walls.

Her smiling face radiated pleasure as we pulled two blue plastic chairs to her wooden table. Foreign travelers are often cheated, said Mrs. Pholudom, and she witnessed it every day on the street where her

bar is located. A former government worker, she now owns Valentine Bar, where she often struggles to fill the tables, but she never takes advantage of tourists. She seeks travelers out with the sole purpose of sharing Thai culture and sharing a piece of her life.

"You pay too much," she said, as she pointed to a discarded menu I had got from next door with prices ranging from 80 to 120 baht. "Too much, too much. I get it for 30 baht, you pay 60 baht."

Upon arriving to Thailand, David and I had quickly discovered that Thais often pay lower prices than tourists. If we had gone to the same stall from where Mrs. Pholudom ordered our food, we would have been charged more money than she. Our hostess then disappeared and reemerged with two cold bottles of water. "For free," she said, and set them down in front of us with two glasses filled with ice.

David and I looked at each other with surprise. Nearly everyone in Thailand is friendly, but nobody offers services for free. As we sat talking to our hostess in broken English and a little Thai, a white 1990s Toyota Corolla pulled up to the curb, and out walked an older man carrying two plastic sacks filled with food.

"My husband," Mrs. Pholudom introduced. As he passed us, he smiled as though seeing two old friends for the first time in years. Mrs. Pholudom followed him to the back of the room, where there was a small round table next to the bar.

"10 baht, 10 baht, 10 baht," Mrs. Pholudom shouted to us while her husband removed five portions of rice and chicken wrapped in wax paper from a plastic sack.

"Cheap, cheap," she said, motioning for us to come and see—and share—their breakfast.

"No, no, we have enough," I said, pointing behind me to where two plates full of steaming pad thai and fried rice had just been delivered. I did not want to take what little food they had bought for themselves, but Mr. Pholudom insisted that we each take a portion of rice and chicken.

For two hours following our meal, David and I sat in the Valentine Bar, which was vacant except for us, sharing photos of Oregon, our home, with Mrs. Pholudom. Her face lit up with each new picture. She was clearly intrigued by the beautiful green landscape and me wearing makeup. "Is that you?" she gasped. "So pretty!"

We talked about jobs in the United States compared to those in Thailand. Mrs. Pholudom told us about her young daughter who was a single mother—"Do you have a friend for her?"—and the differences in food between our country and hers. While we sat talking, Mr. Pholudom reappeared with a plate full of freshly cut, cold watermelon and insisted we eat again.

As the time passed, I remembered we had a train to catch and mentioned to Mrs. Pholudom that we needed to leave to do our laundry. "I have a washer here, in the back," she responded. "Come with me."

David stayed at the table as I walked across the street with Mrs. Pholudom to buy a single-wash box of laundry detergent from a 7-Eleven store. On our way to the store, she handed 60 baht to a

woman at a food cart. "She made your breakfast," Mrs. Pholudom explained.

"*Aroy mak!*" I said to the cook with my warmest smile. Very delicious.

When we returned to the Valentine Bar, Mrs. Pholudom took our mesh bag full of dirty clothes and wandered off to the back. She stepped through a doorway that led into her living quarters—a small apartment connected to the bar.

"David," I said urgently, "she paid that woman across the way 60 baht for our meals."

"So she didn't even take any money from us for herself!" he exclaimed, surprised and humbled by this generosity.

Mrs. Pholudom charged us only 60 baht for two plates of delicious food, two waters, portions of her breakfast, freshly cut watermelon, laundry service, and a ride to the train station. And the entire 60 baht went to the food stall across the street.

When it was time to say goodbye, I handed Mrs. Pholudom 200 baht and told her to keep the change. It seemed too small a token for our gratefulness, but I couldn't see how I could insult this truly amazing lady by offering more.

*Valentine Bar*

The Valentine Bar can be found on Mae Nam Khwae Road in Kanchanaburi. It has no kitchen, but if you want food along with your drinks, Mrs. Pholudom will order in whatever you want—at Thai prices, of course.

# KHON KAEN

## *Danielle Koffler breakfasts like a local in Khon Kaen*

When I first arrived in Thailand, I couldn't figure out what people ate for breakfast here. I was living in Khon Kaen at the time, and like a lot of confused foreigners in this quiet, northeastern province do, I went to a 7-Eleven convenience store to grab a morning meal. I bought mini loaves of bread and ate them while I rode a *songthaew* bus (also called a baht bus) to work.

Unfortunately, my 7-Eleven breakfast wasn't substantial enough to hold me over until lunch. I was suffering from hunger pangs by midmorning every day, until one of my fellow teachers suggested I try *moo ping* and *khao niao*—local breakfast foods that I probably wouldn't have discovered on my own. *Moo ping* is marinated and barbecued pork threaded on bamboo skewers, usually sold along with a small brick of *khao niao*, which is the sticky, glutinous rice that is a staple of northern Thailand.

One of my fellow teachers informed me that street vendors sell this barbecued pork and sticky rice combo during breakfast hours in every marketplace in Khon Kaen, and in fact, there was one vendor very close to my house, right on the road where I waited for my *songthaew* bus every morning. While I wasn't convinced that the dish sounded like an ideal breakfast option, I decided to give it a shot.

It turned out to be a quick, tasty, and easy-to-order meal. The sticky rice was served in a small plastic bag, and the best way to eat it on the go was to fold back the sides of the plastic and take a bite out of the flat, square-shaped brick.

I never got bored of the pork skewers, but if I had, I could have simply switched to the barbecued chicken, liver, and fish alternatives. I quickly became addicted to *moo ping* and *khao niao*, and was soon a regular at the morning barbecue stand. Every day, I would run down to buy my breakfast and practice speaking Thai while ordering my food. The couple who sold my breakfast patiently corrected my slow sentences and mispronunciations, not to mention stopped me from hopping onto the wrong bus each morning.

Depending on the day of the week, I had to catch an "old" or a "new" *songthaew* bus to work. But the sign on these local shared passenger-carrying trucks were in Thai, and by the time I worked out which was which, the bus would be gone. The *moo ping* sellers tried to teach me to read the "old" and "new" signs in Thai script, but quickly gave up and read the signs out loud for me instead.

My interaction with them became such a regular morning ritual, I began to feel guilty on the days when I didn't feel like eating *moo ping*. Just so my barbecue friends wouldn't see me go to work without one of their delicious breakfast packages, I would sneak over to the other end of my block to wait for the bus.

## Vietnamese cuisine in Khon Kaen

When you're not in the mood for *moo ping*, head for the Cactus Resort & Hotel on Pracha Samosorn Road. The hotel runs the small Miracle Coffee, famous for its *kai krata*—a Vietnamese fried egg breakfast dish that is served in the pan in which it is cooked. Two types of Vietnamese sausages (including the distinctive white *moo yor*), are sliced and scattered over the fried egg. The meal is accompanied by toasted buns stuffed with a delicious meat filling.

## Getting around Khon Kaen

*Songthaew* buses are a quaint mode of public transport in Thailand, as ubiquitous as the tuk-tuk and the longtail boat. They are cheap and convenient, and sometimes the only public vehicle you will find in rural areas.

These pickup trucks are easy to spot by their appearance, with two long bench seats in the back, a cover over the seats, and rolled-up plastic sheets on the sides to protect passengers from the rain. If you want a ride in a *songthaew*, all you have to do is flag one down and jump in.

Khon Kaen has an elaborate *songthaew* bus system with different color-coded and numbered trucks. These buses travel all over the city, and you can go anywhere for under 10 baht.

You can look up Khon Kaen's *songthaew* bus routes by visiting the following website and clicking on the "maps" tab on the homepage.

www.khonkaen.com

# PHUKET

## Jamie Monk searches out Phuket's gastronomic secret

Living in Phuket isn't a lifelong vacation, as many would imagine. As an expat settled here, I can tell you there are often times when I feel I have to run away from the holiday-making scene, if only to introduce a notion of normalcy in my life.

Outwitting tourists and discovering quiet, secret bits of Phuket before they get into popular travel guides is a necessity rather than a pastime for a permanent resident like me. But rarely is my "nose" for location as sharp as when I am looking for restaurants that are totally devoid of jet skis, tourists, bikinis, and beach umbrellas.

Over the years, I have ferreted out many restaurants that do great food and are well off the popular beaches. However, if you held a gun to my head and demanded that I choose my favorite, I would probably go for the Lakeside Restaurant.

Six years ago, I used to live on the same street as Nueng, the owner of Lakeside, whose talent for cooking has to be some sort of a divine blessing from the Thai gods. She ran a small, popular eatery called Chili in those days. Now I'd heard that she had opened a new restaurant out in the boonies. Armed with precise directions (postal addresses are of little use out in the sticks), I arrived at this charming thatch-roofed restaurant that seemed to float on the edge of a placid green lake.

There's plenty of fishing in this lake, and the surroundings are idyllic to say the least. A narrow, winding path leads up to the main building, which is sheltered from the direct afternoon sun by a cluster of full-grown coconut trees. I loved the way Nueng had decorated the place—the unpolished wooden furniture and an earthy color scheme had successfully erased the boundary between inside and outside.

But what I loved even more was the duck curry Nueng cooked for my wife. Now, I'm not a big fan of duck curry, but the dish was so aromatic, I had to try some. And once I did, I knew I'd never be able to eat another duck curry in my life without thinking it sadly second-grade. A tofu dish came next— delicate, super soft, and swimming in a piquant tamarind sauce. There was also *pad thai* and a lemony beef stir-fry with crispy basil leaves.

That was my first meal experience at the Lakeside Restaurant. Since then, I have returned again and again to taste more items off Nueng's splendid Thai menu.

I must also suggest Lakeside's unique fish-and-chips, which were recommended to me by a person I had recommended the restaurant to. "Back home in the 'Yookay,'" he said, "I was never a fan of boring cod and soggy chips, but Nueng's take on this British favorite is … a totally different kettle of fish."

I urge you to ignore the bad pun and order the fish-and-chips if you want a non-Thai meal choice at the Lakeside Restaurant. True, it's nothing like the usual British variety that is served with mushy peas on a soggy piece of newspaper. Nor is it like the famous fish-and-chips at Harry Ramsden's in London either. It's typically Nueng—with a remarkably flavorful and subtle Oriental twist.

The remoteness of this restaurant's location is a wonderful thing for regulars like me who come to relish Nueng's food and enjoy the quiet, scenic lakeside ambience. The proprietor, however, has different ideas about this and rues the fact that no tourists ever come this way.

It's an act of extreme gastronomic sacrifice that I am sharing the secret of Lakeside's existence with readers of this book. What's more, I'm even going to give you detailed directions, so you can find Nueng's establishment without getting lost. Be warned that Lakeside is far off the tourist track and quite a drive from the popular beach hubs of Patong/Karon. But once you've eaten there, you'll agree with me that it's well worth the trouble.

## Lakeside Restaurant

This restaurant is located halfway between the airport and Phuket Town. Driving down Highway 402, turn east onto Highway 4027, and head toward the Bang Pae waterfall. Look out for the restaurant's yellow signboard, which will come up within two kilometers on your left. Drive slowly, and keep an eye out, as this signboard is easy to miss.

## Out to lunch

For alternative dining, Jamie adds: The Beach Bar is a humble little restaurant on Phuket's Cape Panwa. Tourists rarely come out this way because the area is too rocky for swimming, but the views of Chalong Bay and Lone Island are fantastic from here. You can enjoy a pretty private afternoon strolling on the beach or simply lolling about in the sand.

The Beach Bar, in my opinion, is an ideal place for a long, leisurely lunch. The menu is made up of simple Thai home-cooked dishes, and the seafood is always fresh. I recommend the sea bass, though my daughter will swear by the fried chicken in garlic, accompanied by copious amounts of fried rice, all of which the owner cooks himself. The atmosphere is informal and homey, and there's never any hurry to eat up, pay the bill, and leave.

To find the Beach Bar, use the Panwa Beach Resort Phuket (on Khao Khad Road) as your landmark. Take the first right turn that comes after the hotel and go down the steep dirt road to the restaurant.

## KOH CHANG

### Ian McNamara savors local flavors on Koh Chang

Despite its name, Koh Chang's Pearl Beach isn't the charming scene that you might imagine. There are no opalescent sands or aquamarine sea, nor any sun-kissed outlines of swim-suited tourists etched out in Gauguin-esque golds and ochres. Rather, it is a fairly unattractive stretch of pebbly shoreline on the island's west coast, where a hodgepodge of recently constructed, cookie-cutter shophouses have come up, along with several pseudo-Western restaurants offering good old English breakfasts and the island's post office. Unless you are dropping off mail or happen to be hungry while you are in the neighborhood, there is no reason to give Pearl Beach more than a passing glance as you whiz by it on your rental scooter.

But head down the concrete track that lies south of the post office, continue past the monolithic apartment block, and you'll arrive at one of Koh Chang's best kept culinary secrets: Saffron on the Sea.

Saffron on the Sea is a small resort with a handful of Balinese-inspired thatched-roof bungalows, built around a mature tropical garden that opens onto the shore. While the bungalows are an excellent value at around 1,500-2,000 baht a night, the real gem here is the seafront restaurant that serves a small menu of the most expertly cooked Thai food you will find on the island.

Saffron restaurant doesn't try too hard to impress; the decor is functional with roughly hewn tables and chairs, the food is unpretentious, and I doubt there is any visionary chef back in the kitchen trying to reinvent traditional Thai cuisine with a lot of fusion and flourish. The success of Saffron, in my opinion, is in its stylish simplicity.

There's an open seating area by the sea, as well as a covered deck with a palm frond roof. A central island in the restaurant, piled high with baskets filled with all manner of fresh herbs and vegetables, is where the dishes get their finishing touches before arriving at your table. Cooking is done on ordinary gas hobs in the main kitchen at the rear.

The menu is a medley of identifiable favorites mixed in with enough lesser-known Thai dishes to make the food seem both easy and exciting. A couple of Saffron specialties that I rarely find anywhere else on the island as the banana flower salad and the *goong hom pha* (prawn in jackets)—both delicious starters. Another signature treat I cannot resist is the *yam pla saffron*, a red snapper so cleverly prepared in a heady blend of lime, green mango, mint, and peanut sauce, I fully understand why the restaurant has chosen to "claim" this dish by lending it its name.

Given that I have probably eaten my way through the entire Saffron menu, I am tempted to recommend more items that I have found to be truly exceptional. But that may take some adventure out of your own food experience at this restaurant. I want you to be surprised—just as I was when I first ate here five years ago.

### Saffron on the Sea
13/10 Moo 4, Hat Kai Mook
Koh Chang
039 551-253

### Worth the wait
Ian adds: As your meal will be prepared from scratch at Saffron, this may entail a forty-five-minute wait before the food finally comes to your table. So as soon as you

arrive, make a beeline for the two bamboo hammocks in the waterfront gazebo. Order your food plus a cocktail or two to tide you over, and then laze on your hammock a while before moving into the main restaurant area to eat.

## GENERAL THAILAND

*David Kovanen interprets Thailand's common tabletop items*

### Beyond the bathroom

"Excuse me, could you please pass the toilet paper?"

It's an odd sort of a question, but you may often hear it when dining out in Thailand.

If you have done any traveling around Asia, you already know to carry a roll of toilet paper for the bathrooms, which are rarely stocked with this much-needed necessity. Where, you might wonder, did all of the toilet paper go? In Thailand, the answer will be that it is sitting on the table of your favorite restaurant!

Napkins are something of a rarity here, and the most common tabletop equivalent is a roll of toilet paper. Even in a fine restaurant, a trusty roll of TP

can be found. You can tell a classy joint from a place for commoners by whether the toilet paper is in a decorative box or merely a plastic holder, or if simply sits naked on the table.

Proper etiquette is to take the tissue, pull a few feet out of the box, and then tear it off. Repeat as necessary. If you forgot to bring tissue with you for the toilet, you may take some from the table, but should then engage in conversation before heading to the toilet so that the connection is lost.

Toilet paper is, after all, not just toilet paper ... at least not in Thailand.

### Mistaken identity

On the tables of Thai restaurants, you will find what look like typical Heinz ketchup bottles.

One of your more sadistically enjoyable experiences could be to watch a novice tourist squirt some of this "ketchup" onto his dinner. You can then sit there counting down: four, three, two, one ... *gotcha!* Try not to laugh as you see the look of pain and terror that uniquely comes from mistaking the bottle of hot chili sauce for ketchup.

You see, in Thailand the tomato ketchup and the red hot chili sauce come in two identical-shaped bottles. They are clearly marked—but in Thai—so you have no idea which is which.

Newbies will always reach for the chili sauce because it has the familiar red label. But the ketchup is in the bottle with the green label, because the tomatoes that it is made from are green in Thailand. So you have to remember that green is ketchup and red is a preview of hell. Most people learn very quickly, by the way, because nobody does hot and spicy like the Thai.

One more detail you might want to remember about Thai spices: there is no antidote to the pain. Water makes it worse. Coca-Cola makes it worse. Vodka makes it worse. Screaming in pain makes it worse. Some research has actually been done on this topic (see Discovery Channel's *Myth-Busters*), and your best option is milk.

You might ask why Thai food is so spicy. There are actually two reasons. The first is that chili peppers are a great preservative. People can tolerate spicy food much more easily than bacteria. The second reason is that the spice causes blood to flow to your taste buds. After a few minutes you will find that flavors really are much more intense. Sweets are sweeter after eating spicy food, too!

**All hail the spoon**

I always thought it was funny how Englishmen use their forks with the tongs down. In Thailand, I found that the Thais have very little use for forks at all, tongs up or down. Mostly, when the fork is unavoidable, the tongs will be sideways facing—an orientation that I had never considered until I visited this country.

The easiest way to spot a newbie tourist isn't so much their preference for using a fork as their always trying to experience Asia by using chopsticks. The Thais care even less for chopsticks than they do for

forks. If chopsticks are placed on the table, they are meant for Chinese and Japanese tourists who haven't yet mastered the primary Thai utensil: the spoon.

The soup spoon, or tablespoon as it's called in Thailand, is the country's do-all, utilitarian table utensil, offering the proper way to eat just about everything from rice to soup. If you observe the Thais eating, you will notice that a spoon is what they primarily use. Westerners tend to be blind to this because the fork is so culturally indoctrinated into us.

That said, the fork is the perfect companion to the spoon. Just remember that the fork should not transport food to the mouth. Use it for poking and sweeping food onto your spoon, but then use the spoon to shovel the rice or soup in.

### Thai *"ketchup"*

One sauce that separates true Thai food connoisseurs from the wannabes is Sriracha. If you love eating or cooking Thai dishes, you must have a bottle of Sriracha in your pantry. So successful is this super hot sauce in the West that it has been nicknamed Thai ketchup.

Like ketchup, you can slather it onto anything from pizzas to *pad thai*. The sharp sweetness of Sriracha lingers in spite of its heat, and these dual flavors can become pretty addictive. If you haven't got your own bottle of Sriracha yet, don't bother buying it in Bangkok. Most Asian grocery stores in your hometown will surely carry the brand.

## Hugh Leong lists his favorite one-dish Thai lunches

A typical Thai dinner consists of many dishes and can be quite an elaborate affair. But lunch is usually a much simpler matter. Nobody has time to sit down to a leisurely midday meal, and they'll grab an inexpensive, one-dish lunch from a nearby food stall or roadside restaurant before rushing back to work.

But your case is different. As a traveler who's in no hurry to get anywhere, you can actually look forward to this meal. And once you know which one-dish lunches to order, you won't be wasting time eating the same old *pad thai* every day either.

To help you make lunch an occasion to explore new one-dish meals, I have put together a sample menu below. These are all standard dishes served almost everywhere in the country. Each one is a full meal in itself and costs less than a dollar. I have also thrown in a few Thai words to make things more interesting.

## Rice Dishes
### Chicken over fatty rice
*(khao man gai)*

I know, the name sounds terrible, but this is my favorite. The clean, simple appearance of the dish conceals a week's supply of cholesterol, so try not to get too addicted to this one. Your clue to a *khao man gai* food stall is the whole boiled chickens hanging off hooks in the shop window. The chicken is chopped into strips and laid over a small mound of rice that has been boiled in chicken fat. The stalls will also have a selection of several sauces in big bowls for you to choose from. Always go for the orange one that has a strong gingery flavor: this is the true *khao man gai* sauce, which takes this amazing dish to a whole new level. If you ask—though I doubt you will—you can also get chicken gizzards, liver, and even a square of congealed chicken blood.

### Fried rice
*(khao phat)*

Most Thai restaurants serve fried rice because not only is the dish popular, it also uses up whatever cooked rice is left over from the previous day. (Old rice makes the best fried rice, in case you're wondering. The grains have time to harden and don't get mushy in the wok.) It is common to add a fried egg to top it off. In Thai, a fried egg is called *khai duw,* or a "star egg." You'll be given a wedge of lemon to squeeze on the rice, and you must remember to do this. Unlike Chinese fried rice, the Thai version is ever-so-slightly sweet, and the lemon is the last essential touch to make the dish pop. When I can't decide what else to eat, I order this.

### Barbecued pork over rice
*(khao moo daeng)*

The name *moo daeng* means "red pork." It is the same red barbecued pork found all over Asia. You'll know which shop sells this when you see strips of red pork hanging in the glass cases in front. Thai red pork is quite lean. Usually some sliced cucumbers will be placed on the side, and a bowl of broth will come with this meal. The whole dish is topped off with a thick gravy.

### Crispy pork over rice
*(khao moo krawp)*

Where the red pork dish is lean, this one is a fat-lover's delight. The pork is roasted (or deep fried) and has a thick, crispy skin. Between the pork meat and the crispy skin lies a thick chunk of fat. You can usually find this dish in the same shop that does red barbecued pork. Thais often order a combination of red and crispy pork on rice, just so they can balance out their fat intake. This dish is also covered with gravy and comes with a bowl of broth.

## Noodle Dishes

### Rice noodle soup
*(kuay teow nam)*

You can find variations of this soup all the way from Japan to Indonesia. The Thai version will have rice noodles of differing thickness, depending on which type you order. The noodles are usually piled in a glass case in front of the shop, so just point to the ones you want. The soup is served with pork, beef, meatballs, or fish balls with large quantities of fried garlic and aromatic herbs stirred in. If you don't want this dish as a soup, ask the cook to make it *haeng* (dry). You'll get all the ingredients, without the broth.

### Wheat noodle soup
*(ba mee nam)*

This is pretty much the same dish as above, except that the noodles are yellow instead of white. And therein lies the difference in flavor. Some people prefer the taste of wheat noodles, while others prefer the rice variety. Lately, *ba mee* is also being made with spinach and other healthy veggies. The color of these noodles is green.

### Rice noodles fried with soy sauce
*(kuay teow phat si-ew)*

Cooked with a liberal amount of soy sauce, this is a broad-rice-noodle dish fried up with meat and fresh greens such as kale. Often an egg will be stirred into the noodles. Although this is a noodle dish, it is not eaten with chopsticks but with a spoon and fork.

### Rice noodles with gravy
*(kuay teow raad naa)*

This dish consists of broad-rice noodles, veggies, and meat served with a thick gravy, as the name indicates. In some restaurants, this dish will have the consistency of a thin soup or stew. This noodle dish is also eaten with a spoon and fork.

## Food courts

Most department stores in Thailand have food courts on the ground or top floor where you can start experimenting with one-dish meals. If the signs are all in Thai, hang around to see what exactly each stall is serving. The food court prices are so reasonable you can try several one-dish meals at once. After that, when you know exactly what you like and feel more confident about ordering, take the adventure out to the streets and tackle the small restaurants and food carts like a pro.

## Table condiments

There will always be a set of condiments placed on each table in the roadside restaurants: fish sauce (*nam pla*) for salt; mild, green chili floating in vinegar for sour; sugar for sweet; and powdered chilies for hot. All dishes, especially the noodle soups mentioned in this essay, are made with a neutral palate in mind, so it is your responsibility to "fix" the dish to suit your own taste buds.

## The heat is on

At most Thai restaurants in the West, you will be asked how hot you want your dish; you will then answer with a star rating going from one to five. Forget about that in Thailand. The cooks at the kinds of one-dish places that Hugh has written about will make each portion the same way they always do, no matter who will be eating it. For your own reference, if something is described to you as "hot," then it's probably way off your usual five-star heat measuring scale, and you may want to give it a pass. And there's no such thing as a one-star dish in Thailand.

## Danielle Koffler masters moo kata barbecue

In Khon Kaen, where I was teaching English to elementary school children, I often passed a *moo kata* restaurant that was always packed with people. There must have been at least a hundred tables in the restaurant, none of which were ever occupied by solo eaters. So I waited for the chance to go there one day with someone.

Tired of eating alone, I finally called a Thai teacher from my school and asked if she would like to have dinner with me that night. As it happened, she was on her way to eat at the same *moo kata* restaurant with one of the male teachers, so I invited myself along.

It was only as we sat down that I realized I was on their date. Nobody had told me they were a couple, but it all seemed to click once I was seated. Thai people are so nice and accommodating that my teacher friend hadn't wanted to say no to me. So all three of us pretended to ignore the fact that I was intruding.

And since I had never been to this restaurant, or anything like it, I was soon able forgot about my social gaffe. I stared curiously at the hole in the middle of our table, as a waiter came over and placed a bucket of hot coals in it. A dish that resembles a Bundt cake pan was then put on top of the coals. There were slits on the top of the pan's "island" so that the coals could breathe. Although this setup is ingenious, I don't recommend leaving your feet below it. Sometimes sparks or bits of coal fall down, and it's unfortunate when your feet are in their way.

Once our coals were ready, my companions led me to the back of the restaurant, where I found an American restaurant inspector's nightmare: trays of raw meat and seafood on ice, with tongs for diners to take whatever they pleased. Vegetables, noodles, fruit, French fries, and a few other fried appetizers were available, as well.

After we chose our raw meat and vegetables, my companions poured broth into the pan and then placed a few pieces of pork fat on the raised island in the center. The fat dripped down the sides, greasing the island and flavoring the soup below. We started placing pieces of meat on the island and dumping vegetables, noodles, and seafood into the broth.

Being a typical American "germaphobe," I was a little concerned that the chopsticks being used to place the raw meat on the pan were the same

ones used to eat the cooked meat. I didn't want to draw attention to this, so instead of using two different pairs of chopsticks, I discreetly dipped my chopsticks in the boiling broth for a little while to sanitize them.

The meat that is barbecued on the heated island in the center of the pan can be eaten as is or with the soup. There were a quite a few different sauces on the table, with varying degrees of spiciness, and the trick to the soup is to add a little sauce once you have poured some into your bowl.

For dessert, the restaurant offered coconut ice cream, fruit, and *nam khang sai*. The latter is wonderfully refreshing and most suited to the hot Thai climate. The fixings for *nam khang sai* were found near the fruit section of the buffet, where I filled a bowl halfway with crushed ice. Then I took my pick of jelly pieces, basil seeds, palm seeds, and pomegranate seeds. I added some coconut milk and one of the flavored sweet syrups, and my *nam khang sai* was ready.

Once you have mastered the art of making *moo kata* in a restaurant, try ordering a *moo kata* takeaway. Restaurants will deliver the coals, pan, ingredients, plates, and utensils to your home and then pick up the dirty cookware and coals when you're done.

### How to moo kata

It can be difficult to recognize a *moo kata* place straight off because there are no signs to distinguish them from regular restaurants. But by asking locals, you'll be able to find one in every major city in Thailand.

*Moo kata* is an all-you-can-eat buffet-style restaurant, where you are meant to enjoy a leisurely meal in the company of friends and family. Groups often spend three to four hours at the *moo kata* table. If you arrive alone, the restaurant will decide whether or not to let you in. If they do, expect to pay at least double the usual per-person rate.

*Moo kata* typically costs around 100 baht per person, not including drinks. If you leave a lot of food behind on your table, though, the restaurant might charge you extra for not eating everything you took. So only take what you know you can finish. After all, you can go back to the buffet line as many times as you want.

### Ban Suan Restaurant

539/3 Nah Muang Road (near Fairy Plaza)
Khon Kaen
043 227-811
Songthaew routes: 9, 19, and 20

## Adrianne Myers
### answers the call of pad thai

The first time I tasted *pad thai*, it came out of a Styrofoam takeout box from a hole-in-the-wall Thai kitchen called Thai Taste, in my home town of London, Ontario. The box was bulging with slick noodles, chicken, shrimp, and tofu, and the lid was marked by a greasy red thumbprint. As I burned my lips with the glorious heat of *pad thai* for the first time, I knew this was something I had to taste at its place of origin. I plan a lot of travel based on food that I feel a nagging desire to try at its source, and much as I love all Thai food, it was *pad thai* that finally took me on a trip to Thailand.

*Kuay teow phat Thai* is the proper name for this dish, which is shortened to *pad thai* to make ordering easier for foreign tourists who subsist on *pad thai* for breakfast, lunch, and dinner when they are in Thailand. The popularity of *pad thai* in the travel circuit isn't hard to understand when you consider its many attributes. For one, it is easily available from countless food carts at every marketplace and most busy street corners. It is a cheap, one-dish meal that is made to order and therefore, always served fresh. Then there is the sublime combination of sweet and lime, and the crunchy texture of bean sprouts and ground peanuts to balance the starchiness of the noodles. And since it's cooked in front of you, you have complete control over how much chili the vendor puts into it.

For someone as obsessed with noodles as I am, the sight of food carts, piled high with an assembly of fresh *pad thai* ingredients, is quite irresistible. Throughout my trip, I randomly tasted portions of *pad thai* from food carts I passed on the road, regardless of the time of day or even how hungry I was.

But my first experience of this iconic dish in its country of origin was not off the streets. It was at a southern island hotel where I was staying. After arriving at the Krabi International Airport, I took a taxi to the coastal town of Ao Nang, where I had to wade into the Andaman Sea to catch a longtail boat to Ao Ton Sai, a climbing destination, isolated from the rest of the headland by sheer limestone cliffs. Weary to the bone from more than thirty hours of travel, I sat at the open-air restaurant of the Tonsai Bay Resort, when my deadened senses were suddenly reawakened by the sight of a heaped plate of *pad thai* being placed in front of me. With a Chang beer in my hand, and the sea stretching out in front of me from the peaceful shelter of the bay, I dug into my noodles as if I had never seen food before.

The joy of eating *pad thai* in a restaurant instead of out in the street is that you get the unique license of customizing it for yourself. Along with my plate of noodles had come several tiny dishes—I added a few drops of fish sauce, a pinch of extra sugar, a sprinkling of dried red chili, and a dash of vinegar, and suddenly discovered to my delight that the possibilities for tinkering with this dish were endless.

The following day, refreshed by a good night's sleep, I took a boat back to Ao Nang and walked east along the beach as far as I could go, to the aptly named Last Café. It was worth every step of the one-kilometer walk to sit on plastic chairs in the shade of trees, within view of a lofty limestone karst, drinking the café's bad instant coffee and eating their heavenly *pad thai.*

Many backpacking tourists associate *pad thai* with food carts on Bangkok's Khao San Road, because that is where they first get fixated on this dish. But my own memories of *pad thai* in Thailand are inextricably linked to the Andaman Sea, as my initiation took place on a beautiful jade green island floating in its calm blue waters.

I have vivid recollections of myself lounging on the beach at Ao Ton Sai, buffeted by warm tropical winds, taking lazy sips from a glass of chilled Chang beer, and eating yet another plate of *pad thai.* My mouth still waters as I remember that startling burst of flavor from the first spoonful—the sweet, lime, and chili ... a perfectly balanced symphony.

### Tonsai Bay Resort
www.tonsaibay.co.th

### Thailand's best pad thai
The jury will forever be out on this one. No two plates of *pad thai* ever seem to taste the same, and every *pad thai* addict has his or her own favorites, so instead of trying to find the best, here is a short list of highly recommended places suggested by this book's writers, who have tasted this noodle treat throughout the country.

## Bangkok

### The Joy Luck Club

Great for vegetarian *pad thai*.

8 Phra Sumen Road
(02) 280-3307

### Suda

A fun open-air restaurant.

6/12 Klong Toey
(02) 229-4518

### Thipsamai Pad Thai

313 Mahachai Road
Samranrat, Phra Nakhon District
(02) 221-6280

## Phuket

### Sea Hag

Soi Permpong
76 341-111

## Hua Hin

### Sawasdee

122/1-2 Naresdamri Road
032 511-935

## Koh Phi Phi

### Papaya

Phi Phi Don
Next to the island's famous
Reggae Bar.

## Chiang Mai

### Pad thai food cart

This cart is located next to the McCormick Hospital on Kaeonawarat Road. You will know which one from the queue that forms around it after 5 p.m.

## Lopburi

### Pad thai food cart

This cart is located behind the Asia Lopburi Hotel on Surasak Road.

## Pattaya

### Da Da's

Tipp Plaza
Off 2nd Road

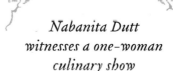

*Nabanita Dutt
witnesses a one-woman
culinary show*

Thais may be very superstitious people, but when it comes to harboring blind beliefs, I'm no slouch either. I wear black on Saturdays to counter the malefic influence of Saturn, carry a piece of amethyst geode in my handbag to control my impulsiveness, and maintain an ever-growing menagerie of three-legged frogs and other feng shui friends to help cleanse the vibes in my living space.

Using the food I eat to release subconscious wishes and desires into the ether, however, is something I had never done, and I have to thank my friend Tek for introducing me to the Thai concept of "lucky foods"—dishes that bring good luck and happiness when eaten during special occasions.

The special occasion in this case was a double celebration of Tek's marriage and housewarming. The actual wedding ceremony had taken place in her native village a month earlier, but Tek's aunt had come back with her to Bangkok to help with the move and cook up a wonderful Thai-style banquet for Tek's big-city friends.

On the menu were several dishes that were laid out on the kitchen counter because Tek hadn't had the time to go out and buy a dining table. There wasn't enough space on the counter to arrange the desserts, and Tek's aunt for some reason had displayed them on top of the fridge. But I don't think anybody minded. It was an informal get-together for a few of Tek's friends, and all of us were more interested in the food itself than how it was presented. I had never eaten Thai food cooked in a Thai home before and was a little anxious about how much of that fishy-smelling powdered shrimp would be sprinkled on top of everything.

Since three of the nine invitees were foreigners, Tek described each item to us, and as she moved from dish to dish, the "lucky" aspect of the banquet slowly started to emerge. Apparently, none of the food here had been chosen randomly or be-

cause her aunt cooked it particularly well. Each item had a special reason for being there.

There was a platter of bite-sized vegetarian treats neatly wrapped up in "golden threads" of fried egg noodles to bring wealth to all of us who ate them. Tubes of sweet bread called *khanom kareaw* had been plaited like DNA strands to indicate the intertwining of two souls. Pounded red sticky rice was cooked in caramel and coconut milk and then shaped into a pretty Valentine heart.

On a silver tray, Tek's aunt had placed small fish curry cakes (*haw mok*) in banana leaf bowls whose edges she had painstakingly scalloped with scissors. The name *haw mok* suggested stickiness or togetherness, and symbolized a close-knit family.

The dish of spaghettilike rice flour noodles was *khanom jeen nam yaa*, served with a pungent fish curry sauce. Instead of being broken up, the noodles were deliberately left long to signify an extended period of time that Tek and her husband would spend as a blissfully married couple. I couldn't taste either of these fish dishes as I don't eat seafood, but I pigged out on the sausages that were salty, sour, hot, and sweet at the same time to suggest the mixed bag of experiences Tek could expect to encounter in this new chapter of her life. Fruits blessed the couple with their lucky colors, and some bright yellow desserts would make sure that the union was truly golden. I especially loved the "money fish," a Chinese cake that looked like a pearly white fish with fake silver coins for scales.

It was certainly a lot of beautiful-looking food. According to Tek, her aunt had taken many days to prepare all of it on her own, though most of the desserts had been ordered from a sweet shop. The complicated recipes were yet another gesture to inform the gods that this was no lighthearted affair. I missed my favorite Thai stir-fries, but I could see how ill-suited those two-minute recipes would have been for an occasion like this.

Tek informed us that there had been many more dishes at the actual wedding festivities in the village, because all the women in her neighborhood had come over to help with the cooking. Here, there was only Tek's aunt, who shyly accepted our congratulations from her low stool in the kitchen for this splendid one-woman show.

## Sampling "lucky" dishes

Food plays an important part in Thai ceremonies, and the ingredients, names, or colors symbolize blessings and good fortune. The preparations mentioned in this essay aren't exclusive to religious functions, and they can be available in restaurants as well. *Khanom jeen nam yaa*, for example, is said to be really good in northern Thailand, where you will find many street stalls selling this noodle dish in the market-places of Chiang Mai and Chiang Rai. And the famous Thai dessert

shops on the island of Koh Kret near Bangkok will surely have most of the lucky sweets mentioned here.

## *John Henderson meets his match in the King of Fruits*

What goes around comes around. Should you ever be tempted to doubt the truth of this proverb, consider this sorry tale.

On a pleasant Sunday afternoon in May, near our home in Bangkok, I finally succumbed to my first bite of durian for the year. The fruit's distinctive yellow pillows looked quite inviting as I walked past the vendor's cart. The durian season might end suddenly, I reasoned. Best to get it now while it's fresh.

The next day at the office, a colleague asked if I needed anything from the lunchtime market. "Sure, a bit of durian would be nice," I said without thinking. The anticipation of tasting that exotic fruit once again must have blocked my common sense.

Thais have a strict code of etiquette where durian is concerned. It may be the King of Fruits, but the strong aroma makes it unwelcome in many settings, such as hotels and office buildings.

In my defense, my accomplice—born and raised in Thailand—should have seen our problems coming and

GENERAL THAILAND

refused my request. Either that or we should have bought enough for the entire floor. An open invitation like that would have evenly spread out the reek—and the blame. But durian isn't cheap. Treating everybody would have set me back by nearly a whole day's wages.

When my coworker showed up with the contraband, I paid him back and suggested that the two of us have a little snack in the midafternoon. But long before the hour arrived, people were darkening my doorway, hands on their hips, giving me a look that said, "Are you out of your mind?"

The odiferous molecules in durian don't simply dissipate, you see. They linger obstinately in the air, like the stench of onions or charred wood. By the time we eventually indulged, everyone within a hundred-meter radius knew of my sin, without having to be told, and had scolded me in no uncertain terms. Worse still, what goes around comes around, in a way I could never have predicted.

Besides this being durian season, the monsoon had also finally arrived. Almost exactly at quitting time, it started to rain, and I went downstairs to see a friend I sometimes commute with, to find out how he was planning to go back home.

It turned out the friend had left early that day. I returned to my office. I had been away for no more than five minutes, but in those minutes, a drainpipe above my bookshelf overflowed, creating an impressive waterfall that gushed out of the

air-conditioner, through my various volumes, and onto the floor. I came back to find half a dozen people furiously bailing, flinging books, and speculating about whether the flood was likely to get deep enough to endanger the computer.

Nobody else's office was touched. And as I stayed till 8 p.m., cleaning up and wringing things out, I thought how, when it comes to the durian, justice is swift. And I wondered why my penance was so high. After all, my intentions had not been evil. Noah, at least, was warned.

### The controversy

Durian is one fruit in the world that people love to hate. Even those who are addicted to the strong taste of it will complain about the smell. Chef and author Anthony Bourdain, for instance, who relishes his durian, says it makes your breath smell as if you've been "kissing your dead grandmother." This large, ugly, thorn-coated fruit is native to Southeast Asia. Thailand has many varieties of durian, of which the mild-tasting *monthong* (golden pillow durian) is probably the one you should choose when introducing your taste buds to this fruit.

No matter how much they complain about it, Thais are mad about durian. Why else would they call it King of Fruits? Come durian season, from April to June, and you will see families in rural Thailand laying out newspapers in their courtyards and breaking open large durians in a messy, juicy celebration of this fruit.

## Durian delights

If you're afraid to jump right in and take a bite out of this stink bomb, cheat and eat durian flavored ice creams or desserts instead. Many Thai restaurants offer menus containing sweet dishes with durian, such as the popular *khao neow durian*, which is sticky rice cooked in coconut cream with bits of fresh durian on the side.

Check out the ice cream displays in shopping malls and grocery stores, and you'll find a durian flavor easily enough. Iberry is a local chain that does a rich and creamy one. You can find iberry outlets in major shopping destinations including Bangkok's Siam Paragon, Siam Square, and Central World.

## Travel advisory

Editor's note: Packing slices of durian in your suitcase may not be such a good idea. I did that one time, thinking my mom would enjoy tasting the strange fruit, but a sniffer dog at the airport zeroed in on my suitcase at security check. The security official opened the bag, confiscated the plastic-wrapped durian that was sitting right on top, and closed it again without saying a word. No doubt some minion was dispatched immediately to get rid of the offensive fruit before it stank up the old Don Muang International Airport. I reloaded the suitcase on my trolley and quickly walked away, feeling very foolish.

## Steven King brews up a guide to popular Thai beers

Less than a century ago, Thais did not drink beer. Now it seems the nation cannot get enough of it. Locally made beer brands, each with a macho animal for a logo, have made the beer drinking culture big in Thailand. As a tourist here, it is imperative that you stay off your Coronas and Heinekens and try something with a lion, elephant, leopard, or tiger on the packaging instead. Even if it is only in the interest of science.

To help you get started on Thai "*bia*," I have evaluated some of the better known local brews. These opinions are not just based on my own (fairly extensive) drinking experience. I have also taken into account the views of hundreds (maybe thousands) of others I have had the honor of sharing a Thai beer with.

### Chang: the wildly popular demon drink

Chang is Thailand's most notorious alcoholic beverage. The beer was introduced as recently as 1994, but within five short years, it managed to grab a major share of the domestic beer market and left Singha, the previous market leader, looking a shadow of its former self.

Talk to any bar owner, and he will tell you there are only two types of beer drinkers in Thailand these days: those who drink Chang and those who don't. The beer has strong brand recognition. Its green logo of two elephants facing each other is instantly identifiable to Thais and tourists alike. Chang also has excellent distribution. It is available in supermarkets, mini-marts, restaurants, and bars—always displayed in prime positions.

The problem I have with Chang is not its super cool image or high alcohol content (6.4%), but the awful "Changover" it gives me the morning after. At precisely 5 a.m., I wake up with a thundering headache and have to hotfoot it to the nearest toilet. The sharp pains in the head I get from a "Changover" suggest that dehydration is not the root cause but perhaps a rogue ingredient in the beer that simply doesn't agree with my system.

In my opinion this brew is not Changtastic, but at least 50 percent of my fellow *farang* beer drinkers will disagree. However, there is no doubt that Chang is a fantastically successful, low-priced beer with a powerful alcoholic kick, and if you don't suffer the same morning-after discomforts that I do, you too will probably love this one.

### Singha: the original Thai beer

Singha is another local beer that many foreign travelers have heard about. For years, Singha ruled Thailand as the premium beer of choice until Chang came along and stole its crown.

I suspect Singha's falling from grace has something to do with its mild 5 percent alcohol content. Thais like their beer strong, and new, cheaper alternatives like Chang are offering them more bang for their baht.

The price of a Singha—positioned somewhere between a Chang and a Heineken—is not really that competitive, but Boon Rawd Brewery, the company that makes Singha, does put a lot of effort into this beer. They use water pumped from deep underground wells before carbon-and-sand filtering it, and their barley and hops are imported from Europe. The result is Singha's distinctively rich taste and strong hop character.

I recommend readers to try this iconic beer, but remember that it is mild. Depending on your desired result, you might have to consider bringing a case of it along to a party.

### Leo: the inoffensive brew

Leo is very affordable, but unlike many dodgy, cheap local brands you will encounter in Thailand, it does not taste like piss, soap, or foam. Its low price, decent alcohol content, and easy availability make it a fairly appealing option. Though the brand is aimed at the Thai market, many *farangs*, including myself, will buy Leo because of all the reasons listed above.

A key to Leo's increasing popularity is its great marketing. Ever since the Thai government banned the use of celebrities in alcohol ads, the company has gone back to more traditional selling tactics, and the Seven Sexy Leo Girls campaign is attracting new consumers by the droves.

One thing I like about this beer is that it can be drunk in quantity without risking a massive hangover. You might feel slightly groggy the next morning if you've been on a major drinking binge the night before, but it normally does not give me a Chang-style hangover. Leo is basically a low-cost version of Heineken—that is, it does not taste like much, and therefore it goes down easily.

Leo, I would say, is my cheap Charlie choice when I am in need of a budget-friendly beer.

### Cheers: probably the worst beer in the world

There are absolutely no redeeming features to this beer. My theory is that nobody bothered to do a taste test before manufacturing Cheers. By the time somebody realized it was disgusting, it was already in the shops, and it was too late to put the stops on the whole thing without a serious loss of face.

While many local beers in Thailand may taste like soap or chemicals, it is rare that a brewery manages to produce a beer that combines both. This stuff is completely undrinkable; I could not even finish a small 320-milliliter can. My suggestion would be to avoid Cheers beer at all costs.

*Beer on ice*

Yes, that is really how people drink it in Thailand. Local beer often has a very high alcohol content, and the ice helps to mellow the harsh aftertaste, not to mention the effects. Putting ice in one's beer is an acquired habit, but a lot of tourists seem to take to it quickly enough.

## Dee Shapland goes (coco)nuts for Thai whiskey

You may have heard three things about local Thai whiskey. First, it is drunk in a "set." Second, it is hallucinogenic. Third, you can only drink it with a Coke.

The first is mostly true: Thais love their sets, and bars rarely serve Sang Thip or Mekhong by the glass. You will have to buy a set, which means paying for an entire bottle, plus a paraphernalia of mixers, ice cubes, and lime wedges.

About the rumors of secret hallucinogenic additives, frankly I have no idea. I too have heard of secret herbal inclusions, but in my opinion, all that rice whiskeys really are is super strong. If you take it nice and slow, and keep a watch on how much your system can tolerate, you should be okay.

As for Coke being the only good mixer for Thai whiskey, I strenuously disagree with that claim. I have discovered a wonderful alternative to drink Thai whiskey with. And if like me you hate shopping, you'll find this piece of advice particularly useful.

Whenever my girlfriend drags me out to the local markets, I put a small, secret bottle of Sang in one of the many zipped pockets of my shorts. Then I innocently stop at the first stall I find selling fresh green-husked coconuts. The vendor will chop off the top, making a small hole before giving me a straw to drink the coconut water with. I offer my girlfriend the first sip, and win brownie points with her for my thoughtfulness. She drinks a good quarter of the tasty coconut water before passing it back. Then I pull out my bottle and pour in as much whiskey as I can fit.

The vendor looks on in amazement while I carefully cover the hole and give the coconut a gentle shake. There! The shopping trip becomes so much more tolerable after that.

I'd much rather mix my Sang Thip with natural coconut water than Coke any day. The thick outer skin of the coconut makes a perfect cocktail cooler, I don't need a brown paper bag to hide the bottle, and I can drink my concoction anywhere I like.

### The truth about Thai whiskey

Thais call this alcohol "whiskey," but it is often produced from sugarcane or molasses and is in fact a kind of rum. Bottles come in two sizes: *klom* (750 ml) and *baen* (375 ml). The most popular brands are Sang Thip, Mekhong, and SangSom, with an alcohol content ranging between 35 and 40 percent.

### Herbal whiskeys

*Yaa Dong* is a potent concoction of whiskey and a variety of medicinal herbs. It is popular in rural communities, particularly in northern Thailand, where the people have great faith in *yaa dong's* curative powers. *Yaa dong* is drunk straight out of little shot glasses, and sellers will tell you that it's okay to drink a shot every day. However, keep in mind that there are no official recipes, and *yaa dong* makers keep their ingredients a closely guarded secret. There's a real element of risk involved in buying *yaa dong* from street stalls, and a lot of tourists keen to try it prefer to make their own *yaa dong* with local whiskey and herbs they purchase from traditional herbal shops. Our advice for staying safe is to not drink ready-made *yaa dong* anywhere.

### Timothy Talen
### Bull gets buggy over his favorite local snacks

You're in Thailand, and you have come face-to-face with a bug cart for the first time in your life. You are tempted to sample one or two of the cart's delicacies, but are not quite sure which ones to try. That's where I come in. I may not be Zagat-qualified to review bugs, but I've eaten my fair share and think I can accurately describe for you the subtle nuances of a barbecued scorpion as opposed to a pregnant water bug.

As most bug carts sell deep-fried insects, your first time shouldn't be a difficult experience if you rein in your imagination and concentrate on the crunchiness. To allay your fears, remember that most insects come with Thai pepper, garlic salt, and special sauces that mask some of the real taste. If that doesn't help, firmly tell yourself that the bugs are a rich source of protein, vitamins, and minerals.

My recommendation after selecting your bugs of choice is to have a good drink at the ready, preferably alcoholic in nature. You will need to cleanse your palate with this drink throughout the bug-eating process. So, here is my critter checklist. To make your choices even simpler, I have star-rated each bug according my personal taste and experience.

### Grasshoppers (tak ga tan) and crickets (jing leed)
5 stars

These little guys come in two sizes, large and small. A professional bug-eater will warn you to pull the lower part of the legs and wings off before eating. A newbie to the scene will do the same, but only after choking on the sharp protrusions on the lower legs first.

Both varieties actually taste pretty good, slightly fishy with a hint of nuttiness. They can be deep-fried or even cooked with chili and lemongrass and eaten with rice. Once you get past the thought that you are eating a bug, they can be a really nice treat.

### Red ant larvae (kai mod daeng)
5 stars

This is truly a Thai delicacy. Small, white, and wiggly, the larvae are usually boiled for a few minutes and then mixed with a little butter or Thai spices. The taste reminds me of nothing as much as buttered sweet corn, and in my opinion, this is a joy to eat. These little nibbles are great all by themselves, but even better when tossed into a soup or a spicy Isaan salad.

### Bamboo worms (rot duan)
5 stars

These delicious insects are known as rot duan or "fast train" because they grow in length as soon as they are dropped in hot oil. It's difficult to fry bamboo worms without the insides spilling out, and the trick I am told is to cook them on a very low flame. Some say the taste reminds them of French fries, while others say it's more like corn chips. Sprinkle Thai spices and seasoning sauce on them, and this will be one snack you'll find hard to put down.

Eating insects is a rite of passage for tourists in Thailand, and the best way to do it is among good friends and traveling companions. You'll laugh, cheer each other on, make faces, and take photographs that will capture the pinnacle of your Thai culinary adventures for people back home.

### Scorpions *(mang pong)*
4 stars

Scorpions are an upgrade to the everyday bug, menacing when alive and equally so when dead, cooked, and waiting to be eaten. I usually start with the claws and chew my way backward. The claws are crunchy with a slightly woody taste, while the body meat has a gritty crablike texture. The Vietnamese and the Chinese favor scorpion over all other insects, because they believe the sting in the tail will make them strong.

The scorpions' mean look and fearful reputation make them hard to consider as something edible. Several doses of liquid courage with a strong alcoholic drink may be required just to get up your nerve.

### Woodworms *(non mai)*
3 stars

Woodworms are like the Twinkies of the Thai insect-eating world. Their golden brown exterior encases fluffy, tender meat inside. They can be gently roasted over hot coals or fried in oil.

While they have a good taste to them, they are one of the harder insects, psychologically, to get into your mouth. Extra palate cleansing may be needed to smooth their journey down your throat.

### Giant water bug *(maeng da)*
1 star

First, I have to explain that I'm not talking about the run-of-the-mill variety found all over the world. No, I'm talking about the free range (rice paddy) variety that is quite large— Madagascar hissing cockroach large.

I was taught how to eat water bugs by a professional bug eater: a little Thai girl. First, I had to pull off the meaty pinchers and eat them. Then I grabbed it by its head, inserted the thorax into my mouth, and bit down slightly while trying to scrape the thorax away from the body and head. I have to say this was the bug I had the biggest problem with.

The meat, however, turned out to be quite sweet and flavorful. Pregnant female water bugs are considered a delicacy and highly prized for their abdomen full of succulent eggs. Pounded giant water bug is a common ingredient used in making the *nam prik* chili paste that goes into so many Thai dishes. So whether you know it or not, you've probably eaten some already.

In my opinion, the average Westerner will feel the most reluctance eating this bug.

## Buggy beginnings

Insect eating is a tradition that has spread from Northeast Thailand to the rest of the country. If you're traveling in the northeastern provinces, you might see locals using UV tube lights outside their houses at night to attract insects and collect them in buckets. What the families don't consume themselves, they deep-fry and sell in the markets. To supplement income, northeastern Thais migrate to big cities like Bangkok and Phuket, and sell insects on the streets. Usually, their bug-laden carts can be found in busy market areas and entertainment centers, and are frequented by shop assistants and bar girls craving a tasty snack.

## Safety first

Only buy from vendors who have fresh, golden oil in their woks. If the frying oil is old and dark in color, the insects will lose their individual flavors and end up tasting all the same.

## Getting buggy at Aroon Rai

Aroon Rai is a no-frills restaurant in Chiang Mai, just south of Thapae Gate, that is famous for its signature chicken curry. But it also has a menu full of delicious fried insects, and many travelers go there for their first bug-eating experience.

45 Kotchasarn Road
Chiang Mai

## Geena Fife
### seeks convenient sustenance in local 7-Elevens

My alarm clock wakes me up to another gorgeous day on Phi Phi Island. Back home, I would hide my face under the pillow and snooze for an extra few minutes before dragging myself out of bed and off to work. But I am not at home, so I stretch pleasurably and then jump up to put on my swimsuit. Grabbing all the essential items for the day—sunscreen, towel, book, and sunglasses—I run out the door to grab a hurried breakfast, so I can swim while the tide is still high.

Not wanting to waste any beach time by ordering breakfast at a café, which would offer good food but on notoriously slow "Thai time," I head to one of Thailand's countless 7-Eleven convenience stores. On Koh Phi Phi alone, there are three to choose from. Part of my initial exploration of the island had been to identify which of them would become my "local" food source during my stay.

"Sawatdee ka!" I greet the friendly 7-Eleven staff cheerily as I head, almost on autopilot, to all corners of the store, assembling my quick and delicious first meal of the day. After asking one of my new pale-green-shirted friends to cook up a 29-baht ham-and-cheese toasty, I pour myself a 13-baht "small" cup of iced coffee. The smallest size is about the equivalent of a large McDonald's cup—this will certainly kick-start my day! A prepackaged banana "cake" for 10 baht completes my three-course way of breaking fast for the ridiculously low price of about $1.50. A big *kop khun ka* to the staff, and I'm out the door, on my way to the beach to enjoy my food sitting under a coconut tree, reading a book with the background music of waves lapping against the shore.

Can it get any better? Oh, yes it can! After finishing eating, I put my rubbish into the 7-Eleven plastic bag (to dispose of in a bin later) and head into the clear blue water for a swim. Alternating between sunbathing on the beach and cooling off floating on my back in the water, I blissfully lose all sense of time, until the overhead sun and intensifying tropical heat tells me that it is around midday. As the shade of my coconut tree slowly creeps away and then disappears entirely, I know it is time to escape for a while to grab lunch and some air-conditioned relief.

Having worked up quite a sweat, looking at various restaurant options throughout the main village, I nip into my trusty air-con sanctuary to escape the oppressive heat—yes, that's right, my beloved 7-Eleven. As soon as I walk through the automatic doors, the annoying "bing-bong" signaling my entry to the staff, a blast of deliciously cold air hits me full in the face. I feel my overheated body almost sighing in relief.

Unlike this morning, I am not in any hurry, so I take my time looking at the many different brands of bottled water, opening, closing, and then reopening the fridge doors, pretending to struggle with my choice of the right water, while secretly just enjoying the extra coolness that hits me each time I open the fridge door. After I take about fifteen minutes to choose my water, the staff starts looking a bit concerned, so I move over to the toiletries section, wondering if I'm running out of anything.

Eventually, I remember that I am low on sunscreen. This is great because there are a lot of sunscreen brands, and I so can dawdle for a long time. I want to make sure I don't get one with whitening cream in it. While I'm doing this, my stomach admonishes me for not having eaten lunch, so I reluctantly make my selection and head to the counter to join the long queue of tourists and locals procrastinating in the cool atmosphere.

After lunch, I am exhausted by the day's activities (so stressful!), and decide to nap in my room until I feel sufficiently cooled and rested to join a longtail boat tour in the late afternoon.

When I return from snorkeling in clear aquamarine waters, the sky has turned pinkish with the promise of a spectacular sunset. Wrapping a sarong around my waist, I go to the 7-Eleven to buy a couple of cheap Chang beers to drink on the beach while I watch the closing of another day on the island.

Once the sun and moon have properly swapped places in the sky, I wander along the beach to find the nearest restaurant table, where I can dig my toes in the sand and tuck into dinner and a couple more beers. After my meal, I head to a nearby bar and immediately spot something out of the corner of my eye that has become so familiar to me—the 7-Eleven logo. Although this time it is not above a building, signaling the portals to a little air-con heaven, but emblazoned across an Irish backpacker's chest!

Yes, my love affair with 7-Eleven is not something unique to me. In fact, the 7-Eleven is an institution in Thailand, especially amongst tourists, and therefore any decent night market will sell you tops and T-shirts that you can proudly wear to show your support for this pervasive brand.

After a fun couple of hours exchanging travel stories over cocktails with the aforementioned Irish backpacker, I decide it's finally time to head home to bed. But not before I make one last visit to my local 7-Eleven to get some dessert.

Feeling a little more confident than usual, thanks to my indulgence at the bar, I head to the section of the shop that has some of the more interesting edible products I haven't tried. The pink and white sponge sandwich looks delicious, but I finally decide to settle for a familiar ice cream product. The ever-smiling staff are incredibly patient as I struggle to find the correct amount of baht. Once I manage to pay for my dessert, I bid my 7-Eleven friends a fond farewell and promise to see them all the next day.

Which, of course, I do. I wander in sometime in the midmorning with a throbbing headache, feeling very sorry for myself, and go straight to the stock of paracetamol.

### How convenient

Thailand has more 5,500 7-Eleven stores, the third-largest number after Japan and the USA. A lot of foreign tourists depend on 7-Eleven for all of their traveler specific shopping, and people who don't have a taste for Thai food go to 7-Elevens for quick meals. The Smoky Sausage Bites and steamed pork bunc available at Thai 7-Eleven stores are particularly popular with tourists.

# SEEING THE SIGHTS

*Fresh perspectives on must-see attractions*

This chapter may come as a bit of a surprise, because I have deliberately struck the most popular sites in Thailand off the list. As a fan of Thai religious art, I could have easily taken you on a temple tour to some of my favorite spots around the country—for example, the famous mirror-encrusted Doi Suthep in Chiang Mai, but you're an informed traveler, and I expect you've already heard about that. And about the Emerald Buddha and the Grand Palace and the Floating Market ...

All of these well-known tourist attractions are impressive, and ought to be right on top of your travel itinerary. But if you're a frequent visitor who has already seen them, or if you want to customize your Thai experience by adding a few new places that are slightly off the tourist trail, then this chapter has a wealth of offbeat options in store for you.

The experiences our authors have shared are so diverse, I find it hard to categorize and describe them in a few sentences. There are some great ghost stories, like the one by Adam Mico, who visits a haunted house standing morosely at the edge of a village near Ayutthaya, an unhappy tomb for a restless entity whose presence weighs heavily on Adam as he explores the abandoned building. Mick Shippen, on the other hand, enjoys a nice social visit with hundreds of ghosts and spirits who condescend to attend a festival organized by the local people of Dan Sai to honor and appease them.

In Mike Rose's essay, you can read about what is possibly the strangest market on the planet, located on an active railway track in Samut Songkhram. The hawkers set up makeshift stalls, and then periodically rush about removing their merchandise from the direct path of oncoming trains. Once the trains have passed, it's back to business as usual—the stalls are set up again and people continue buying and selling, as if nothing unusual has just happened. Oliver Fennell also suggests "cultural immersion" in a for-Thais-only bazaar at

the edge of an infamous slum in the capital, provided you're okay with the sight of skinless pig heads and mounds of cow intestines lying exposed for flies to surreptitiously lay eggs on.

Relishing the advantages of getting lost, Jenny Beattie does just that in the labyrinthine lanes of Bangkok's colorful Thon Buri district, where few tourists ever have a reason to venture; on the flip side, she practices the art of "finding" as she geocaches with her husband in a Bangkok park. And moving away from busy, urban neighborhoods, Ryan Humphreys invites readers to discover the capital from a new perspective while biking an island paradise floating on the Chao Phraya River.

Because local festivities are as much a part of sightseeing as monuments and museums, the annual rituals of the hill tribe people of northern Thailand are represented in this chapter, with wonderful essays by Nicholas Towers and Stu Lloyd that illustrate the simple joys of celebration—a time when supplementing meager everyday sustenance with a bottle of Sprite is a rare treat.

There is so much going on in this chapter, I'll just have to leave off here and let these highlighted essays serve as a sampler to whet your appetite for many more fascinating sights and experiences our authors have written about. While none of them can quite compete with the scale and grandeur of well-established hot spots that attract thousands of foreign tourists every day, they certainly inspire you to probe deeper into the country, and chart your own course through the many wonders of Thailand

# BANGKOK

*Jenny Beattie
wanders off the map
in Bangkok*

Some people carry a compass around in their heads. Me? No, I'm not one of them. Let me turn twice, and unless I've laid a trail of breadcrumbs, I don't know which direction I've come from. Going "off piste"—off the map, in other words—is an occupational hazard for me, especially if I'm walking around unfamiliar neighborhoods in Bangkok.

I had been living here about a year when I needed to buy some wax-covered thread for a craft class. My teacher drew a map and pointed at it saying, "The shop is over the river, somewhere in those *sois*..." Back at my apartment, I looked at her drawing and then at my bilingual map—the roads she'd drawn were sparse in detail. In fact, they were not even on my map. But I wanted the thread, so I had no option but to follow her vague directions into Bangkok's Thon Buri district, praying all the while that I'd be able to find my way back home afterward.

From the Saphan Taksin Skytrain station, I hopped onto a cross river ferry boat, and within minutes I had reached Thon Buri on the west bank of the Chao Phraya River. So far so good. Thon Buri, very briefly the old capital city of Siam and now integrated into Bangkok, greeted me with delicious smells of barbecuing fish, overlaid with the thick organic odor of rotting weeds and wet litter. I was observed with interest as I disembarked and paid my 3-baht fare. Out in the dappled sun, two motorbike taxis and a street dog lazed. A park next to the ferry building housed an outdoor gym in which three men were working out. One of them grinned and flexed his muscled arm at me.

At the top of the *soi*, I photographed the road sign as an insurance policy. If I lost my bearings, I could show it to a taxi driver. Then, following the map my teacher had drawn, I headed for Krung Thon Buri Road. It was boiling hot, around lunchtime, and there were food vendors everywhere. I stopped at a stall to buy some fruit, but the seller and I, despite several attempts, didn't understand each other's Thai. On my side of the river, I'd pay 20 baht for such fruit, so I just gave him that.

Workers from nearby offices and shops poured out onto the street and formed queues around the vendors for fish balls, sausages, and eggs impaled on sticks. Next to the food, a man had set up a sewing machine; a cobbler resoled shoes, and a blind lottery ticket seller sat with a wooden box of tickets opened hopefully on his lap. Two motorbike taxi men played checkers on a "board" marked in pencil on the flagstone.

Nibbling on my fruit, I turned right at the huge intersection on Somdet Phra Chao Taksin Road, feeling smug that I hadn't got lost yet. But the self-satisfied feeling didn't last long; the road turned quite unexpectedly into a bustling seafood market, and I walked between rows of stalls feeling somewhat disoriented. Ice melted off stall counters heaped with fish, crab, and lobster, and the fishy-smelling water sloshed onto the pavement. Alongside the fish market, a row of permanent shops hawked a variety of Wellington boots, and with my feet feeling wet and vulnerable in sandals, I could see why.

This market was what is commonly referred to in Asia as a wet market—an open place where meat, fish, and produce are sold in bulk. The fish stalls gave way to exotic vegetables that sellers had arranged artistically into piles. The market traders scrutinized me as I took photos of rattan containers full of ruby red chilies, and they talked about the *farang* to their neighbors. Platters of cooked food, stir-fries, salads, and curries were spread out on tables with canopies above to thwart the out-of-season rain that had been falling on the city over the past couple of days.

With so many unfamiliar vegetables, fruits, and fish to look over and photograph, I didn't realize how far I had walked until Wongwianyai, a colossus of a roundabout, loomed up in front of me. At its center stood a statue of King Taksin poised for battle on his horse.

Taksin was the last king before the present Chakri Dynasty began. He established Thon Buri very briefly as the capital of Siam. His reign ended badly—in madness followed by his execution—and nobody cared to remember him until the 1950s, when Italian sculptor Corrado Feroci commemorated his achievements with this sculpture, which now keeps watch over traffic movements in the Wongwianyai roundabout.

Coming face-to-face with King Taksin's statue wasn't good news in the least. It meant I had gone too far. My hand-drawn map stopped here, and not knowing what to do next, I retraced my steps. Dodging a motorbike piled high with leather hides, I plunged into Charoen Rat 1, the nearest *soi*.

This *soi* turned out to be yet another marketplace, laden with goods like zips, threads, and ribbons that spilled out of the shops and onto the pavement. I went into one of the stores and asked, "*Poot phasaa Angrit dai mai?*" (Do you speak English?) The shopkeeper gazed back, impassive, as though I was speaking a language he did not recognize. I scrambled inside my bag and pulled out a piece of waxed thread. "*Mee mai, ka?*" (Do you have this?) Heads shook. I tried more shops and was met with the same blank stares.

Zigzagging across the *soi*, I spotted leather, chains, buckles, and studs being sold. In one window, I saw rows of tiny sculptures neatly arranged on shelves. Finally, the penny dropped and I realized where I was. The sculptures were in fact high heels without their shoes. I had stumbled into a cobblers' market.

On the opposite side of the street there was one last shop left to try. I went there to show my sample without any real hope of success. Incredibly, I hit pay dirt! The shop girl pointed at a shelf full of waxed thread. One shop among hundreds in the area had what I was looking for; and I, who was helpless as a baby even with a map in hand, had managed to find it.

Feeling jubilant, I bought the thread and attempted to retrace my steps, but it was no good; I had turned around too many times. My luck for the day, thankfully, held up, and help soon came in the shape of a woman selling oranges, a food vendor, two motorbike taxis drivers, and a university student who spoke excellent English.

Between the five of them, they managed to direct me back to the pier, from where I took a return ferry to my familiar Saphan Taksin station and waited for a train. I was back on the map again, and feeling ten feet tall. Not only had I hunted down the elusive waxed thread shop, but I was going home with my senses filled with the sights, sounds, and smells of ordinary Thai market life in the old streets of Thon Buri.

### Getting to Thon Buri

The Skytrain network will now take you all the way to Thon Buri. The line from Saphan Taksin has recently been extended to two new stations—Krung Thon Buri and Wong Wian Yai—on the Thon Buri side of the Chao Phraya River.

### Chao Phraya Express Boat

All of the resources you need to travel confidently up and down the Chao Phraya River can be found at the following website. In particular, make sure to check the boat schedules and pier location map before setting out.

www.chaophrayaboat.co.th

### Oliver Fennell explores a neighborhood market in Bangkok

To think of Asian markets is usually to think of hectic, smelly, noisy sprawls of shacks and stalls peddling oddities sourced from the surrounding seas and farms. Sure enough, you can find that in Bangkok, but not if you stick to the tourist trail of Patpong and Chatuchak. The latter has appeal in its own right, but I'd never recommend the aggressive, overpriced Patpong market stalls. If you really want to see a local Thai marketplace—cheap, authentic, and frenetic, with a side order of strange—head for Klong Toey Market.

There you can dive into the city center's premier, straight-from-the-farm shopping destination and prepare to get thoroughly lost—but that's all part of the fun, isn't it? While attempting to navigate the haphazard layout of Klong Toey, you will have to take care not to slip in piles of discarded vegetables, puddles of sludge, and hosed-down walkways as you go. You'll be dealing with a sensory onslaught, both pleasant and uncomfortable.

The sounds are as you'd expect in an open market—squawking fowl and screeching vendors—while the smells range from the delightful tang of fresh herbs and fruits to the hold-your-nose pong emanating from raw meat and flyblown fish sitting under the tropical sun. Visually, the bountiful array of colorful fruit and vegetables, some of which you may never have seen before, is offset by tables laden with guts, buckets filled with unidentifiable (but allegedly edible) brown slop, and peculiar delicacies such as entire pigs' faces skinned from the skull and stacked atop each other, flattened so that their mouths are spread in hideous and lopsided piggy grins.

Beyond the foodstuffs, plenty of other things are for sale, albeit arranged rather incongruously. DVDs can be found next to a squid shop, sneakers are for sale alongside giant tree fungus, and there's even a hairdressing salon and a mechanic's garage tucked somewhere inside that melee.

Foreigners may be greeted with curiosity. The vendors almost certainly won't know any English. That means the epic bouts of haggling one would normally associate with Thai markets are out. But not to worry, as the goods are cheap enough to render that unnecessary. In any case, do you *really* want to take home that punnet of chickens' feet or half kilo of blood cake?

To make specific retail recommendations would be pointless, as giving directions would be an exercise in futility, but if you want to take a walk on the wild side, follow the directions given below and keep left from that point, parallel to the main road, until, after two or three minutes, you come to a covered area that runs between the road and the canal. Here, you will find trays of slithering eels, bowls of live tortoises, large helpings of snails, a variety of edible insects, and a veritable wealth of frogs—bagged by the dozen (live or dead) and skinned, minced, or ready-cooked on a stick.

All this, and not an overpriced Singha T-shirt or elephant-themed trinket in sight. Yes, Klong Toey Market may be light on health and safety regulations, and may sometimes offend Western sensibilities, but it's entirely authentic and intriguing, and worth a photograph every ten seconds. Go on, take a look, and start clicking away.

### Getting to Klong Toey

Take the subway to Queen Sirikit Convention Center station and take Exit 1. From there, walk straight ahead and then up the footbridge and over Rama IV Road. Go down the first set of steps after you've crossed the road, and you'll be at one corner of the market. Alternatively, hop into a taxi, and, if the driver does not speak English, ask for "Talad Klong Toey."

### Klong Toey slum

The eastern end of the market backs onto the infamous Klong

Toey slum, one of the largest slums in Bangkok, where more than 120,000 of the city's poorest residents live in crammed tenements next to open drains, filthy rail tracks, and garbage dumps. Drugs, prostitution, and all sorts of poverty-induced crime are rampant here, and though there are NGOs such as Mercy Centre working to help residents find a more hopeful future, it isn't advisable for tourists to casually wander around the area. You'll know you have reached the slum when the market stalls give way to tin shacks. Stop right there, turn around, and walk away.

www.mercycentre.org

### Better safe than sorry

Sanitary concerns dictate that you probably shouldn't eat at any of the "restaurants" in the Klong Toey Market. Even if street food doesn't usually upset your constitution, the market itself is generally dirty and attracts rats and vermin.

### Jenny Beattie geocaches for hidden treasures in Bangkok

"It's so impersonal," I say, giving the evil eye to the GPS unit nestled in my husband's grip. "Why can't we explore someplace that's in the Bangkok guidebook?"

Although I have tried to suspend my cynicism, the excitement of geocaching is still a mystery to me. This hobby, as my husband David has explained to me numerous times, is a kind of high-tech treasure hunt in which adventurers seek caches around the world with the help of a GPS, and hide them for other geocachers to find.

The cache might be a small container with only a logbook and a pencil to record your find, or it might be a bigger box holding gifts or trackable items like "geocoins" and "travel bugs." All geocachers, including David, are members of geocaching websites where they interact with each other and report their finds, but I just can't get excited about sharing a hobby with people who don't even know each other.

"It'll be fun," my husband assures me. "We're going to some parks around Bangkok; you'll enjoy it."

David, his colleague Roger, and I climb into a cab. David asks the taxi driver to take us to the junction of Ekamai and Rama IX Roads, which is a warren of concrete structures. It doesn't look at all like the green space he promised me.

Underneath Rama IX Road's concrete expressway, we climb out of the taxi. "This park we are going to is called Suan Phan Phirom," David says, shouting to be heard over the noise of traffic. My map shows the roads crossing and looping over the page

BANGKOK

like cursive handwriting, with a small green space squeezed in between.

As soon as we enter the park, the men fix their eyes on the GPS's display screen and set off on their hunt. I watch their receding backs, and then turn away to take in my surroundings. Each province in Thailand has its own species of tree, and Suan Phan Phirom contains an example from all seventy-six provinces, planted randomly across the park. Four concrete columns from the expressway cut right through the center, but the gardeners have built a frame around them, decorated with boxes of foliage and flowers as a kind of disguise. As parks go, this one is pretty idiosyncratic.

I make my way toward the men, past a basketball court, an outdoor gym, and some picnicking Thais. David greets me at the edge of the jogging track. Some way off, Roger is dancing—a leg-slapping, British Morris dance. He must be very excited at finding the treasure, I remark. "No, it's big red ants," David says with the wisdom of a man who has been here before. "They have a nasty bite."

After a bit of rooting around where X marks the spot, they cheer; they've found the cache, and they bring it over to share it with me. It's a tube, about six inches long with a piece of paper and tiny stub of a pencil. "We sign the logbook," David explains, "and then we log on to the website and let the geocaching community know that we've found it."

Huh? Is that it? I am underwhelmed.

With the first mission accomplished, we move on to our next hunt at Wachirabenchatat Park, located next door to the famous Chatuchak weekend market. It used to be a golf club, and its undulating landscape echoes the fairways and bunkers of its previous life. This park, I gather from the men, is home to multiple caches. Oh joy!

David and Roger hurry off along a path. Oblivious to a glimpse of Thai life, they pass a Buddhist monk counseling a man near a copse of trees. I leave them to their caching and head for a small humpbacked bridge nearby, from where I can see four separate groups having their photographs taken. Clearly, Wachirabenchatat Park is a backdrop to wedding and graduation pictures galore. Nearest me, an impossibly cute Thai girl in a floral skirt gazes at lily pads in a pond for her father's picture. David and Roger double back past me. "Wrong way," they say, watching the GPS screen as a group of Thai students swerve their bicycles to avoid hitting them.

I tag along, and we go about a hundred meters before stepping off the road and plunging into a wilderness not intended for the public. "The rules say geocachers mustn't be spotted by noncachers," David explains, "so quite often the treasure is hidden away from busy areas." Under a huge tamarind tree, David and Roger scuffle about, poking with sticks, for another cache. Some ten minutes later, the cache is declared not found.

We move on, dodging bikes, lovers, friends, and families taking photos in front of blossoming Rosy Trumpet trees. The men march and I wander through a mock-up of Bangkok's roads where small children can learn to ride tricycles safely. Scale models of the Rama VIII Bridge and Victory Monument add authenticity to this miniature Bangkok tableau, and all that is needed to complete the picture is a recreation of the city's traffic jams.

We stop at a small playground in the park, where the men believe a cache could be under a miniature bridge. They assign themselves on either side of it to search for the treasure, trying hard to look inconspicuous, but the location yields no cache.

The last hunt before lunch takes us over the old golf course fairways, through a cool, lime green grove to the very edge of the park's boundaries. The GPS leads us to the hot spot, a tree, leaning over a stream.

This time, we really hit upon a treasure. As well as the usual logbook, there's a geocoin that one member has registered and is tracking on the website as it makes its way around the globe. At last, I feel a frisson of excitement, thinking of the tiny role we will play by sending the geocoin on to its next leg of the journey.

There's another gem in the cache: a postcard placed nearly a year earlier. The geocacher, a student at the University of Vermont, has requested we write on the postcard and return it to him.

Holding the postcard in my hand, I feel a sudden spiritual connection with the student who buried it here with so much hope. I imagine him waiting patiently for a year now, for it to arrive in his mailbox. What was buried as an ordinary postcard will now go back to him as a precious keepsake.

I glance at David with a silent apology for misjudging his hobby, and for not appreciating his excitement in discovering new places in Bangkok and hiding and finding caches. How, I now wonder, had I ever imagined this hobby to be anonymous and impersonal?

## Geocachers unite!

The world's geocache community is growing every day, and the following website is their favorite virtual meeting place. For a newbie, the website is very easy to navigate, with step-by-step instructions on how to get started. Register as a member, get hold of a GPS unit, and you're in the game! For clues to caches in Thailand, search on the website by country name. In the Forum section, you can meet fellow cachers in Thailand, who are always ready to help with tips and suggestion

www.geocaching.com

## Closer to home

On the above website, click on the "Hide And Seek A Cache" tab on the homepage, and enter your postal address. The website will throw up a list of the caches hidden near where you live—unless you're extremely unlucky, there should be at least a few. This is a great way to get into the excitement of caching and preparing for the experience before your trip.

### Geocoins and travel bugs

Geocachers use special coins and dog tags that have unique tracking numbers. Using these numbers, the owner of a geocoin or a travel bug can follow the progress of his or her cache as it hitchhikes around the world.

## MUANG BORAN

### Caroline Fournier leaves Bangkok to do Thailand in a day

People never seem to linger very long in Bangkok. Businessmen come in for a few days to do what businessmen do. Tourists make a hurried stop to see the major attractions and then quickly move on to explore other parts of Thailand. As I checked in to my hotel, the young man at the desk seemed surprised that I was staying for ten days in the city—an eternity in his eyes!

I think it's a bit of a shame that most people miss out on really getting to know Bangkok. In these ten days, I found many obscure sites within the city that were just as interesting as the famous ones. With the luxury of time on my hands, I was able to visit a handful of these lesser-known attractions, many of which became the best experiences of my trip. This included places like Muang Boran (also known as the Ancient City) where very few foreign tourists ever seem to take the time to go.

Muang Boran, to put it simply, is a miniature Thailand that squeezes the country's 514,000 square kilometers into a 240-acre plot. Shaped like the map of Thailand, Muang Boran contains replicas of 116 of the country's best constructions, laid out among picturesque hills, rivers, and forests. It goes without saying that I was skeptical when I first heard about Muang Boran, expecting the site to be nothing more than a kitschy theme park or akin to seeing the Eiffel Tower in Las Vegas. But, although it was a good distance away from the center of town and therefore necessitated a long cab ride, the experience was well worth it.

Once I arrived at the gates, I paid my entrance fee, and armed with a map and a bicycle—both included in the fee—I started making my way down the pathways that wind throughout this property. You can visit Muang Boran on foot, but considering the heat, sun, and sheer vastness of this property, I do not recommend it. A car is also an option, but it would be a shame to simply look at these beautiful structures from behind glass windows and not take the time to enter and fully experience them.

Muang Boran's half- and full-scale constructions of famous *stupas*, *chedis*, wats, and Buddha images are realistic. Thailand's ancient art, history, culture, and way of life have been distilled and presented with such close attention to detail, I quickly forgot that I was looking at replicas. Instead, I felt transported to the many corners of this beautiful country, and all within a few hours.

In addition to the ancient heritage sites, Muang Boran also has recreations such as a typical northern Thai village, an old market town, and a floating market. The Northern Thai village takes you back in time with its small wooden homes on stilts. The paths that run through the old market town are lined with shophouses where artisans work at their handicrafts, stall owners sell traditional products, and snack vendors make fresh sweets and savories. The floating market emphasizes the importance of rivers and *klongs* (canals) in the daily lives of the Thai people.

This market was my last site of the day. Cycling through 240 acres of Thailand's history under a hot sun meant that by midday I had worked up quite an appetite. I stopped there for a steaming bowl of soup from a woman simmering two huge containers of it on her small boat.

For tourists short on time or with a fixed itinerary that explores only a small pocket of Thailand, Muang Boran is an easy way to round out a trip and feel that you have seen more of this country. It is also a great place to visit if you are traveling with children.

Even on weekends, there are few tourists, and the sheer vastness of the property never makes it feel crowded. Just be sure to come early, as there's a lot of ground to cover in a single day. And don't be put off by the fact that it's a recreation—the experience, I can assure you, is as real as it can get.

### Muang Boran (Ancient City)

Samut Prakan
Kilometer 33
Old Sukhumvit Road
Bangpu
(02) 709-1644
www.ancientcity.com

### Getting to Muang Boran

The most convenient way to go to Muang Boran is by taxi. But if you want to take a bus, hop onto bus 511 (Pinklao-Paknam) to the end of the line and then catch minibus 36, which passes by Muang Boran's entrance gate.

### Transportation tip

If you have never cycled in Thailand, as you make your way around Muang Boran, stay on the left-hand side and remember that the traffic circles run clockwise. Caroline learned this the hard way—she almost had a close encounter with one of the maintenance trucks coming at her from the opposite direction in one of the traffic circles!

# BANG KRA JAO

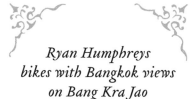

## *Ryan Humphreys bikes with Bangkok views on Bang Kra Jao*

"*Farang, farang*, you!" a local resident called out, smiling and pointing to an empty seat.

I had come to what looked like a dead end, and the guy was inviting me to join him and his friends for a drink. I mimed back that drinking would make me lose control of my bicycle. The men raised their glasses and waved goodbye as I cycled deeper along the pathway into the mangrove forest.

I was on the island of Bangkachao—or as the locals call it: Bang Kra Jao—a secluded oasis of tropical forests, swamps, and meandering canals, located bewilderingly close to Bangkok. This proximity—just a short river taxi ride across the Chao Phraya—to all the noise and pollution of the big city made Bang Kra Jao's existence a little hard to believe. It was as if some invisible barrier around the island held the miasma of civilization at bay, preserving the fresh woody fragrance in the air I was breathing as I pedaled down a network of raised concrete paths that crisscrossed the island.

These raised paths gave Bang Kra Jao a unique character of its own. It also made the island an ideal place for bicycling. At times, the paths became really narrow with the marshy forest floor lying a good distance below on either side, but that added more thrill to the ride, as long as I was careful, refused friendly offers of a drink, and watched where I was going.

Happily, I pedaled past Thai houses on stilts, some built close to the elevated path and some set deeper in the forest. I watched women stoking the fires under their woks, and girls in calf-length skirts chasing each other with the unfettered joy of being done with school for the day. I saw a fisherman, knee deep in the water, a cigarette hanging from his mouth, casting his line.

I felt like an intruder, an uninvited guest cycling in and out of the lives of these people, and smiled my apology if we made eye contact. I knew there were temples, markets, farms, and parks on the island, but it did not matter to me if I found them. I was not looking for anything in particular.

As I pedaled through the mangrove forests of Bang Kra Jao, I caught glimpses of Bangkok's skyline bristling with tall towers and high-rise buildings. It felt odd and enervating at the same time, cycling along a concrete path in a tropical jungle with the modern outlines of the glitzy city hovering so close in view.

### *Getting to Bang Kra Jao*
Travel companies such as Spice Roads offer eco-tours to Bang Kra

Jao. But if you want to go it alone, take a river taxi from the Municipal Pier next to the Klong Toey port in Bangkok. Even if you don't cycle, you can explore the island by hiring a motorcycle taxi to show you around.

www.spiceroads.com

### Roll your own

As you meander around Bang Kra Jao, you are sure to come across an incense workshop. You can observe how the local artisans make scented cones and joss sticks, leaving them to dry in the sun. You can also try rolling a few joss sticks yourself or buy some as a souvenir.

---

## AYUTTHAYA

### Adam Mico photographs a ghostly presence in Ayutthaya

We were all at lunch when my brother-in-law Raywat suggested we go visit a haunted mansion called the Green House, a short distance away from the city of Ayutthaya. My brother-in-law can always be counted upon to come up with unusual ideas for family day trips. Moreover, he is an amazing storyteller, and he had us enthralled with his account of this century-old mansion, built by a wealthy merchant named Khun Pitak Bori Harn.

Apparently, the merchant fell ill one day and was taken to Bangkok for treatment. When the doctors told him that his days were numbered, he elected to return to his beloved mansion and die in the presence of his family. Alas, he perished in the boat that was bringing him back to Ayutthaya, and his final journey home remained incomplete. Harn's grief-stricken widow refused to go on living in the ill-fated mansion and sold it off to the government immediately afterward.

The Green House has probably remained unoccupied from the day the merchant's family walked away from it. And though there are no documented deaths that have occurred here, the local people talk of photographed *winyarn* (souls) and unexplained physical contact.

It was midafternoon by the time we reached the Green House, a short one-hour drive from Bangkok. We found some villagers entertaining themselves with a cockfight in the front yard of the mansion, and the occasional cawing of their birds in the pit seemed to reinforce the warm, sleepy silence that typically hangs over rural Thai neighborhoods at this time of day.

Approaching the two-storied mansion, we could see how the Green House got its name. Most of its exterior paint had been leached away, but many shuttered doors and windows had somehow managed to hold on to their minty green color. These wooden panels were wide open, as if trying to shield as much of the rotting, moss-covered outer walls from view as possible, but the sloping roof lay exposed, missing tiles in patches through which the wooden rafters were now peeping through.

Clearly, nobody had bothered to keep up with maintenance work at the Green House, but the building still exuded an architectural arrogance that forced us to stop and contemplate its grand past.

There were no signs of life around the mansion, certainly no one to seek permission from, so we cautiously stepped inside, our footsteps sounding unnaturally loud on the ancient teak wood floor. The front room of the Green House was a dark, cavernous, empty space. Once my eyes had adjusted to the dim light, I saw a yellowing piece of newspaper tacked to one wall, carrying an article about a television crew's spooky experiences in this house. Apparently, a female reporter had actually felt an invisible hand touch the small of her back, giving credence to local legends about paranormal "touching" incidents here.

But it was broad daylight outside, and we weren't going to be scared off by a newspaper clipping now that we had come this far. We moved from room to room on the ground floor, finding a sparse collection of items that had been pushed well back against the walls: ancient display cases filled with dusty mementos; garlands of dried flowers; a framed photograph of merchant Harn; and holy shrines—several, in fact, as if reinforcement was required to fight the powerful demon in residence. A headless mannequin wore an expensive, pink, traditional costume with a golden belt wound around the waist. A long scarf of crimson brocade was casually thrown across its shoulders, and it was suspended off the floor as if it had been hanged to death.

This sight made my stomach turn with fear, and I quickly followed the others up the stairs to the mansion's second floor. No way was I going to be left alone with this mannequin.

Upstairs, the layout of the rooms was pretty similar to that of the ones below, but the air carried a heaviness that was making all of us feel uneasy and short of breath. The atmosphere was getting claustrophobic. If there was indeed any spirit living at the Green House, it had to be here. One room was dedicated to Mrs. Harn's shrine, and items that may have been her personal belongings lay around it. A rocking chair made of wicker was directly opposite Mrs. Harn's shrine, and I couldn't help feeling that her dead husband's spirit often sat there and watched her.

I asked my son if he would like me to take a photograph of him next to the shrine. The boy flatly refused. He didn't want to go anywhere near Mrs. Harn's possessions, and only agreed to stand close to it when my wife offered to join him in the picture. Snap. I took one photograph. Snap. I took another. I checked the two photos I had just taken, and noticed something very odd. The first photo had a translucent spherical shape toward the top. The second photo, shot immediately after the first, showed no such irregularity.

Something wasn't quite right, and I couldn't stand being inside the Green

House a moment longer. Gathering up my family, I left posthaste.

When we returned to my in-law's farm, Raywat called the workers over and told them what had happened. None of the farmers had been to the Green House themselves, but they paled when Raywat mentioned the translucent sphere in my picture. It matched the description of other *winyarn* activities at the Green House they had heard of over the years.

So what had really happened to my first photograph of the upstairs shrine? Could the mysterious spherical shape simply have been a lens flare or some trick of light? Of course. But was it also possible that the mansion was indeed haunted and I had unwittingly captured a manifestation of it on my camera? Frankly, I don't know anymore.

If you asked me this question as I was rushing out of the Green House that day, I would probably have said yes. But now that I have established some mental distance from the incident, all I am going to tell you is that visiting the mansion was the eeriest experience of my life.

It took me days to get over the Green House, especially the spooky mannequin that looked so out of place and creepy in that decrepit, dusty building. I could not stop wondering: who had put it there, and why? Since I have no plans to return to the Green House anytime soon, I guess I'll never know.

### The Green House

This mansion sits on the bank of the Noi River in Tambon Ammarit in the Phak Hai District of Ayutthaya Province. The locals call the mansion "Baan Kaew" (Green House), and you will be able to locate it easily with their help. If you're visiting on a weekend, stop by the Lat Chado Market and ask for directions there.

### Lat Chado Market

This hundred-year-old market has recently been revived as a weekend affair. It is the latest hot shopping destination in Ayutthaya. Walking around Lat Chado, with its quaint wooden architecture and well-preserved shophouses laden with handicrafts and locally made sweets and savories, is a wonderful way to extend your day trip to the Green House.

# LOPBURI

### Laura Bartlett
### Jurica monkeys around in Lophuri

Before I arrived in Lopburi, I had heard strange stories about the hedonistic life led by the town's huge population of resident long-tailed macaques.

Apparently, these monkeys liked to fine dine on exotic foods and had a discerning eye for fashion. They promenaded around the town's historical ruins with the confidence of ownership and passed their time socializing with tourists. And when they needed a break from the grind of daily life, they hopped onto a train and holidayed in Chiang Mai.

I almost expected to hear next that they paid for their train tickets and charged a fee for entertaining travelers. But no, they were simply Lopburi's biggest tourist attraction, and the locals took great care of them. Plus, they were in the business of petty thievery: stealing hats, handbags, and anything else that caught their fancy.

As we were driving into Lopburi, we were told that our first stop was going to be Prang Sam Yot, an ancient Khmer shrine that is a playground for the Lopburi monkeys. Our guide, Nok, advised us to leave all our belongings in the bus. The monkeys were very attracted by shiny golden things, so along with the hats, sunglasses, and bags, the little pieces of jewelry we wore had to come off too.

When we disembarked in front of Prang Sam Yot on Wichayen Road, I squealed with delight. This was the first time I was seeing monkeys that were not in a zoo. There seemed to be hundreds of them, and they were all so busy, ducking in and out of entryways, sliding down walls, climbing up poles, and swinging from the electric wires.

Nok led us to the front of Prang Sam Yot, an imposing structure with three corncob-shaped towers that looked like something out of an Indiana Jones movie. The years, and possibly the

monkeys, had been hard on this ancient temple, and much of its carved stucco surfacing had leached right down to its skeleton of brick and sandstone.

Nok was taking our group to see a Buddha statue that had miraculously remained intact inside the bowels of this grand relic, but I hung back to watch the antics of Prang Sam Yot's simian population instead.

Making my way back to the entrance, I almost walked into a female monkey sitting on the ground with a baby latched onto her chest. She made eye contact with me and then held my gaze until I felt impelled to reach into my pocket and pull out the pear I had bought earlier on from a street vendor. The monkey took the fruit gently from my hand and started to eat with great relish.

It wasn't long before "word" spread around Prang Sam Yot that something tastier than the peanuts other tourists were giving was available on the grounds. Another mother and baby arrived on the scene, and wanted a share of the fruit. My little friend wasn't sharing, but the pieces of pear she dropped were quickly picked up by the second mother.

Both of the monkeys were enjoying the fruit so much they didn't even realize that the sticky juice was drenching the poor babies clinging to their chests. At that moment, I wished I had brought a ten-pound bag of pears.

My husband, Cory, came by to tell me that the monkey scene was even livelier on the other side of the temple. When I got there, I was delighted to find hundreds more monkeys in all shapes and sizes. The speckled sandy color of the temple was such a perfect camouflage for their brown little bodies that I jumped every time some of them moved and made their presence known.

I became totally unaware of my surroundings as I took one photo after another. Everything here was a photo opportunity. The monkeys didn't seem to mind the intrusion of my camera; in fact, they patiently held their poses long enough for me to finish taking their pictures.

I was kneeling on the ground, composing a shot with three female monkeys lined up against a wall, when I felt a light tap on my shoulder. Before I could even turn to see who it was, a flash of sharp pain ran through my skull. Owww! One very young monkey had come up from behind and pulled a bunch of hair right off my head!

Things happened so fast after that. A local Thai boy suddenly materialized from nowhere with a slingshot and pinged the young monkey with a pellet. The monkey retreated at once onto a high ledge on the walls of the temple. There he sat with a wounded expression on his face, flossing his teeth with my hair!

It was all so bizarre I started to laugh in spite of the stinging pain in my scalp. Especially when I was told that my mane of long, golden hair had caused this unusual act of aggression. I had washed my hair that morning, and it had dried under the hot sun into a mass of thick, shining curls. The inexperienced monkey was dazzled by the sight of the golden hair and couldn't resist stealing a handful.

When I looked around for the Thai boy to thank him for his help, I was amused to discover that my knight in shining armor wasn't above reproach either. With his slingshot and a cohort in tow, he was frightening the monkeys into surrendering anything of value they had stolen. If the monkeys refused to be frightened, he and his friend bribed them with food.

We boarded our bus soon after that, and Cory regaled our tour group with the story of my encounter with the Prang Sam Yot monkeys. If it wasn't for the boy with the slingshot, he said, I might have left Lopburi bald.

He was joking of course. The monkeys at Prang Sam Yot were perfectly comfortable around human beings, and my young molester had meant me no harm. Nevertheless, the incident made for a good story.

"Now wouldn't that be a great shampoo commercial?" a member of the group remarked. "Hair so shiny, even monkeys can't resist it."

Oh, if only Cory had been there to capture my Lopburi hair robbery on camera! I wasn't sure about commercials, but it certainly would have been the most viewed among all the Thailand travel videos I uploaded on YouTube.

## Lopburi Monkey Festival

On the last Sunday in November, the residents of Lopburi hold a popular festival in honor of the city's monkeys. Thousands of people come to watch and photograph the monkeys as they dine in style off an elaborate Chinese buffet. The meal is funded by the people of Lopburi who believe the animals bring good luck and prosperity to the city.

### Helping out

More than a thousand monkeys live in Lopburi, and they are constantly in need of medical care. Accidents and injuries happen every day, and many are suffering from hernias and other ailments caused by the unnaturalness of their urban existence.

To help the monkeys, a hospital has been set up in Lopburi. The institution runs several programs, such as monkey care and monkey training. Any donations or volunteer aid from visitors will greatly assist this hospital in carrying on with its work

www.warthai.org

## SAMUT SONGKHRAM

### Mike Rose discovers a secret railway in Samut Songkhram

I was shopping in the Mae Klong market in Samut Songkhram, a pleas-ant port located sixty kilometers west of Bangkok. Walking around, idly looking at products, I saw some railway tracks cutting through. Since the market stalls actually covered the tracks, I figured it was an old, disused line.

Suddenly, the stall owners—in unison, it seemed—began to move their stalls to the side of the railway tracks. As I stood there, watching them hurriedly clear the tracks and wondering what on earth was going on, a distant whistle sounded. A few seconds later, a diesel rail car appeared and actually *ran through* the bustling market before disappearing into the distance. Once the train had passed, the stall owners set up their shops again and carried on trading as if nothing had happened.

This strange sequence of events led me to my discovery of a part of a commuter railway line that I now know runs from Bangkok to the town of Mahachai and onward to Samut Songkhram ... after passing through the Mae Klong market.

The reason I call the railway "secret" is because you won't find any mention of this route on the schedules of the State Railway of Thailand. For sure the local people know this line, which they call the Mae Klong–Mahachai railway, but to most foreigners it remains an unseen part of Thailand.

The line was opened in 1905 to ferry fresh produce from the two sea ports it serves to Bangkok, but it was never connected to the rest of Thailand's rail network. Over time and with the advent of a better road system, the freight traffic on the line declined, but passenger trains continued to use the tracks, providing a commuter service between the capital and the two towns.

The Mae Klong–Mahachai railway is actually two lines separated in the middle by a river. The trains on this route begin their journey from a small station called Wong Wain Yai in Bangkok's Thon Buri district and travel on the first leg to Mahachai town. The Tha Chin river flows through the town, and as there's no railway bridge, passengers have to alight from the train and cross the Tha Chin River by ferry to the rail terminus on the opposite bank. From here, the line picks up again and continues to its final destination of Samut Songkhram.

Traveling on the Mae Klong–Mahachai railway is a comfortable mean der through the Thai countryside with each leg of the journey lasting about an hour, with a five-minute ferry crossing in between. The first half consists mostly of urban scenery and glimpses of a fish market, but after crossing the Tha Chin River, things get more interesting.

If you're lucky, the train will slow just outside Mahachai, and you can join the local passengers in throwing bananas to a troupe of monkeys waiting eagerly by the tracks. Not long after this simian feasting point, you'll pass through an area that is the heart of Thailand's salt farming industry. Fields or "pans" are flooded with seawater, which is then allowed to evaporate, leaving behind a large residue of pure salt. You will see many mounds of this salt, raked into piles for collection by armies of workers toiling under the hot sun.

And finally, there is the ride through the Mae Klong market as the train approaches its last stop. Viewed from inside the train, these scenes are just as memorable as when viewed from outside. The day I discovered the secret railway, I had witnessed the nonchalance with which stall owners dealt with the nuisance of a train running regularly over their business space. When I rode the train into the market on another occasion, I had the unsettling experience of being within touching distance of stalls and piles of goods pushed just far enough from the track to avoid damage. For regular commuters and the Mae Klong market folks, this may be just an everyday event, but for someone like me, who is used to taking every safety precaution when near a moving train, it was nothing short of a recklessly daring stunt.

*Riding the rails*

Several trains run the Mae Klong–Mahachai route every day, but timetables are difficult to find, since they do not appear on the State Railway of Thailand's schedules. The practical thing to do would be to contact the Wongwian Yai station (02 465-2017) or the Samut Songkhram station (03 471-1906) for exact times.

*Double vision*

A half-day trip on the "secret" railway from Bangkok is a rewarding experience on its own. But you may consider an overnight stop at Samut Songkhram to explore the floating market, eat at the fresh seafood shacks, and visit some of the beautiful riverside temples.

You can also visit the statue of Chang and Eng, the first conjoint twins the world had ever seen. Chang and Eng were born joined at the chest in 1811 in Samut Songkhram. They were spotted loitering near the port by some American sea captains, who took them back to America and promoted them as the "Siamese Twins" in a traveling show. A statue in Samut Songkhram depicts the twins as adult men of the world, standing proudly in their smart Western suits. To learn more about them, read *Chang and Eng* by Darin Strauss.

## KOH KRET

### Robert Carmack potters around on Koh Kret

I knew nothing about Koh Kret, a seemingly remote island in the middle of the Chao Phraya River, until the topic came up during lunch with some of my Thai acquaintances. We were dining in Nonthaburi, just north of Bangkok, savoring a Thai noodle dish that my friend Jerawat said could be traced back to the Mon people. The same Mon who fled from Burma to Thailand and now made pottery on Koh Kret, an island that was just across the river from where we were eating.

The designation word "Mon" is not Thai for the generic word for the people of Myanmar: Burmese, or Bamar. Instead, it applies to one specific ethnic group in Myanmar (formerly Burma). Living predominantly near the city of Moulmein, the Mon people once ruled the country prior to the Bamar kingdom's rise and were regular allies with the Thais against Burmese subjugation. Since the eighteenth century, however, they have become a stigmatized minority. Some of the Mon, victims no doubt of the royal pogroms of ancient Burma, migrated to Siam as guests of the Thai king at that time.

"Today they live on Koh Kret and make pots. They kiln," explained my Thai friend. "And they make many sugar dishes." Both understatements, as I would discover during my subsequent trip to the island.

An interesting piece of history about Koh Kret itself is that it did not begin life as an island. Rather, it was a bend in the mighty Chao Phraya River that somehow inconvenienced an early king during one of his boating pilgrimages. The meandering river detour caused such royal outrage that a canal was dredged in 1722, and eventually widened so that it became part of the river itself, creating an island. Not so accidentally, it also isolated the Mon foreigners and kept them from contaminating the locals.

For years, the Mon people lived on Koh Kret without any Thai influence to dilute the island's essentially Mon characteristics. So when tourists go to Koh Kret today, they can still hear the Mon language being spoken and see traces of Mon heritage, which is quite different from mainstream Thai culture.

The main attraction on Koh Kret is of course the pottery that Jerawat mentioned. The inhabitants of the island make unglazed pottery in a unique Mon style that is renowned in the region, the finest pieces fetching hundreds of dollars for the intricate floral motifs etched onto wet clay. Locally made pots are so plentiful that I saw visitors being given a pot for free whenever they bought a soft drink, iced tea, or coffee. Simple urns and vases, but a nice souvenir nonetheless to take back home.

The secondary attraction, which incidentally got me more excited than anything else on the island, was the food. I saw the locals deep-fry edible flowers, deliciously dipped in a wet rice-powder slurry, and knew I had come to a good place.

There are numerous restaurants in Koh Kret serving up all the local Mon specialties for tourists to try. One of them is *khao chae*, a dish so well-known that it has since been adopted into the royal Thai cuisine repertoire. The rice is delicately scented with a candle, then steamed and tossed in ice water. Accompaniments to *khao chae* are many, ranging from fried sweetened shrimp paste to stuffed

capsicum and a jerkylike sweet beef or pork floss. These are eaten in tandem with the chilled iced rice and are particularly popular during the sweltering summer months of April and May. Another specialty I love is the *kao maw*, fermented sweet sticky rice cakes, which were literally dripping with natural alcohol.

But perhaps the best of all are the variety of Mon desserts—most made simply with sugar and colored agar agar and shaped into delicious bite-sized morsels. No trip to Koh Kret is complete without a stop at one of the island's specialty dessert restaurants dotting the coastline.

The island is not big. You can do it on bicycle or cover most of it on foot in just a few hours. There are several *wats* to explore, notably Wat Paramai Yikawat, celebrated for its nineteenth-century mural paintings, which is an innovative blending of Thai and Western Renaissance art.

With its abundance of food and pottery shopping, Koh Kret can be a nice, short getaway for tourists who need a break from the bustle of Bangkok. Just make sure to go on a weekend, as the Mon expect visitors on Saturdays and Sundays and set up their shops accordingly. That is, unless bicycling around a crowd-free island is just the kind of quiet day trip you're after.

### Getting to Koh Kret

The quickest way to reach Koh Kret from Bangkok is by Chao Phraya Express Boat. Leaving from Sathorn Pier, it goes directly to the island on Saturdays and Sundays. On other days, you will have to take the boat to Nonthaburi and then do the rest of the distance on another (green flag) river express boat or hire a longtail boat. A river cruise to Koh Kret from Maharat Pier is another option.

## Hiring bicycles

Once you have reached Koh Kret, you can hire a bicycle on an hourly or per-day basis from Wat Paramai Yikawat.

## KOH SICHANG

*Mick Shippen examines the squid-fishing culture of Koh Sichang*

The view of Koh Sichang from Sriracha's boat-lined pier doesn't look promising. Heavily laden barges, freighters, tugs, and ocean-going tankers sheltering between the mainland and the island make it more like a maritime industrial zone than a scenic holiday spot. However, if you take the forty-five-minute ferry ride to the Koh Sichang harbor, you will find that the unattractive approach hides

a delightful squid-fishing town and beaches that still attract relatively few foreign tourists.

As you get off the ferry, you will be met by very curious-looking local taxis (a combination of a *tuk-tuk*'s rear and a motorcycle's front end) waiting to take you into Koh Sichang, a lazy, laid-back town that wears its typical ramshackle Thai charm with ease.

The small haul of fishing tackle shops dotting Koh Sichang's streets, stocked to the gills with rods, lines, weights, hooks, and fluorescent lures that no self-respecting squid could resist, confirms the town as a popular weekend destination for sea anglers. Piers and rocky outcrops are favorite spots to try to land a catch. Although stocks of crab and clams are now considered to be dangerously low, squid fishing is still a major industry here. As you come up to the island, you may notice the brightly colored squid boats pushed up against the wave-worn jetties. Their bows are adorned with garlands and flowers to placate the spirits of the sea, as they patiently await sunset before venturing out in search of a catch.

The repeating patterns of drying cephalopods, carefully arranged on blue canvases stretched across wooden frames, decorate the main street like an impromptu art exhibition. Highly prized for quality, Koh Sichang dried squid is the perfect chewy accompaniment to an ice-cold beer when roasted over a barbecue.

For hundreds of years, long-distance seafarers have sought safe anchorage at Koh Sichang, and the discovery in these waters of a Chinese junk dating from 1290 AD and loaded with porcelain confirms that the island was a significant port on the ancient trade route. Then, when the Chinese Taechiew fled their homeland in the early 1900s and sailed into the Gulf of Thailand, they settled on Koh Sichang before moving on to other parts of the country.

The temple of Chao Phor Kao Yai on the northern end of the island confirms the town as an important early settlement for a sizable Chinese community. Dragons guard the steep flight of steps that lead to the recently renovated temple, and the original shrine is housed inside a cave at the rear of the site. Legend has it that shortly after the porcelain-laden junk went down off the coast, sailors reported seeing a golden light emanating from the cave. Inside, a large stalagmite in human form was discovered. Now covered with gold leaf, this mysterious figure continues to act as a Siren, drawing Buddhist devotees from far and wide.

Koh Sichang attracts its fair share of sun worshippers as well. A narrow concrete road winds its way through rocky, shrub-covered terrain, over to the western side of the island, where it drops sharply down to Haad Tam Phang—a beautiful cove of white sand and clear water. Here, in the shade of a small grove of beach umbrellas, there is good seafood to be eaten and a warm sea to enjoy. With only the occasional fishing smack to break the horizon line and sunsets as vivid and intoxicating

as a Bloody Mary, this area seems far away indeed from the industrial eastern shore.

Despite its diminutive size, Koh Sichang has enough of interest to keep visitors pleasantly occupied for several days at a time. For an island a mere hundred kilometers from Bangkok and only a hearty cast north of Pattaya, the fact that Koh Sichang has remained largely unscathed by tourism seems nothing short of a miracle.

Beyond the freighter-strewn waters is an island of character and charm, a place that has little in common with other Thai resorts and beach towns. Unsullied by mass tourism, it remains a rough-cut diamond cast into the Gulf of Thailand.

### Getting to Koh Sichang

This island is located twelve kilometers off the coast of the fishing town of Sriracha in Chonburi Province. From Bangkok, buses leave from Mo Chit and Ekamai stations every thirty minutes and will get you to Sriracha within two hours. Get off opposite the Robinson Department Store in Sriracha and take a short tuk-tuk ride to the quayside. Ferries bound for Koh Sichang leave every hour from here and take forty-five minutes.

### Getting fresh

Koh Sichang has some good seafood restaurants, but there's nothing like fishing for your own or choosing a bucket of the day's catch at the market by the pier and grilling it at the beach. The squid are succulent and sweet. Make sure to buy a small bag of the chili sauce the locals make to eat them with.

## BAAN AYO ANAMAI

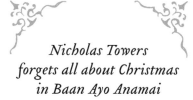

### Nicholas Towers forgets all about Christmas in Baan Ayo Anamai

Many people will tell you that the wandering Akha hill tribe saleswomen, known as the Frog Ladies because of the croaking wooden frogs they sell, are little more than a novelty or a nuisance. Wearing gigantic silver headdresses and a profusion of gaudy jewelry, they startle you with their dramatic appearance, and then seize on that split second of confusion to try to sell you a frog that croaks if you rub its back with a wooden stick.

It was quite by chance that I got friendly with a group of Frog Ladies who hustled their wares around Bangkok's Khao San Road. Patrick, a drunken Irishman who was staying in the hotel where I worked, had invited twelve Frog Ladies to sit with him at an outdoor bar, and he was buying

round after round of drinks and food for them. When he saw me pass by, he asked me to join them and act as translator because neither he nor the women had any idea what the other was saying. Over time, this acquaintance blossomed into friendship, and the Frog Ladies invited me to visit their village anytime I wanted.

I decided to take them up on their offer during Christmas. December in Bangkok was searingly hot, and with most of the population being Buddhist, it wasn't going to be much of a holiday here anyway. The Akha tribespeople, on the other hand, had been converted to Christianity, so I suggested that I celebrate with them instead. The Frog Ladies were delighted and told me all about the pig they would kill for the Christmas meal.

From Bangkok, I traveled north to Chiang Rai and took a bus on to Mae Chan town, where my friends came for me in a pickup truck. They took me high up a mountain to Baan Ayo Anamai, their small village nestling in the mist. News of my arrival spread like wildfire, and children and adults alike gathered to stare at me with ill-concealed curiosity. Cool-looking local youths dressed like Thai pop stars in tight jeans and gravity-defying hairdos pulled up on their motorbikes to give me the once-over. After this initial inspection, I was escorted inside the village, where to my surprise I saw no celebratory lights or decorations to mark this day as Christmas Eve.

It was December 22, and for reasons I did not understand, the

Akha villagers celebrated Christmas on December 23, two day earlier than the rest of the world. Their Christianity too, as I discovered later, was tempered with animistic beliefs in ghosts, spirits, and superstitions. Though the Christian missionaries had succeeded in converting the people of Baan Ayo Anamai to Christianity, they had only really gone so far as getting them to accept Jesus + The Ten Commandments + God. The birthday of Jesus Christ, as a result, was a low-key affair.

I explored the village and couldn't help but note the poverty of the people. Most owned a few livestock and farmed to feed themselves. Though handicraft was a modest source of income, the villagers didn't seem to be making any themselves. I guess the croaking wooden toads that had facilitated my visit here were sourced from other Akha villages and sold by the Frog Ladies in Bangkok. The richer folks had modest brick houses to live in, while the others had huts and hovels made of straw and bamboo. In each home I peeked into, I saw women and children wearing heavy jewelry and black Akha garments with colorful aprons and sashes. I was surprised to see that they didn't take their unwieldy silver headdresses off even while they worked around the house.

Because the church service was about to begin, I hurried off to join the villagers and hear a Thai pastor give a short Christmas Eve speech. A banquet followed for the adults, including mostly standard dishes that they probably ate every day. While we grown-ups enjoyed the food, the children hummed in the background, delirious with anticipation for the main Christmas Eve event, which would be all about them—a raffle that only the kids could participate in.

I decided to check out the prizes that were causing so much excitement, and my heart almost broke when I saw what they were: tubes of toothpaste, packets of Lay's potato chips, and wads of chewing gum. The star prize was a 1.5-liter bottle of Sprite.

I marveled at the difference an expenditure of 3,000 baht would have made to this humble cache, and then admonished myself for thinking like a typical Westerner. Toys and goodies beyond the village means would only upset the balance of this society and give the kids something that would later make their everyday existence seem joyless and bleak in comparison. They were so happy at the possibility of winning the bottle of Sprite—who was I to measure that happiness in material terms and say it wasn't good enough?

With the raffle, the Christmas Eve festivities ended, and the villagers began to disperse into the night. It had been a great celebration this year, I heard them say to each other, and I wasn't going to quibble with that statement this time. I just felt grateful and honored that they had let me share it with them.

I woke up next morning after a great night's rest in the hut of one of the Frog Ladies. It was 7 a.m., but the household was already up and about. I washed my face, gave the hostess's little grandson a quick lesson on how to say "good morning," and took my tea out onto the porch.

A weak winter sun had risen today, and the village looked clean and tidy with the morning dew keeping the constant dust down. Invigorated by the freshness of the mountain air, a few roosters were still clucking their 5 a.m. wake-up calls. In neighboring huts, the Akha women were already at work, sweeping their front porches, mending old clothes, or beating the chaff off rice grains that would be boiled later for the midday meal. Somewhere in the distance, I head the croak of a wooden frog as a stick was rubbed up and down its back to check for sound quality. It was back to life as usual in the Baan Ayo Anamai village.

As I stood on the porch enjoying my tea and watching villagers as they walked down the unpaved path in front of my hostess's hut, I was startled to see an elderly woman with a tattered red Santa hat, which she wore at a jaunty angle over her Akha headdress. The sight made me almost choke on my sugarless tea. How could I have forgotten? *Today* was Christmas Day.

### Getting to Baan Ayo Anamai
To reach Baan Ayo Anamai, take a bus from Chiang Rai to Mae Sa-long, and then hire one of the blue pickup truck–taxis from the bus stop to cover the fifteen-kilometer distance to the village. Baan Ayo Anamai is signposted along the way, and you're unlikely to get lost because there are no turns on the road until you reach the village.

### Wooden frogs
If, like countless tourists in Thailand, you have fallen prey to a Frog Lady's sales pitch, here's what to do with the wooden frog once you get home. Place it near the main entrance door of your house, looking inward, and make it croak anytime you go on an important assignment. The guttural, lifelike sound the frog makes when you rub its back apparently brings good luck, and the placement is a feng shui–approved method of inviting wealth into your home.

## DOI LAAN

### Stu Lloyd raises a toast to "big bottoms" in Doi Laan

At the invitation of my Lisu friend— "Mimi from the Mountains," as she calls herself—we are in Doi Laan (*doi* being the Northern Thai word for *mountain*) to attend the New Year festival of the Lisu hill tribe people. The Lisu originated somewhere near Tibet and live mostly in China's Yunnan Province, although a few have filtered down to Myanmar, Laos, and Thailand over the centuries.

"This festival is a good chance for all the Lisu in Thailand to meet," Mimi tells me. "They choose this month because of the school holiday, so that students can join the festival."

Somewhere between 500 and 750 Lisu (plus five *farang* guests, including us) have descended on this spartan mountain village, about forty-five minutes southwest of Chiang Rai city. Every spare corner in Doi Laan's homes, shacks, and mud huts is occupied by guests. We can tell those who've come back from the "big smoke" of Chiang Mai—they're the ones sporting dyed, Korean-style hairdos and using cell phones.

The method of imparting Lisu history to the gathered crowd is song, and dancing can go all night, for three or so nights. But this is no Full Moon rave. To the untrained eye (mine) it looks like "Ring Around the Rosie." "Dancing in a circle around the holy village tree is our way of showing respect to it," explains Mimi over the rather discordant rasp of the *fulu* bamboo flutes.

But before someone wades into the mosh pit with abandon, it pays to know the strict rules of the game. "Any man can hold a woman's hand, unless she is the man's relative or cousin or shares the same last name," says Mimi. "It is forbidden to hold a relative's hand; it is taboo. If it is necessary, then women or men must have something like a handkerchief in between, so that their hands will not directly touch each other."

During the dance, only men can ask women to hold their hand or to join the dance. "Except if that woman is a bit drunk or wanted to make a joke to some men," laughs Mimi with her trademark glowing smile.

Indeed, corn whiskey has a lot to answer for in these festivities. It is served up in liberal lashings. Not too dissimilar to the worst Scotch I have ever tasted, but with a burnt, earthy aftertaste—clearly, it'll be a while before I get a job in PR with the Lisu Corn Whiskey Marketing Board. The Lisu, when toasting for prosperity, have a curiously endearing expression. Rather than saying "cheers," they say, "*Bobo laay,*" which means: "Here's to your big bottom."

Mimi ushers us into her mum and dad's house (which doubles as the village clinic), where we sit on tiny wooden stools raised just inches above the dirt floor. The meal they serve is stunning, a mixture of spicy vegetable and meat dishes, all courtesy of the jungle. "We don't go to market for anything except sometimes meat," declares Mimi proudly. Chickens tiptoe gingerly through the house. Pot-bellied pigs bask in the sunny pen outside. She is momentarily distracted by a call on her mobile phone.

The only other modern intrusion here seems to be Crocs shoes. I spy several fluorescent pairs competing for visual attention with the rest of the blindingly colorful outfits. But no clothing item is richer than the hats called *u-thue*, each garnished with hundreds of red strings and beads.

Imagine Liberace in a Foreign Legionnaire's cap, and you get the idea.

"The hats are more like a fashion now with all the color," Mimi says. "In the past we used knitting wool. The strings hanging down are to please the spirit. The spirit likes to see the color. It is springtime for the Lisu, so the spirit would love it and be happy to see spring as well."

It is a real privilege to experience this cultural life from the inside as we have. But I have just one marketing suggestion for the Lisu if they're trying to promote their festival as a tourist attraction: how about adding some snappy break beats to the raspy music and packaging this festival as a—wait for it—Fulu Moon Party!

## Flower children

Most of the Lisu hill tribe people who migrated to northern Thailand over the last eighty years are known as Flowery Lisu (Hua Lisu), because of their brightly colored and stunningly embellished everyday clothes. In China, on the other hand, they are known as Black Lisu (He Lisu) because they wear stark, black traditional costumes. During the New Year festival, the colorful Flowery Lisu people dress even more elaborately, bringing out silver ornaments, robes, and accessories they save to wear only on this special annual occasion, which is partly a religious event, partly a fashion show, and largely an opportunity to strike up romances and initiate marriage alliances.

## Lisu New Year festival

Held on a rotational basis in different Lisu villages in Northern Thailand, the Lisu New Year festival takes place during January or February, corresponding with the Chinese New Year. The date changes every year according to the lunar calendar, so you will need to check with the Tourism Authority of Thailand to find out when and where it will be held on a particular year. In earlier days, the Lisu did not allow tourists to attend their festival, but foreign participation is no longer considered taboo.

www.tourismthailand.org

## Getting to Doi Laan

The village of Doi Laan is a two-hour drive north from Chiang Mai or a forty-five-minute drive south from Chiang Rai on Highway 108.

# DAN SAI

*Mick Shippen gets into Dan Sai's ghost party spirit*

I had always been under the impression that the northeast region of Isaan was flat and barren. Yet here I was on the road to Dan Sai, a district in Loei Province, traveling across a range of rolling mountains that pushed up from beneath a thick carpet of bottle-green foliage. As I rounded a corner, the rice paddies on the fertile valley floor came into view, spread out like a patchwork tablecloth decorated with cocktail-umbrella houses and Christmas cracker novelty animals. It was apparent that I was being carried toward a town that promised to be different from anything I'd seen before.

For three days each year, Dan Sai transformed into a town full of ghosts. Under the guidance of headman and shaman Jao Paw Guan, the residents welcome the return of the spirits and join with them in boisterous celebration. The day before the festivities were due to begin, I sat with the headman at the Wat Ponchai temple, and while his followers listened attentively, this strikingly calm man answered my questions about the Phi Ta Khon ghost festival.

"Nobody is really sure how or when this festival came to Dan Sai, but it is the only town in Thailand in which it takes place," he told me.

It is up to Jao Paw Guan—and the spirits—to decide when the festival actually begins. Although it is usually held sometime during the fourth lunar month (June or July), the exact date often isn't announced until just before the event. Claiming to be in direct contact with the spirits, the shaman patiently waits for word from them before giving notice.

On the first day of the festival, I watched the locals come out as *phi ta khons*, or "ghosts wearing masks," to conceal their identity as they accompanied the spirits in a colorful parade through the town.

From daybreak, the rice whiskey flowed freely, and to the uninitiated such as myself, it appeared that perhaps all the tradition and ceremony was merely an excuse for a damn good party. It was evident that I didn't have a ghost of a chance of avoiding it, and sure enough, a glass of the town's finest brew was soon thrust unceremoniously into my hand by an enthusiastic reveler. I was in no position to refuse, and fortunately my good-natured host was as free with information as he was with the liquor.

"Twenty or thirty years ago, the masks that people made were very plain," said my increasingly animated bartender. "We used sticky rice baskets and drew simple faces on them with soot and turmeric paste."

Apparently, people used to discard the masks after the festival, as it was considered bad luck to keep one in the house. Today, however, they have become prized possessions, and the best ones can sell for thousands of baht at the end of the festival.

As the procession began, I could see for myself that cheap throwaway masks were no longer in vogue. Members of the present-day ghostly cortege now took their craft seriously. What were once simple, almost childlike creations had evolved into an elaborate form of artistic expression. The sticky rice basket still featured in the construction, but for the main elongated face, a dried frond from a coconut palm was used. Over the years, the facial features, particularly the nose, became more exaggerated. Beautifully painted, the highly stylized masks were no longer tossed out once the festival was over.

By midday, the previously sleepy provincial town had been well and truly jolted from its slumber. Curiosities were plentiful. Men plastered with mud and adorned with necklaces of oranges and limes filed past, followed by groups of young boys painted black from head to toe. The sight of thousands of people in kaleidoscopic costumes and ornate masks was a visually arresting, spiritually uplifting, and, it must be said, somewhat surreal experience. Here was the entire population of Dan Sai town in joyous pursuit of the unseen!

To even the most casual observer, it would be obvious that the festival was a thinly disguised fertility ritual. It was a dramatic attempt to provoke the clouds into unleashing the season's rain. The procession was led by the *phi ta khon yai*, a pair of enormous ghost effigies, both of which stood stark naked. In addition, many of the villagers carried with them wooden phallic symbols, the belief being that if a touch of good-humored vulgarity is brought to bear on the proceedings it will encourage *fon tok fa pa*—rain and thunder.

Day 2 of the ceremony included a rocket festival, when firecrackers ripped through the sky over Dan Sai and exploded with what was hope-

fully some strong, cloud-bursting salvos. And on the last and final day, the festival took on a much more sedate and serious air when the town's older residents made their way to the local temple and listened to sermons.

Meanwhile, the Phi Ta Khon spirits slipped quietly back into the forest, where they would protect the people of Dan Sai from a distance, until they could come out and show themselves again at the festival next year.

### Getting to Dan Sai

The nearest airport to Dan Sai is fifty kilometers away in Loei. From Loei, board a bus bound for Phitsanulok, and get off en route at the Dan Sai stop.

### Dan Sai Folk Museum

Located inside the Wat Ponchai temple, this museum offers a record of the town's history going back four hundred years. The Phi Ta Khon is a major part of the display, and you can learn all about this unique festival here. You can also see live demonstrations of Phi Ta Khon masks being made every weekend. The museum runs a little souvenir shop where you can buy Phi Ta Khon merchandise such as masks and ceramics.

### At the movies

*Phi Ta Khon: Ghosts of Isan* is a documentary by Robert Mills and Richard Bishop, filmed during the ghost festival in Dan Sai in 2004. Available on DVD, the film manages to capture the raw frenzy of this extravagant costume show with strong visuals and haunting, catchy Molam country music.

# PHUKET

*Raaj Sanghvi photographs his favorite Phuket shophouses*

I love Phuket's historical Old Town. It's a world away from the city's popular beach scene, and not many tourists come this way. Phuket's image as a holiday resort is so well ingrained in the visitors' psyche that I guess it's difficult for most to even imagine that the city has a wealth of cultural attractions to offer, as well.

But the fact is that Phuket was a boomtown long before the first tourist ever set foot here. It was an exciting destination— not for pleasure seekers, but job seekers, who came to get rich quick by working Phuket's lucrative tin mines. Immigrants arrived in the early 1800s from China, Penang, Malacca, and other parts of Southeast Asia, and with the settling of each community, Phuket's multicultural heritage was further enriched. Over the next hundred years or so, fancy residences, busy markets, and gorgeous temples were built in styles that reminded the wealthy immigrant traders of their homelands on distant shores, and foreign languages, food, religion, and artistic ideas intermingled to create a unique "Phuketian" way of life.

When Phuket's tin industry finally collapsed, on account of a sudden drop in global tin prices, the buzz around the city gradually died, too. What remained from its heyday was a living legacy of a multiethnic society, fantastic examples of Sino-Colonial architecture in the Old Town area that still connect the city to its once-glorious past.

Every time I visit Phuket, I take myself off on a walking tour of the Old Town. I roam its eight main historical streets, stopping to admire the well-preserved Chinese temples, browse in secondhand bookshops, enjoy a hot and spicy Baba-style meal, or simply sit in a café and laze away the afternoon sipping endless cups of the strong local coffee.

Recently, I even added a mission to my aimless wanderings: I took a camera along and made a photo tour of Thalang Road. This is my favorite street in the Old Town, running east-west right through its center. Thalang Road was the commercial hub of Phuket during the height of the tin-mining boom, and its Sino-Colonial architecture, along with its closely-packed buildings, impressive facades, and charmingly latticed entryways, offer great opportunities for photography.

SOUTHERN THAILAND

My plan was to concentrate on Thalang Road's "shophouses"—buildings that were literally a combination of a shop and a house. Built narrow and long like railway boxcars, these hybrid structures go back to British colonial times, when traders used the front to conduct their business, and the back to house their families. An interesting design feature in most Old Town shophouses is an open-to-the-sky courtyard built inside them. In all probability, the families in residence would gather here to relax and enjoy some fresh air after sundown without being seen in public. A surprisingly large number of the existing shophouses still carry on with traditional trades, while others have been converted into restaurants and bars.

Usually, I linger around these shophouses to see how work and life coexist within these quaintly designed buildings, but today I was on my photography tour, and so without wasting any time, I went to one of my favorites: Guan Choon Tong, the oldest Chinese herbal medicine shop in Phuket.

For nearly a century, the same family has been in residence here, grinding up medicinal herbs that they store in a warren of cubbyholes lined along the wall or in hundreds of tin containers that surely must have been made during Phuket's tin-mining days. I shot several pictures of the exotic interiors, breathing in the aroma of dried fruit, bark, and roots that must have been hanging in the air ever since the store first opened. There was a long line of customers waiting patiently to be served, but the owners of Guan Choon Tong graciously posed for a quick picture for me, looking as ancient and reliable as the cures they were selling.

My next stop on Thalang Road was its most attractive shophouse: China Inn Café. Unlike the Guan Choon Tong herbal store, which probably hadn't seen a lick of paint in the last hundred years, China Inn had been grandly renovated inside and out. A colorful, wood-carved entranceway led me into the elegant interiors of the restaurant that looked almost like a museum, with owner Supat Noi Promchan's sentimental collection of old Phuket memorabilia strategically displayed on every available wall, mantel, and tabletop. Walking deeper into the restaurant, I photographed a cozy little garden that had now replaced the shophouse's open-air courtyard and made a mental note to return with a book someday to spend an afternoon here among the trees and shades.

By the time I emerged from China Inn, it was almost noon. The hot July sun propelled me in the direction of a small lane off Thalang Road called Soi Romanee, where I could get more shophouse photos as well as a pint of chilled beer at the Glasnost Law & Notary Public Bar.

I always enjoy strolling up and down Soi Romanee—a lyrical name that somehow goes well with its notoriety as Phuket's red-light district during the mining boom era. Though the brothels closed long ago and the pleasure girls have disappeared, many of the shophouses standing shoulder-to-shoulder along this *soi* have been converted into bars and restaurants, and so the entertainment continues.

The facades here are as attractively colored and decorated as many others scattered around Old Town, but the lack of busy traffic on Soi Romanee gives you the chance to admire them in peace. I took a few photos of the impressive paintings and woodwork that embellished the entrance doors on this *soi*, and then headed toward Glasnost for the cold beer I had promised myself.

The appeal of Glasnost is its reputation as a "lawyers' hangout"—a watering hole where the lawyers of Phuket come to relax and talk shop. You're welcome at Glasnost even if you don't practice law, though, and sometimes it's fun to just sit inside this refurbished shophouse, have a drink, and soak in the warm, friendly atmosphere that often characterizes a place patronized by regulars. Puchong Tirawat, the proprietor, has captured the essence of old Phuket in his interior decoration, and even the tea and coffee services are presented with a touch of traditional ceremony.

But I had no time to hang around and do my usual Glasnost people-watching. My family was flying in from New Delhi to join me, and I had to hurry back to the hotel. While I waited for a cab that would take me to the Laguna Beach Resort, I looked over my Old Town photos, glad that they hadn't come out too badly. They were my own compositions—not perfect, but personal, just like the neighborhood itself.

## Walking Old Town

Before you embark on a walking tour of the Old Town, pick up a free copy of the Phuket Town Treasure Map. The map offers a comprehensive two-kilometer walking route through the Old Town's eight main roads. Hotels, restaurants, shops, temples, historical sites, and everything else of tourist interest are clearly identified in both English and Thai. The map is published by Art & Culture Asia, and can be downloaded from the company's website. To find the Old Town map, click the "maps" tab on the homepage and choose Southern Thailand from the drop-down menu.

www.artandcultureasia.com

## Guan Choon Tong

16 Thalang Road
Old Town, Phuket

## China Inn Café

20 Thalang Road
Old Town, Phuket

## Glasnost Law & Notary Public Bar

14 Soi Romanee
Old Town, Phuket

## Book lover's paradise

Another Old Town treasure, South Wind Books is a great

place to buy secondhand books and magazines. The attraction of this bookstore is that it sells books in all major European and Asian languages.

3 Phang Nga Road
(Opposite the Kasikorn Bank)
Old Town, Phuket

*Palate pleaser*

The Kopi de Phuket restaurant started life as a coffee shop, and to this date serves the best strong *gafae boran* (traditional sweetened coffee) in the Old Town. Its Baba food—a fusion of Hokkien Chinese and Thai—is unapologetically home-style and completely authentic. The small, carefully crafted menu offers a selection of unique dishes. Look out for the daily specials.

61 Phuket Road
Old Town, Phuket
www.kopidephuket.com

# PATTANI

## Karen Coates notes the quiet beauty of Pattani

The sun falls over this dazzling town, and silence emerges with the moon. By day, Pattani's yellow-painted shops and homes absorb the sun as only tropical walls will do. Everything gleams until the hours grow dark and the streets go bare. Then, the only commotion is that of a thousand swiftlets fluttering their way home after a day in flight. Nothing else stirs.

It's the quiet that emerges amid disarray. Since 2004, thousands have died in violence across southern Thailand's largely Muslim provinces of Songkhla, Yala, Narathiwat, and Pattani. It's called an Islamic insurgency, but no one knows precisely what's happening or why. And the people, both Muslims and Buddhists, have suffered.

I sit on a wooden bench as dusk comes with the birds. Their soothing song is everywhere. Their flurry paints the sky like a Jackson Pollock painting in motion, all stripes and squiggles and splotches of feathers. I chat with an old woman who has gray hair and a fine complexion. She's lived here forty years. She watches the birds' routines and talks about the trouble.

"Now no one can stop it," she says, though her neighborhood has seen no disturbance. "There is no problem here." This is her home, and year after year, she remains.

Pattani wasn't always this way. The city beckons with brilliant sun and the scent of the nearby sea. The air is spiced with clove cigarettes and stubborn heat. This is a region more Muslim than Buddhist, more Malay than Thai, with the local language of Yawi dominating conversations on the street. Yet a sizable Chinese population takes root here as well. This area belonged to the independent sultanate of Pattani, until Thailand annexed the land in the early 1900s. A policy of forced assimilation left scars that never healed. Cultures and ideologies have clashed ever since; separatists have fought for an independent land.

But the people of Pattani exhibit a pride in their history and who they are. My guide, a beautiful young Muslim woman named Wilaiwan, tells me Thais everywhere love to smile. "In the north people speak very sweetly," she says. Around here, she says, the sincerity of a person's face runs deep. "In the south, people smile with their hearts and mouth."

Wilaiwan shows me her Pattani. She takes me to an area where Chinese men gather at a little café, sipping orange Thai tea. They chat within view of the Leng Chu Kiang Shrine, a rainbow-colored attraction that was once the destination of Buddhist pilgrims from distant lands. It's surrounded by Chinese medicine shops and pleasant vendors selling dried fish. There are no customers. No smog, no filth, no traffic, no crowds. Only colors and light. It's like stepping into a storybook written for you, the only reader, to enjoy.

I travel with Wilaiwan to the local market, the liveliest avenue in town. It's a cacophony of sensations— grilled pandanus treats, bananas and oranges, chili sauce and fish sauce, long beans, glittery eels, big messy butcher blocks and the repetitive *zhhh zhhh zhhht* of a coconut shaver, creating a mound of white flakes.

Yet I am the spectacle here. Heads turn and shopkeepers stare. Women in long flowery veils ask Wilaiwan about her new friend. "People here rarely meet foreigners," she says. But they're eager to share their food, and it is through the flavors and textures of Pattani that I come to know it best.

Wilaiwan takes me to a local restaurant, and we eat fried crabmeat with black pepper and shiitake mushrooms. The manager offers a plate of clams and mussels—a gift. We share this dining room with only one other customer.

At night, we eat Melayu food on the street leading toward Prince of Songkhla University. The hour is early; the street bustles with young people. It is an oasis of life in the otherwise quiet night. We stop for plates of *kao yam*, "the most nutritious dish," Wilaiwan says. Vegetables, herbs, *budu* fish sauce, fish powder, coconut, and chili mixed with blue rice colored by the tranquil hue of a pea flower plant. The dish fills my mouth with such an intriguing combination of sweet, salty, fishy, hot—it leaves me wanting more.

More time to explore this place, more time to eat bamboo curry and crab sausage and crispy fried *krue poh*, a local snack of fish on a stick. I'd like to follow a fleet of colorful boats as they head to sea, then back again as the men unload their catch. I'd like to linger beneath the evening stream of swiftlets, then visit the old gray-haired woman again to see what she has cooking in her kitchen. Perhaps another time, I will return. After the silence lifts, when Pattani is beautiful—and as free as its birds.

## Exploring Pattani

Located in southern Thailand and reached from Bangkok by bus, Pattani is a former Portuguese, Dutch, Japanese, and British trading post (during the 1600s). Today it gives travelers a glimpse of daily life for the country's Muslim population.

## GENERAL THAILAND

## Stu Lloyd joins friends on a trip down memory lane

My first trip to the Kingdom was as a young lad in early 1988. After a three-day sojourn exploring the fabled pleasures of Bangkok, I marched into my boss's office in Hong Kong and promptly requested a transfer. "*Everyone* wants a transfer to Thailand," he said, "join the queue behind me."

But as the saying goes, if you hang around the pond long enough, you're bound to fall in someday. That plunge, feet first and with boots on

and all, happened in 2009, when I sold up everything in Australia and moved to Chiang Mai.

My only regret is I didn't make the move earlier. My friends regaled me with stories about the "good old days" in Thailand—-the rip-roaring Vietnam War era, the hedonistic pre-AIDS decades, the days when Phuket was just a few shacks along Patong Beach. And for every person who said, "You shoulda been here ten years ago," there was another who declared, "You shoulda been here twenty years ago."

But twenty years is not much in the great scheme of things. I have been lucky enough in my travels to meet three *farang* personalities who generously indulged my curiosity as I listened slack-jawed to their stories of how Thailand used to be ... more than sixty years ago.

Brigitte Opfer, who lived in Bangkok from 1948 to 1958 as the wife of a Lever Brothers' factory manager, still has vivid recollections of the legendary Railway Hotel, which in its heyday epitomized the exclusivity of Hua Hin as a beach town for the royals, the rich, and the famous. "It was lovely; you could sit looking out at the topiary garden and play solo all day long. But you could only go to the beach before nine in the morning, and then again in the evening. At other times, the sand flies would come and eat you alive." The topiary still stands at the Railway Hotel (now the Centara Grand Beach Resort & Villas Hua Hin) with its surrealistic menagerie of elephants, deer, birds, and other exotic animals. But there is no sign of the pesky sand flies these days.

The hotel, built in 1923, has had a long and proud history of pampering its customers with elegant, Western-style hospitality. Its colonial-era architecture—despite a thoroughly modern overhaul—echoes with nostalgia the same way the Oriental in Bangkok or the Raffles in Singapore do. The airiness of its lobby, the tinkling of the piano as you arrive, the blue and cream silk outfits of the dainty front office staff who come forward to greet you, all recall a bygone era when the Railway Hotel was the favored playground of celebrities, millionaires, and high government officials.

Brigitte's fond memories of the oysters sold in Hua Hin in extra-large portions are still as fresh as the oysters themselves. "We had to order a hundred, because it wouldn't be decent to ask for less," she says. "They were so cheap ... about 10 pence for a hundred oysters. We all ate as much as we could, and the rest had to go in the bin because we couldn't keep them."

Seafood is still a huge draw in Hua Hin, with many good seafood restaurants porched on the wharves along Narosdamri Road. The "10 pence for a hundred" bargains may be a thing of the past, but the oysters remain very cheap: huge, succulent, and buttery, served with chili and lime and toasted garlic. Sensational!

As for the famed Oriental (now the Mandarin Oriental Bangkok) on the Chao Phraya River, Brigitte was less enamored by it, though she was a reg-ular guest there anyway. "The Oriental was the best at the time, but it was still a dump," says Brigitte of Thailand's first and most famous hotel. "The rooms were fantastic though. They were enormous, and you had a very large balcony as well. But you had to walk for ten minutes down that long corridor—if you forgot something in the room, that was too bad. Also, you couldn't use their towels. The maids dusted the rooms with those towels, I think, and then vaguely washed them before putting them back in the bathroom. We used to spend a lot of time socializing in the garden, with the big black-and-white awnings drawn against the sun. The mosquitoes would be out in full force, and we had to smell that peculiar smell the wind blew in from the Chao Phraya."

Around that time, a former architect-turned-OSS operative from Delaware named Jim Thompson went into partnership with the photojournalist Germaine Krull to buy over and renovate the Oriental Hotel. While this partnership soured, it set the hotel—originally built as a doss-house for seafarers in 1876—on a course that would see it voted the best in the world, several times over.

Harold Stephens, a former U.S. Marine who arrived in Thailand in 1959 and has basically never left, concurs with Brigitte Opfer's summation of the Oriental. "The property was nothing; just a really rundown, nondescript hotel on the river—the *only* one on the river."

But he appreciated the low cost of everything. "We'd go into the Oriental, and the beers there were 8 baht a bottle. So nothing was expensive. The Oriental used to have the Bamboo Bar in the old wing, not the one that's there now. They would have first-class entertainers, like Shirley Simmons from Australia, who would come up and do contracts for them. And they had really, really good floor shows. We'd go and meet the entertainers, and write about them. The Oriental would be their warm-up act. Then they'd go to Vietnam and make vast fortunes. They'd get $400 a show, and they could do three or four shows a night!"

Jim Thompson, meanwhile, went on and made his name for himself with something entirely different: revitalizing the fading Thai silk cottage industry before disappearing in Malaysia in 1967 in what remains an enduring mystery. Harold met the man a few times before his disappearance, socialized with him at his now-famous Ayutthaya-style house on Klong Maha Nag in Bangkok, and even wrote a book about the mystery.

While Brigitte never met Jim Thompson, she remembers his first shop "next door to the tailor" in Suriwong. "You paid shillings there. And you could have *any* shade or color of silk fabric you liked if you wanted to match it with something." Interestingly, though the Jim Thompson silk empire has grown to include at least twenty-five stores in the country today, plus many overseas, the brightly colored silk fabric he produced was in great contrast to the prevailing fashions of the day in Thailand. "The women wore little white blouses and black sarongs. The chaps

wore ducks, white trousers, and shirts. It was a while before the Thais started to venture towards bright colors."

Another man with early memories of Bangkok is Major Roy Hudson, a Royal Engineer who first arrived in 1945 from Burma. With World War II barely wrapped up, he quickly made the city his home. Now over ninety, and still with a glint of mischief in his eyes, he recalls a lot of dance halls and clubs cropping up in the city. "We enjoyed a huge amount of hospitality. Dances were being held at Enfong Gardens, and people were attending them in their best clothes. Mind you, nobody had any money. But there were young girls who had beautiful dresses, and they were always inviting us officers to drink."

Not that life in Bangkok was all play for Major Roy Hudson, of course. Work-wise, the first thing he had to do was mend the Rama VI Bridge. Built in 1927 and the first bridge to cross the Chao Phraya River, it had been damaged during the war.

"One of the bridge's bascules was standing like that," he told me, gesturing with his hand pointing up at an angle, "while the other bascule was completely missing. They said, "You're a sapper, what're you going to do about it?' When Bangkok had been bombed, the second bascule had dropped into the river, about thirty meters deep at that point, and there was no way I could retrieve it." The repair project got increasingly complicated, but Hudson somehow rose to the challenge. "Then they said, 'Sometimes we want to open the bridge.' Okay, so I marked with white paint the spot where the rollers should be, and said, 'You tell me when you want it open, and I'll come down and open it for you. It will only take about twenty minutes.' So the bridge was finally repaired against all odds, and it's still in use today." He says this with immense pride, and rightly so. At 440 meters, it remains the longest railway bridge in Thailand, ten meters longer than its nearest rival, the so-called "Bridge on the River Kwai."

Like myself, and probably many of you readers, that first taste of Thai life was enough to give Major Roy Hudson "the bug" for Thailand. But the seeds had unwittingly been sown years earlier. "Everything in my life seems to be roads that led to Thailand," he says. "The first time I ever heard about the country was when I was at school in Buenos Aires. The singing master said, 'Right, the lesson today is to sing the Thai national anthem. It's not very difficult. The first words are "O Wattana Siam," and you should sing it to the tune of "God Save the King."' So we all stood up and started singing "O Wattana Siam, O Wattana Siam" until we were red in the face."

The second event for Hudson—a pretty momentous one—was at boarding school in Surrey, England, at the age of fourteen. "We went out for a walk one Sunday and saw a dark-complexioned gentleman strolling toward us with a walking stick and a homburg hat, dressed very well and wearing nice, brown shoes. He stopped in front of us, and we raised our caps in re-

spect. He asked some ordinary questions, like which school we went to, etc. I was very interested to know who he was because he was obviously a *poo yai*, a "big noise." Later I found out, he was staying at a place called the Knole House, which he had rented, and he was the king of Thailand. He had not abdicated at the time. So the very first person from Thailand I met was His Majesty the King Prajadhipok or Rama VII himself!"

When Hudson retired from the army in 1959, he could finally realize his dream of spending the rest of his life in northern Thailand. "The plan right from the start was to make a beeline for Chiang Mai," he says, "because Chiang Mai was paradise. It was the last paradise on earth." Within a year of moving there, he married his English student, Khun Arpawn, and fifty years later they still remain happily ensconced in their peaceful mountain paradise.

To Thailand with love, indeed.

*Centara Grand Beach Resort & Villas Hua Hin*
www.centarahotelsresorts.com/chbr

*Mandarin Oriental Bangkok*
www.mandarinoriental.com/bangkok

*The Jim Thompson House*
For more about Jim Thompson, go to page 159.

www.jimthompsonhouse.com

# SPIRITUAL THAILAND

*Exploring Buddhism and beyond*

Spiritual life in Thailand is delightfully complicated. At the most visible level there is Buddhism, a religion imported from India in the sixth century AD and practiced by the majority of the people in the country. But look closely at the belief system of Buddhist Thais, and you'll find that they also pray to select gods from India's Hindu pantheon and borrow freely from Hindu legends and mythology (venerated Hindu epics like the *Ramayana*).

Two separate religions of Indian origin don't merely coexist in Thailand; they blend seamlessly together in a way that is uniquely and peculiarly Thai. Now, add to this mix a third element—deep-rooted animist beliefs in superstitions, magic, souls, ghosts, and afterlife—and it isn't hard to see why Western tourists find the heavily nuanced mindscape of the Thai people so hard to decode.

The authors who have contributed to this chapter do not attempt to decode it either. Instead, they share their firsthand experiences of Thai spirituality that only serve to reinforce its fascinating complexity.

Michael Roberts writes about Bangkok's famous Erawan temple where Brahma, a Hindu god of high status, takes a hiatus from his traditional role in Hinduism as creator of the universe to put good-luck stamps on lottery tickets, watch Thai dances, and bless people who release caged birds in his honor. As teacher in a Buddhist religious school near the capital, Lauric Rhoads has a rare opportunity to see the sweet, human side of child monks from whom she has to maintain a respectful physical distance at all times and remember not to even pass a book or a piece of chalk directly into their hands.

Joe Shakarchi witnesses a Buddhist initiation ceremony, where he cannot fully understand the proceedings but feels deeply moved by the beauty of the occasion and the friendliness

of complete strangers who warmly invite him to be part of their congregation. And Laura Bartlett Jurica spends a quiet, relaxing afternoon "making merit" at Wat Prayoon, feeding bits of sausage and fruit to hungry turtles and wondering how a religious activity like this can be so much fun.

When our authors encounter certain deep-rooted superstitions in Thailand that defy their Western sense of logic, they willingly set aside their disbelief for the moment and go along with the experience to see where it leads. At the request of his Thai girlfriend, for instance, Mike Rose visits a Buddhist fortune-teller to solve a recent business of theft, fully expecting the guy to be some spiritual con artist. Instead, the fortune-teller not only identifies the thief but, as an afterthought, reveals a few secrets about Mike, as well. In another instance, Mike—who never seems to come off well from his run-ins with Thai superstition—nearly has his manhood sucked out of him by Phi Tani, a nasty female ghost, after he relieves himself under her banana tree.

Apparently, the ghosts in Thailand are hard to please, and we learn how finicky they can be from Chang Noi's essay about the travails of installing a new spirit house at his residence. Most travelers have seen these beautiful spirit houses throughout the country, inlaid with tiny mirrors and festooned with colorful ribbons, but who could ever guess what a production it is to cajole spirits to take up residence in one of these accommodations?

Thai ghosts, as you will also discover in this chapter, don't just live in banana trees and spirit houses. Going by Scott Earle's account, they inhabit tattoos as well. Scott, who is the proud owner of a Buddhist tattoo, is invited to an annual festival at Bangkok's Wat Bang Phra, where he is amazed to see other tattoo-owners completely overcome by the spirit of the animal they have chosen to have inked on their bodies.

It is nearly impossible to find a logical explanation for such interactions with the otherworld. But for tourists, the pleasure of these exotic experiences is simply in taking them at face value. So keep your mind wide open and let the irrepressible Thai spirit of *sanook* (fun) infuse your encounters with the mystic dimensions of the country. Marvel at the spiritual diversity of Thailand, let your hair down, and if you're around during the Songkran New Year festival, get yourself a good water pistol and join the enthusiastic water fighting on the streets, as Geena Fife did and writes about in this chapter. Or dance the night away at a village temple get-together, hoping you're belle of the ball like Robert Tilley, who is chased by hordes of adoring women and at least one mustachioed male, all willing to pay for a chance to shake a leg with him.

## BANGKOK

*Michael Roberts befriends a Bangkok lord*

For reasons that are too detailed to get into here, there are very few temples dedicated to the Hindu god Brahma in India. During my travels around the country, I had found only one, so I was quite taken aback to see the Erawan Shrine in Bangkok.

I had been misled by many people who told me the God of the Erawan was a four-faced Buddha. This is a common mistake foreign tourists make by ascribing one god to Thailand. The Thai people have combined Buddhism with Hinduism and animism to create a seamless belief system that works very well for them, though it leaves us confused sometimes as to who's who.

The exquisite golden image gracing the open-air altar at the Erawan Shrine is Brahma the Creator, whom the Thais call Phra Prom. He sits on a lotus and has a swan as his totem animal. The fact that he wears a long, white beard and holds no weaponry in his four hands has always led me to regard him as a kind, old grandfather. Perhaps that is also the reason why the Thai people feel comfortable bringing all their troubles to his door.

**BANGKOK**

The shrine itself is small but spectacular. The monotony of the overall golden color of both the altar and the statue is broken with tiny blue mirrors that twinkle in the sun, making the shrine impossible to miss if you're driving through the big four-way intersection in Ploenchit.

Legend has it that the open-air Erawan Shrine was built in 1956 as an antidote to a series of terrible accidents taking place at the construction site of a hotel right next to it. Brahma's presence drove away whatever evil spirits were dogging the hotel project, and since then he has been reigning over this important intersection, receiving prayers from thousands of people who visit him every day.

Since I regularly stay at a hotel right across the road from the Erawan Shrine, I go there at least once during each of my trips to Thailand. It has become something of a ritual. I feel a strange sense of disquiet on the rare occasions when I have been in Bangkok and not visited the shrine.

The customs and ceremonies are a little difficult to understand right away, and it took me several visits to figure out how things are done here. For example, I often wondered why people were standing by the gate with cages full of little birds, until somebody explained they were a means to make merit. Buying the birds and then setting them free earns you good karma. The lottery-ticket sellers, also stationed near the gates, sell tickets to pilgrims who can have them blessed by Brahma for good luck.

A third interesting presence, this time inside the shrine, is the troupe of dancing girls. There are usually about eight of them, in full theatrical makeup and traditional costumes that include tall, conical crowns resembling the *prangs* seen on many temple tops. Sometimes I saw the dancers sitting idly around the raised platform built to the right of the altar, looking hot and bored. At other times, I caught them dancing gracefully to live music provided by the shrine musicians. I was curious to know why they did this, and I soon gathered that these dancers too were a means of making merit. A worshipper can buy a dance for the pleasure of Brahma, and choose the number of girls he or she wants. Last time I checked, a platform filled with dancing girls would cost somewhere around 1,000 baht.

The offerings made at the Erawan altar are a matter of personal choice. I usually buy a basic set for 25 baht from the stall inside the shrine: garlands, candles, and a package of incense. The prayers sent up to the Lord of the Erawan Shrine differ from person to person, as well. Many Thais come here to make wishes. In trade for their wishes coming true, they promise to give something special to the shrine or do some special good deeds.

I have my own version of prayer: after setting the garlands, incense, and candles in front of the deity, I chant the short *beej* (basic) mantra for Brahma: "Om Sat Chit Ekam Brahma."

If I do it the correct way—that is, repeat the Brahma mantra 108 times—I can go into a temporary meditative state that makes it possible to stand under a scorching sun for more than five minutes without choking on the thick plumes of incense and candle smoke snaking around the altar. Then, as soon as my prayer is done, I rush out of the Erawan Shrine in search of air-conditioning and a blessedly cold can of Diet Coke at any of the nearby shopping malls—the loud drumbeats of the temple dance music still ringing in my ears.

I know I ought to be less cavalier with my dealings with the God of the Erawan, but over the years, we have come to a friendly understanding: as long as I keep my appointment with Grandfather Brahma on every trip to Thailand, he grants me the only wish he knows I'll ever ask from him.

### Erawan Shrine

The Erawan Shrine is located at the junction of Ploenchit and Rajadamri roads. The nearest Skytrain station is Chidlom, which has a covered walkway that overlooks the shrine.

### Hands-free worship

With both hands loaded with offerings of flowers and candles that you cannot place on the ground, you'll need to know this little trick to get the incense sticks out of their plastic wrappers without breaking them. Look for the "fire stands" (for lighting candles) scattered around the shrine. Stick the tip of the incense package into the fire. Allow the top of the plastic to burn off, and then push the sticks out. The flame can be shared—that is, more than one person can light their candles or incense from it at the same time—so don't stand in the sun waiting for others to finish before you.

## Laura Bartlett Jurica improves her karma one turtle at a time in Bangkok

Much as I love turtles, my encounters with them so far have always gone off badly. I nearly lost a cheek to a common snapping turtle I tried to adopt when I was a child in Missouri. And I almost caused my dad to lose a finger trying to get a dinner-plate-sized alligator snapper to the safety of the side of the road.

Now I am in Bangkok, at the Wat Prayoon monastery near the Memorial Bridge, courting turtle troubles all over again.

Wat Prayoon is a sleepy little monastery complex built in 1828 during the Rattanakosin period. While it is neither as grand nor as often visited as the celebrated Wat Arun located nearby, it has a beautiful pond filled with all kinds of good-luck turtles. The locals in the area released these reptiles into the Wat Prayoon pond as an act of compassion, and feeding them gets a person good karma.

A quiet afternoon spent feeding the turtles sounded like an idyllic break from the bustle of Bangkok, and I dragged my husband Cory there, promising to be careful not to risk another turtle attack.

As soon as we walked into the Wat Prayoon monastery, we came face-to-face with what was possibly the most fascinating manmade structure I had seen so far in Thailand: a miniature hill that resembled a hardened mass of molten volcanic lava. When I discovered later that the mound was designed to look like a huge melting candle, I was amazed at the craftsmanship that had gone into creating such an accurate depiction of dripping wax.

The mound was covered with tiny spirit houses, grottos, shrines, and even dollhouses, all sumptuously decorated with golden filigree work and tiny mirrors that sparkled in the afternoon sun. At its base lay a large shallow pool filled with the good-luck turtles I had come to see.

The hour was a little past noon, and Wat Prayoon had no visitors other than Cory and me. There was only an old woman selling turtle food near the entrance, chatting with a monk who lounged under a tree.

We approached the pair to see what we could buy from the wooden food cart. There was chicken mixed with bits of sausages and also pa-

paya. The woman smiled in greeting and asked what we wanted in Thai. Cory gestured that we would like one plate of each, and the monk clapped his hands in approval. The more food we fed probably meant more good fortune for us.

When we returned to the pool and sat down by its edge, a school of turtles was already waiting for us with their waxy necks sticking out of the water. Looking down into those wide-open mouths, I felt a moment's apprehension at the thought of getting my fingers anywhere near them, but Cory showed me the long bamboo skewers the woman had given him along with the food plates. All we had to do was stick a piece of fruit or meat to the end of the skewers and hold it out to the turtles. They rose up to the surface, straining as far as their shells would allow, and gently sucked the food off the skewers.

Countless turtles came and went in the half hour we spent feeding them. The old and wizened ones had a layer of moss on their shells. They were too slow to latch onto the bamboo sticks, and more often than not, the young turtles darted out and snatched the food from right above their noses. Soon, I could identify the newcomers in the pool; they joined the crowd with great enthusiasm but weren't smart enough to grab the tasty tidbits before the others did.

Feeling sorry for them, Cory threw the last of the sausage bits directly into the water. A noisy scuffle ensued as the turtles rushed this way and that, trying to swallow a piece of sausage before it floated away.

When all the food was gone, the turtles became quiet again. A few swam around near us, hoping for seconds, but the others went off to clamber up on rocks and enjoy an afternoon nap in the sun.

When I turned around, I saw the monk had disappeared and the woman with the cart was nodding off in her chair. Cory decided to go explore the towering white *chedi* we had spied from our boat on the Chao Phraya River, but I was content to just sit there and delight in the beauty of my surroundings. The mound with its miniature ghost shrines, the pool and the little bridges over it—everything was manmade here. And yet, like a Japanese garden, this little oasis of peace hidden behind Wat Prayoon's great boundary walls was so perfectly in tune with nature.

Cory soon returned, and I said my goodbyes to the turtles and prepared to leave. On our way out, we ran into a young Thai boy in a Mickey Mouse T-shirt, coming to feed the turtles after school. He seemed startled to see a pair of foreigners at Wat Prayoon, as tourists rarely came this way to take part in the local animal-feeding ritual. We exchanged shy smiles, and on an impulse, I took out the sheet of Mickey Mouse stickers I had in my bag and gave it to him.

The good fortune Cory and I had just accrued by feeding the turtles might take its time in coming, but it was nice to know that the young boy would

certainly be taking home a return gift from Wat Prayoon this afternoon.

### Getting to Wat Prayoon

Wat Prayoon, also known as Wat Prayurawongsawat Worawiharn, is located near the Old Portuguese Quarter in Thon Buri. If you're going to Wat Prayoon by boat on the Chao Phraya River, get off at the Memorial Bridge pier, and walk over to the Thon Buri side. The wat's distinctive white spiraled *chedi* is clearly visible from the river.

### *Joe Shakarchi sees himself in Bangkok's Emerald Buddha*

The day before I left for Thailand, my friend Sandra told me that the Temple of the Emerald Buddha was the most spiritual place she had ever seen. Anywhere in the world. It's hard for anything to live up to a buildup like that, and the temple had the added burden of my own high expectations: I wanted to see it not as a tourist, but as a Buddhist visiting a historic site.

My first few moments in the temple, unfortunately, fell far short of what I had hoped for.

Of course, I admired the art and architecture, to the extent that I was awestruck by the beauty of the many shrines and spires within the complex, the exquisite inlay work of multicolored glass chips glimmering in the sun, and the murals of scenes from the Hindu epic, the *Ramayana*. But the spirituality that I had come in search of completely escaped me.

Making my way through a row of grinning lion statues, I entered the main temple sanctuary, only to be swallowed up by a mass of people. Pressing myself against the other tourists, I managed to glimpse the altar and the small jade Buddha perched on top of a high throne. But overly loud conversations about cameras and DVD purchases robbed me of any opportunity for introspection. Many of the tourists had come to see nothing more than an architectural attraction and were behaving accordingly. I struggled to connect with the divine in this melee, and after a few minutes, I gave up and decided to leave.

While walking out of the temple, I noticed the image of a lion on a mirrored surface in front of the exit. The large frame had several interlocking mirror panels, reflecting several angles. Wondering why it was there, I looked into the mirrors. To my surprise, what I saw was myself—*and* the Emerald Buddha—together in the same frame.

I believe my life was changed in that instant. For the first time I understood the Buddhist saying "Look inside: *you* are the Buddha." For as Buddhists, it is not the Buddha we are seeking. It is ourselves.

I also realized the reason why there are multiple statues of the Buddha in every temple: to remind people that there is no single Buddha. Everyone is a Buddha, or a potential Buddha—and that included me.

The understanding flooded over me. Every time a Thai uttered a *sawatdee*, bowed his or her head, and smiled the gracious smile that Thailand is so famous for, they were following the path shown by the Buddha himself. They were expressing an unwavering respect for the Buddha residing within every individual.

A simple glance into a mirror had explained this crucial Buddhist belief, and I sank into meditation and stayed like that for a very long time, quietly ecstatic. When I finally rose and passed the mirror on the way to the exit, I pulled out my notebook and wrote a short poem to remember the moment:

*I first saw myself
in the mirror
Looking at the green
Emerald Buddha
looking at me*

### Reflecting on Buddhism

The image of the lion on the interlocking mirror panels can be found right in front of the exit door at the Temple of the Emerald Buddha (Wat Phra Kaew). The temple adjoins the Grand Palace.

## *Jan Polatschek discovers Bangkok's vibrant Jewish community*

As my plane descends toward Suvarnabhumi Airport, Wat Sothon Wararam Worawihan appears below. Since the population of Thailand is primarily Buddhist, a temple complex near the airport is not unexpected. What is unexpected is the large Aeyatul Muslimin Mosque that towers beside the airport expressway en route to downtown Bangkok. Most Thai Muslims live in southern Thailand, near Malaysia, but there is a sufficient population in the capital to support more than a hundred local mosques. In addition, the country's members of the Hindu faith maintain several *mandirs*, and Christians of every denomination attend large churches or smaller neighborhood assemblies.

As an American Jew who has retired to Bangkok, I hoped to find a semblance of Jewish life in this city. But what took me by surprise was the vibrancy of the small yet devoted community. I met Jews from the Americas, Israel, Australia, France, England, Romania, Hungary, South Africa, Afghanistan, and the Middle East.

Temple Beth Elisheva is the center of Jewish spirituality in Thailand, and synagogue services are conducted every weekday morning. The traditional Friday evening and Saturday morning Sabbath services are always well attended by young families with energetic children, single men and women, and faithful Jewish travelers. Our prayers are comforting, and our songs are spirited. The temple meals overflow with strictly kosher Thai specialties, Middle Eastern salads, and platters of roast chicken and brisket just like our mothers used to make.

The heart of Jewish ritual and education in Thailand is Rabbi Yosef Kantor, the leader of our congregation. I always enjoy his sermons. The Rabbi weaves current events, modern cultural trends, personal anecdotes, professional experiences, the teachings of the Bible, and the wisdom of the Talmud into his cheerful, warm, and thoughtful messages. The Rabbi may speak for five or ten minutes, sometimes longer, and always without any notes.

Rabbi Kantor is a Hasidic Jew from Australia. He follows all the commandments of this tradition. I don't believe, for example, that he has ever shaved his beard, which is long and reddish brown. He lives a strictly Orthodox Jewish life, yet he never suggests that we follow him. Nor does he insist that we come to synagogue regularly or even that we join as members. The Rabbi's message is always positive as he simply encourages us to do the right thing in this world and to live our life in accordance with G-d's hopes and expectations.

My own expectations for a Jewish life here in Thailand are fulfilled during my favorite holiday, the springtime festival of Passover. Thousands of Jewish citizens, residents, retirees, international students, and travelers attend the community Passover Seder and ceremonial meal. Seders are conducted in Bangkok, Koh Samui, Phuket, Chiang Mai, and other popular retirement and tourist areas. Prayers and songs, stories and discussion, wine and food — oh, so much food!—are the ingredients of this joyful retelling of our exodus from bondage in Egypt three thousand years ago.

Who knew that here in Thailand I would find such a welcoming and vigorous Jewish community? Who knew that I would befriend a distinguished and inspiring rabbi? Who knew that as a member of a tiny religious minority, I could live a satisfying spiritual life halfway around the world from home? Who knew? Baruch HaShem.

### Beth Elisheva synagogue
121 Soi Sai Nam Thip 2
Sukhumvit, Soi 22
Bangkok
(02) 663-0244

### Learning curve:
A note from the editor: Certain words and phrases in this essay were unfamiliar to me at the time of editing. Jan sent me explanations, and I am noting down a couple here in the hope that they will answer any questions that you might have, as well, if you are not conversant with Jewish customs.

G-d: Jews always hyphenate this word, so that His name can never be erased.

Baruch HaShem: "We use this phrase instead of 'Thank G-d,' so as to not speak G-d's name too often or in vain," writes Jan. "If I ask a Jewish man, 'How is your family?' he will respond, 'Baruch HaShem.'"

### Spiritual Bangkok
For more about Judaism in Thailand, as well as information about churches, mosques, and temples around Bangkok, visit the following websites.

www.jewishthailand.com
www.bangkok.com/other-places-of-worship.htm

### Joe Shakarchi participates in a Bangkok initiation ceremony

I have a talent for getting lost. I'll go in the wrong direction, arrive at the wrong temple, eat dinner at the wrong restaurant, maybe even spend the night in the wrong hotel. This talent, however, has also taken me to places that I would never have found on a tourist map—offering up memorable experiences that only revealed themselves to me because

I was lost. The following story is a perfect example.

It was my first trip to Thailand, and I was depending on my guidebook to find the most spectacular sights around Bangkok. Wat Arun in the city's Thon Buri district was obviously on my list, and I set out one day to see the ivory-colored temple on the west bank of the Chao Phraya River.

From a distance I could see Wat Arun's enormous *prang*, a Khmer-style tower that dominated the riverside view, and on an impulse, decided to walk down the bridge that connected Chao Phraya's two banks instead of crossing the river on a ferry. It would be fun to wander through the streets leading up to the temple, and if I kept Wat Arun's tall *prang* in view all the time, I couldn't possibly get lost.

Thon Buri is not a tourist area, and as I wended my way toward Wat Arun, I passed quaint neighborhoods populated by Thais tending their stores, frying fish in small stalls, hawking clothes, and pushing food carts laden with grilled meat and fruit. And when I finally reached the *prang*, it turned out to be the tower of an old, dilapidated neighborhood temple.

The red and green rooftop and spiraling wall decorations had fallen into disrepair. The exterior wood planks were slimy from having weathered too many Thai monsoons, and the paint was peeling off. Though this temple was a far cry from the majestic Wat Arun I had set out to see, it was interesting nonetheless, because it seemed like a "real" temple where local people came to pray, rather than a tourist attraction.

"Can I help you? Are you lost?" A young monk dressed in saffron robes had stepped out of the temple, and seeing me standing there, had asked the question.

"Yes, I am lost, but really, that's okay," I replied, and then added, "May I visit your temple?"

In broken, heavily accented English, the monk informed me that they rarely got any visitors, as this was just an old neighborhood temple. However, he would be most happy to have me look around. As he escorted me inside, he asked where I was from. When I said "America," he told the other people there that I had traveled ten thousand miles to visit their shrine. It was an honor for them that I had made such an effort.

The temple was very busy that day. People were sitting in groups, chatting amiably, and passing around orange juice and Pepsi. I discovered that a ceremony was about to start—my new monk friend's brother was about to be initiated into monkhood, and I was welcome to stay and observe the ritual if I wanted.

Of course, I was delighted by the invitation and asked if there were any customs I needed to follow. "Just take your shoes off," the monk said, "and sit on the red carpet with the other people. The only 'rule' is to not point your feet at the Buddha."

The others quickly made space for me on the carpet, their smiles and glances conveying genuine warmth. I was quite surprised by this friendly acceptance of my presence. It was only the third day of my first trip to Asia, and here I was in a Buddhist temple, about to witness the sacred initiation ceremony like a true member of the community.

The temple's altar had been decorated especially for today's occasion, with fresh flowers surrounding the statue of the Buddha. Sticks of incense also encircled the statue, their fragrant smoke curling softly around the Buddha's meditative face before spreading through the air to instill a meditative quietness in all of us.

I couldn't help noticing two household objects sitting next to the Buddha: an electric fan tied with a pink ribbon and a blue water cooler. They looked quite out of place in this religious setting. I was even more puzzled when a monk picked them up and displayed them to the gathered crowd, who started murmuring excitedly.

The ceremony began soon after, and everybody settled down to watch the head monk and the novice sit down at the altar. The monks recited incantations and made ceremonial movements to welcome the initiate into their brotherhood. After a few minutes, when the prayers had been read and blessings had been given, all the attendees stood up to form a procession. They marched toward the altar carrying colorful decorations, flowers, and religious ornaments. Suddenly, my monk friend walked up behind me, placed a long-handled ornamental fan in my hands, and firmly pushed me into the procession. Instead of merely

watching the ceremony, I was now a part of it!

The procession concluded with the attendees presenting the new monk with gifts: sandals, an umbrella, a radio. Simple items to suit the simple life this boy was about to embark on. Now I understood the fuss over the fan and cooler; in the heat and humidity of Bangkok, they were very valuable gifts indeed.

Finally, the initiate and his family gathered for photos. They surprised me by asking if they could include me in the pictures. As I smiled and posed for the camera, my mind whirled with confusion. Why should they want a complete stranger in their ceremony photographs? Had this been America, would I have allowed *them* to intrude like this on a private family affair?

The monk's family wanted to know my name and address, so they could send me the photographs. But not only could I not remember my address, for a moment I couldn't remember how to spell my name. This was not just a momentary lapse in memory. Thrown into a strange ceremony in a foreign culture, I was for the moment no longer sure who I was.

I thanked the family for all their kindness before leaving the temple, feeling emotional and overwhelmed, and also very glad that my talent for getting lost had brought me here. I didn't get to see the architectural wonder of Wat Arun glistening in the sunlight that day, but I did experience something that I believe has changed me significantly as a person: the expansive spirit of Buddhism.

### Initiation ceremonies

Everybody is allowed to observe a Buddhist ordination. If this is of interest to you, simply go to a temple and ask when the next ordination ceremony will take place. Many young monks are ordained at the start of the rainy season, just before the auspicious period of Khao Phansa (also called Buddhist Lent) near the end of July.

The best temple in Bangkok to visit for this purpose is Wat Bowonniwet, located on Phra Sumen Road in the Banglamphu area. You can walk there from the Phra Athit pier on the Chao Phraya Express Boat line. Many monks choose Wat Bowonniwet for their ordination, as do members of the Thai royal family.

When making your request and attending the ceremony, be sure to dress modestly.

## NAKHON PATHOM

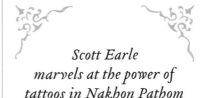

*Scott Earle marvels at the power of tattoos in Nakhon Pathom*

Last year in January, my wife and I went to Ayutthaya with her family to *tham boon*—make merit. Among the several temples we visited was one called Wat Ayodhya, where there was a monk doing tattoos. We got talking with the monk, and while touching up a huge artwork on the back of someone who was obviously a regular visitor, he explained what these ancient Buddhist tattoos symbolized.

In the room with us were a couple of other people who had waited all day to get their tattoos. Apparently, this monk worked here very infrequently, as he was a teacher at another temple called Wat Bang Phra in Nakhon Pathom province. I had never heard of Wat Bang Phra, so I had no idea then that it was the place in Thailand to get "powerful" religious tattoos done and blessed by Buddhist monks.

While we were in Wat Ayodhya that day, the monk gave each of us an "invisible tattoo." He used a clear perfumed oil instead of ink, and a needle that doesn't go very deep into the skin, so the tattoo is only visible until it heals. The temporary status, however, didn't make the tattoo any less painful. It definitely stings—and pretty hard too. After our tattoos were done, we took the monk's phone number and went away, thinking that was that.

But a tattoo isn't the sort of accessory you can just get and forget. After a few weeks of discussions, my wife and I decided we would like "proper" tattoos. I was a little surprised at her enthusiasm, because her pain threshold, unlike mine, is very low. The invisible oil job had been a tough experience for her, and the monk had said that the "real" (ink) tattoo was much more painful. But I was game if she was, and we both chose the *ha thaew* or "five-row" tattoo, as it supposedly brings prosperity and good fortune, as long as you follow the five rules it prescribes.

My wife called the monk to set up an appointment, and surprisingly he remembered us. He said we could go to his temple that weekend and get our tattoos.

On Saturday we went to Wat Bang Phra, which is a large temple about an hour's drive west from central Bangkok. When we got there, we found the monk in a little air-conditioned room, surrounded by hordes of people, most of whom were covered in tattoos.

I don't think I need to tell you that getting a tattoo by hand with an eighteen-inch needle, instead of by modern machines, is an extremely painful experience. My wife wisely

let me go first. The fact that I bled quite a lot and whimpered from time to time allowed her to mentally prepare for hers.

It took about forty-five to sixty minutes for the monk to do my tattoo, which was actually quite large. My wife's smaller version took about thirty minutes.

Since we've had them done, we have gone back to the temple several times with friends who also wanted tattoos—usually the invisible ones. We've also had ours retouched on the monk's advice, to make sure they are just right and fully charged with positive, mystical "powers."

Then, at the beginning of February 2010, I received an unexpected call from the monk. The temple was having a tattoo festival, and he said he would like us to come. I had no idea what this festival was all about, and I said sure.

On the day of the festival, we woke up at 4 a.m. and took two of our tattooed friends with us to Wat Bang Phra. When we got there, the place was already crowded with several hundred people waiting for the proceedings to begin a few hours later. We found ourselves a spot at the back of the forecourt, not knowing what mayhem was about to unfold. At around eight, we heard some screaming behind one of the buildings, and soon the refrain was taken up by others in the crowd.

Covered in tattoos, people were being possessed by the spirits of the animals tattooed on their bodies! As far as we could tell, nobody was faking it. The possessed individuals would start screaming, and then stand up and run full pelt toward the raised area at the front where the monks would soon be sitting.

As more and more people surrendered to the power of their tattoos, rolling their heads and flailing their arms and legs about, the situation started looking dangerous. By now, the forecourt was packed with ten thousand people at least. There was no place to move, and no hope of avoiding a collision if we fell in the path of a possessed individual charging in our direction. What's more, there was no hope of getting out either, as we were near the back, and a sea of humans separated us from the exit in the front.

There were quite a few clashes, and I saw at least one person get slightly injured. None of us was hurt, though, and I got trodden on only once. We watched in amazement as four people became possessed right next to us—their companions brought them back to their senses by grabbing hold of their ears and rubbing them!

This went on until the devotions were over and the monks directed the crowds to move forward to be sprayed by holy water. Things calmed down after the water blessing, and the festival officially drew to a close. Before we left, we met our friend the monk and sat talking with him for half an hour in his air-conditioned room, recovering from the heat and the mind-boggling scene we had just witnessed outside.

The Wat Bang Phra tattoo festival was a strange and confusing experience for a Westerner who has never seen a mass trance like that before. Parts of it were fun, and parts of it, I have to admit, were terrifying. Would I go to watch the festival next year? I'm not sure. Maybe, if the monk's phone call comes again, though this time I'd try to stay in a safer position on the fringes of the crowd. Or maybe I'll decide that once was enough and politely tell the monk that I'm very busy that day …

### Beyond body art

The tattoos done by monks in Thai Buddhist temples are called Sak Yant. Unlike ordinary tattoos, Sak-Yant are not merely a form of body art. Believers go to Buddhist monks rather than to a regular tattoo parlor because the Sak Yant apparently have strong protection powers. When applied and "charged" with good energy, they bring health, wealth, virility, and other good things into the owner's life. Each type of Sak Yant motif—often a combination of Hindu animal symbols and script —has a particular power, and prospective tattoo owners choose them according to their individual needs. From time to time, the tattoos need to be re-charged with fresh energy by the monk who created them. And the owner has to follow a few rules prescribed by the monk to keep their power alive.

For an illuminating and informed look at Sak Yant, read *Sacred Skin: Thailand's Spirit Tattoos* by Tom Vater and Aroon Thaewchatturat.

## Wat Bang Phra festival

The tattoo festival takes place once every year, usually on the first Saturday of March. The annual festival at Wat Bang Phra is the biggest of such gatherings that take place in most Thai temples where Sak Yant tattoos are done. During this time it is customary for Sak Yant tattoo owners to go and pay respect to the monks who drew the mystical talismans on their bodies.

It is believed that the animal tattoos can become so powerful on the auspicious festival day that they can possess the mind and body of their owners for a period of time. People start behaving like the animal their tattoo represents (crawling like a snake, growling like a tiger, etc.) and rushing toward the monks who created them. Usually, after the holy water blessing, the trance is broken, and the tattoos become calm and energize.

www.wat-bang-phra.com

## Invisible tattoos

Invisible tattoos are favored by Thai women and some men who don't want their talismans to be noticed by others. Although the invisible tattoo heals and disappears from plain view, its mysti-cal powers are said to remain intact, protecting their wearers in the same way an ink tattoo does.

# BAN PHE

## *Laurie Rhoads peeks into the life of child monks in Ban Phe*

It is typical for most, if not all, males in Thai society to spend a period of their life as a monk. For some, it is just a few days or months; for others it could be their entire school life, or even longer. Apparently, even Thai kings are not exempt from this age-old tradition.

I was in Ban Phe, a small fishing village near Bangkok, to teach a group of young monks, ranging in age from twelve to eighteen, at the village temple school. I was there as an English-language teacher, but I was a student too, constantly taking notes, knowing this would be a rare opportunity for me to study the formative training process according to Buddhist philosophy.

The boys studied all the usual academic subjects, plus daily lessons in Dhamma (Buddhist teachings). Their routines were more or less the same as that of fully ordained monks: waking up before sunrise, abstaining from food after noon, wearing saffron robes and ordinary plastic sandals with no accessories such as watches or jewelry of any sort.

On the face of it, these were pretty regular students with a range of personalities you'd find in any classroom—some were shy, and some were outgoing; some were serious, while some were outright clowns. I was surprised how many of them spoke English well and had a healthy curiosity about things going on in the outside world. They were interested in U.S. politics (especially the nomination of Obama) and followed European league soccer. My favorite photo of them is one taken from the back, in which you can't see any of their faces, but you can see the name of the American band Linkin Park clearly written in indelible ink on one of their robes!

As a counterpoint to this ordinariness, there were strict rules to be observed around them, and these, more than anything, made me constantly aware of their special child monk status.

Avoiding physical contact was one such rule. The boys couldn't touch or be touched by any woman—not even a sister. I couldn't hand them anything, and if I had to pass on a piece of paper or chalk to write on the blackboard, I would have to set it down in front of them. It was awkward at times, because not only was this conduct pretty counterintuitive to me, the teaching model we were using relied a great deal on handing out and then taking back pictures of key vocabulary terms. But I did my best to adjust, with just the occasional slip-up that usually elicited some nervous giggles from both parties involved.

Before every full moon, my students had to have their heads shaved—not just their skulls but their eyebrows too. I remember walking into class one day to find the little monks looking unusually pale. When I inquired into this sudden change in their appearance, I learned that the practice symbolized the renunciation of worldly vanities, following the example of Gautama Buddha when he renounced his life as a prince and left home in search of enlightenment. The boys looked so sweet and innocent with their freshly shaved heads and eyebrows—and much younger than they were.

Unlike in a typical school in the United States, nobody was allowed to wear shoes inside, and I taught my class barefoot. And yet, there were no objections to dogs and cats roaming around the classroom during lessons. We adored these free-range animals, especially the puppy pile outside the school building with ten adorable pups in it. We christened our favorite cat "student" Mr. Kittios, though he was in fact a she.

The three weeks I spent at the temple school seemed to fly past, and though it had felt strange at first to be in the constant company of the young monks in their saffron robes, I soon began to acculturate. The small adjustments, like not pointing my feet at the holy boys, became an instinctive thing the moment I took off my shoes at the school entrance and started my workday. The complete immersion I experienced by participating in the day-to-day lives of the child monks gave me more insights into the Thai way of life than I could ever have expected as a Westerner touring this fascinating country.

### Teaching in Ban Phe

Ban Phe is a peaceful fishing village with lovely beaches, 180 kilometers south of Bangkok. Teaching experiences at the temple school here can be arranged by TEFL International.

www.tefllife.com

## LAMPANG

### Robert Tilley becomes the belle of a Lampang ball

The monks at our local village temple invited us to shimmy at their place. This invitation came in the usual way—announcements on the village loudspeaker system (which I slept through), and a domestic process that I have dubbed "reading the signs." In my household, that means keeping a very sharp eye on my partner, Pan, and her movements—if there's any departure from routine, then something's up.

In this case, Pan was busy preparing sweetmeats, and my hand was briskly rapped when I reached for one. These were for the monks, she said. That meant a merit-making festival was about to take place at the village temple, after which there would be a *ramwong* dance party. During this festival, the monks would accept alms such as packets of sticky rice, sweetmeats, and ordinary household items including toothpaste and Lux soap, and then look on impassively as the locals took over the temple compound for merry-making that would continue far into the night.

This festival was being held in the grounds of a half-built temple perched on a hill above our village. The usual food and drink stalls had been set up in front of the partially completed temple, but right in front of the monks' quarters was a makeshift discotheque, where a couple of electric guitars, a synthesizer, and a line of chubby singing girls were hammering out the latest Thai hits as if there were no tomorrow.

Around the perimeter of the roped-off dance floor were crowds of onlookers. And why weren't they dancing? The reason rapidly became clear when a very pretty young woman grabbed my arm and hauled me off to dance. "I've paid 20 baht for you," she said in the triumphant tone of a housewife who's just got a good bargain. She pointed by way of explanation at a table set up at the entrance to the roped-off area, where a team of young women and schoolgirls were dropping 20-baht notes into a silver-colored chalice, the kind used to present temple offerings.

So, now a temple offering myself, I shimmied around, bumping and grinding to the shrieks and wails of the miniskirted chorus line fronting Thailand's version of the Spice Girls. It was a warm night, a crescent moon lazily recumbent in a black sky, and the temperature in the open-sided, tent-roofed dance hall was high enough to bake a cake.

The dance over, I stumbled off for a beer, but had an ice-cold can thrust in my hand by the trim little guy in torn jeans who attaches himself to me at all parties such as this one. "I got three dances with you," he hissed between broken teeth and a ragged toothbrush mustache. Then he waved his program of booked dances to prove it.

What? He'd paid 60 baht for the pleasure of my company? Could I perhaps make a living out of this?

From what I could decipher from Pan's translation and my own by now sharpened curiosity, this appeared to be the Thai version of society balls best described in the novels of Jane Austen and William Makepeace Thackeray. You really were expected to book—and be booked—for the evening's program of dances. Those wallflowers on the other side of the ropes had either no money to dance or no suitors.

I didn't have to part with a bean to dance, however, and was whisked off time and again to go through my disco routine. My name peppered the announcements of the MC: "And now

Mr. Bob has been asked to dance again, this time by Mr. Rambutan." In the center of the throng, my mustachioed pal held up two fingers to remind me I still had obligations to him.

When Pan decided to call it a day—or a night—I was feeling like Cinderella bumping down the dirt track home in my Japanese version of a pearly coach. It was not going to my head, I assure you, but I had seen some really disappointed faces back there as I waved a tipsy goodbye and followed Pan into the night. Like Mr. Rambutan, my most devoted dance partner, grimacing with chagrin behind one raised finger.

### Joining the party

Although parties like this one are common during major festivals such as Loi Krathong and Song-kran, they take place randomly all through the year at village temples. Check with the local tourist office or even your hotel to find out where the nearest temple festival is occurring and whether or not a *ramwong* will be a part of it.

## KHORAT

### *Chang Noi shifts his resident spirits to a new house in Khorat*

Due to an auspicious occasion, my wife promised our residential spirits a new house. "Is that okay?" she asked me.

The Spirit Houses we had in the garden must have been as old as the house we were living in (about fifteen years). I had just wanted to renovate them, but building—buying—new ones was also okay with me. I didn't worry too much about this because I thought the old ones would be removed and the new ones installed in the same place. How mistaken I was! As I soon learned, the old Spirit Houses were actually in the "wrong" place.

It should be noted that I am writing about spirit "houses." Yes, there are two varieties, something you might have noticed while traveling in Thailand. They are for two different kinds of spirits. One stands high on a single pole (or leg), while the other is a little closer to the ground, on four or six legs.

Since our old Spirit Houses were wrongly positioned, my wife said that a new place had to be chosen. To do this, we needed a specialist. My wife had a chat with one of the neighbors who knew somebody in another village who knew all about Spirit Houses. Conveniently, they also sold Spirit Houses. So the next morning, a Thai boy of about twenty came to our house to see where the new Spirit Houses must be built.

After making some calculations, the young spirit specialist pointed at a place right in the middle of the garden. This was the moment for me to politely interfere in the decision of the new location. I had found out a bit about the "rules" of good positioning and said, "So actually, this would *also* be a good place?" I pointed to a location a bit closer to our home. The young spirit specialist understood I wasn't going to ruin my garden and agreed that the place I pointed out was actually the best place.

The next question: how big must the "floor" be for the new Spirit Houses? The specialist told us three meters by three and a half meters by about seventy centimeters high. Wait a minute! We weren't building a guesthouse! I suggested fresh figures. These too he found acceptable, and the size decreased dramatically.

With the structural plans all set, we had to choose the best day to bless the new Spirit Houses. The young specialist did yet more calculations and declared May 21 to be a very good one. At 7 a.m. that day, he would come to bless the new Spirit Houses—and also ask the spirits to move in to their new house. The symbolic price of this blessing was 6 baht. As for a "donation," that was of course up to us. My wife decided she would donate 1,000 baht.

Now we had to buy new Spirit Houses. The young spirit specialist did not have much of a selection in his shop, but he offered to take us to the factory from where he buys his stock. Far? No, just on the other side of Route 36. "Just on the other side" was a trip of twenty-five kilometers. We arrived at the factory and saw hundreds of Spirit Houses in different colors and sizes on display. My wife and I have different tastes, but they are her spirits, so "up to you" was my contribution to the selection process.

For 5,500 baht, she chose two Spirit Houses and two tables, all made of cement and painted in a kind of red/brown with gold-colored flowers. They would be delivered on the day before the blessing.

After that, we found a small crew of Burmese workers who agreed to build the floor of the new Spirit Houses for 2,500 baht. They showed up the next day, and I hovered around as they worked—we foreigners may have a plan, but locals usually have their own agenda. The floor was finished later than promised, but when the job was over, it was actually not as disruptive as I had thought it would be.

All that was left to think of now was getting ready for the blessing day. We needed to buy accessories for the new Spirit Houses from a special shop under a large, old tree in the local market. Each Spirit House needed figures of a horse, an el-

ephant, a young lady, and a man; two vases for fresh flowers; two candle stands; one cup of sand to stick incense in; one yellow plastic flower; and one drinking glass. For the four-legged Spirit House, we needed additional figures of an old man and an old lady. And cigars. And also food such as chicken, fruit, sweet dessert, and a bottle of *lao khao*.

Our new Spirit Houses were delivered a few days earlier than expected. They were installed on the new floor, and they looked good. On the morning of the big day, my wife woke up at 5 a.m. to cook food for the spirits (which of course would be eaten by herself and her friends). At about seven thirty, the young spirit specialist arrived and the ceremony of blessing the new and old Spirit Houses began. Ritual water was sprayed on the new Spirit Houses and all our invitees. The old Spirit Houses were blessed, too, and the young specialist asked for forgiveness for replacing them.

After the ceremony was over, he took his 6 baht and the donation envelope and left. But we still had to deal with the old Spirit Houses. How to dispose of them?

This is when I learned where the old Spirit Houses I saw under big trees by the roadside were coming from. We loaded ours into the back of my truck. Behind a nearby temple was a small lake, and next to that lake was a big, old tree. There were many old Spirit Houses under it, and we added ours to the collection.

We now live happily together with our new Spirit Houses. The spirits are very comfortable, my wife is no longer afraid to be alone at home, and our cats are delighted with two new places to play around in.

## Spirit Houses

The beautifully ornate structures you see in front of houses in Thailand are not birdhouses or garden decorations, but homes for spirits to live in. The Thais believe there are incorporeal beings everywhere, and naturally, some inhabit their private living spaces. To coexist peacefully with these entities and stop them from causing any trouble, people handle them with kid gloves. They are given exquisite Spirit Houses to live in and are kept well supplied with regular offerings of prayers, incense, food, and flowers. In return, it is expected that the contented spirits will act as guardians of the household and protect its members from danger and misfortune.

## Spirit House graveyards

Discarded Spirit Houses may appear to be empty shells, but they cannot be dumped unceremoniously in the trash. Often, families will decide to leave the old ones where they are for fear of angering any spirit that may still be lingering. However, if the old Spirit Houses have to be disposed of, this is done with respect by leaving them under a shady tree or near a temple—preferably in the company of other dead, old, or broken Spirit Houses, which creates a surreal graveyard.

## To buy or not to buy

Editor's note: The small, elaborately carved Spirit Houses sold in Thai handicraft shops are such beauties that you may find it difficult to resist buying a miniature to take home. I bought one on impulse, and then suffered from severe bouts of postpurchase superstition because I didn't know the rules of installing one correctly. Finally, I made my peace by informing the Spirit House that under no circumstance was it to keep any spirits inside; it would be just a decoration piece. By doing this, I believe I broke its association with spirits, and ever since, it has been sitting on my bookshelf without causing any mischief.

## NONG HIM

XXXXXXXXXXXXXXXXXXXXXXXXXXXXXXX
ooooooooooooooooooooooooooooooo

### *Mike Rose escapes the clutches of a feisty ghost in Nong Hin*

It was a perfect day to be out cycling in the Thai countryside. It was sunny but not too humid, my shirt wasn't sticking to my back, and I didn't have to constantly wipe sweat off the handlebars. My Thai friend and I were pedaling at a leisurely pace, past coconut groves, shrimp ponds, and banana plantations on a flat road with no traffic to distract us from the charming mellowness of our surroundings. Having recently arrived from the gray, frigid wetness of United Kingdom, I was thawing out quite pleasurably in the tropical weather.

But then the call came, as ill-timed and inconvenient as ever.

I tightened my abdominal muscles to dull the impact of the bumpy road on my bladder, but it was no use. The more I thought about it, the more the urge grew. Finally I had to stop, make my excuses, and go, leaving my friend to hold the cycle for me.

The area I had chosen was fairly devoid of houses, but there was thick undergrowth off the side of the narrow road. Afraid of hanging around in

case something was lurking in there, I found a banana tree and quickly finished my business.

When I returned, feeling much relieved, I found my cycle on its side on the ground. My friend was crouching next to it, her hands clasped in a prayer!

Had I broken some rules of propriety here? Was there a protocol for going al fresco in the company of a Thai lady? Was there something euphemistic in nature that I should have said before running off like that?

My friend was looking so disturbed, I thought better of questioning her right then. We got on our bikes and resumed our journey. From time to time, I gazed at her bent head, feeling wretched about upsetting her like this.

Later that evening, when we were sitting on the verandah, sipping tea as a full moon rose high over our heads, I finally found the courage to broach the topic of my unscheduled rest stop. "Why were you in such a rush to get home today?" I asked tentatively, hoping she'd understand what I was getting at.

"You shouldn't have gone behind the banana tree like that," she said, quickly coming to the point. "You could have been attacked by Phi Tani!"

A venomous snake or a nasty local reptile? Oh no, Phi Tani was something much, much worse, my friend assured me. She was a ghost!

It turned out that I had risked a ghost attack in broad daylight, and that too off the side of a road where any number of cars or people could be passing by. As a Westerner coming from a culture where ghosts usually slink up from behind, in lonely spots on dark moonless nights (in the movies, that is), I found her claim fantastical.

But once she told me all about this lovely, female ghost, I realized that Phi Tani could be very wicked indeed, especially when the victims were handsome male specimens such as myself.

Though not as famous as Mae Nak, Phi Tani was still a top-rung ghost in the Thai pantheon of spirits, who haunted a particular variety of banana tree called Kluey Tani. Kluey Tani banana trees have a lot of commercial uses, but no Thai householder would ever allow one to grow in his or her compound. Letting Phi Tani live anywhere close to you is just asking for disaster to happen.

The ghost enjoyed torturing males, and she was particularly dangerous when the tree was in bud. She would lure men to come close to the banana tree, so she could rob them of their spirit and strength. Countless men all over Thailand fell prey to this wily ghost all the time, and woke up to find themselves hugging the banana tree.

It was getting close to nightfall as we sat there on the verandah, and my friend was looking quite frightened as she told me the tale. Her fear was infectious, and so yes, I admit I was feeling pretty scared myself. There were dark shadows of tall vegetation all around us and there could easily be a Kluey Tani tree among them. I could clearly imagine the Phi Tani ghost sitting on a high branch, swinging her legs as she listened intently to us talking about her. Oh, why was

I so stupid as to go and pee behind a haunted tree!

But then, like most Thai ghost stories, the Phi Tani saga took a somewhat comic turn. The ghost could be fooled, it seemed! Her weakness for men made her susceptible to their romantic advances, and if any man could put up a convincing act of loving her, he could use her toward his own end.

A lot of Thai men used Phi Tani to know more about their future wife, for example. They went to the banana tree and professed their love and a curiosity about the woman they would eventually marry. They cut a piece of the tree root and carved it into the shape of a woman, and sure enough, Phi Tani would appear in their dreams that night and spill the beans. To appease the spirit— like any woman, she mustn't be scorned—the men then had to seek her permission to marry elsewhere.

I shook off my fear and laughed with relief at the absurdity of it all. So Phi Tani was basically the nonhuman equivalent of a high-strung, insecure, and lovesick woman with a loose set of morals.

My close brush with Phi Tani, however, made me realize just how deeply the Thais feared the occult world. After that incident, I made it a point to ask all my Thai neighbors about ghosts, and each time, I heard horrifying stories of haunting and exorcism that needed the intervention of a *mo phi* (witch doctor) to be set right. Sometimes, it would be too late and the victims would die before they could be helped. By those standards, my own Phi Tani seemed almost benign in comparison. If our paths crossed again, all I had to do was wear a moony expression and serenade her to keep her happy and harmless.

## Up a tree

Phi Tani belongs to a subgroup of spirits called Phi Ton Mai, which means "ghosts that live in trees." To save passersby from being attacked by a Phi Ton Mai, monks often tie holy cloth and various symbols of the Buddha around the trunks of trees that are known to be haunted.

## Ghostly superstar

Mae Nak is Thailand's celebrity ghost, the subject of four films and many operas, books, and TV shows. According to legend, there was once a woman named Nak whose husband was away on military duty for a long time. In his absence, she died at childbirth, but her spirit didn't want to move on. The ghost took a human form and continued to live as Nak, fooling her husband until he figured out she wasn't real and abandoned her. Furious at being spurned, the docile Nak turned into a malevolent spirit, wreaking havoc on her village until she was "tamed" and brought to rest by a Buddhist monk.

There is a temple devoted to Mae Nak in Bangkok, at Wat Mahabut (located off Sukhumvit Soi 77, also known as On Nut Road). This is a curious, somewhat eerie sort of a shrine with a gold leaf–covered figure of a hideous-looking Nak wearing a badly made wig. The temple walls are covered with sketches and painted portraits of Nak, with her looking slightly different but extremely beautiful in each. People who come to pray at Mae Nak's shrine bring her gifts such as perfume, lipstick, hair spray, clothes, and accessories. For her baby they bring toys, milk, and sweets.

## Mike Rose submits to a Buddhist fortune-teller in Nong Hin

Thais may be obsessed with lotteries, but one thing they won't gamble with is their future. And why should they, when they have holy soothsayers to guide them through every crossroad in life? From marriage alliances and new businesses to family feuds, travel plans, and extramarital affairs—the Buddhist fortune-tellers are the agony aunts of Thai society, privy to all sorts of confidences. Serene, neutral, and nonjudgmental, they listen to their clients, and then, with the divine guidance of their all-seeing eyes, they make wise predictions about the future.

Now, I'm not the sort of man who's likely to ever go to a fortune-teller on his own, but when my Thai friend said she was going to visit one at a nearby temple that I hadn't been to, I thought I might as well tag along, and if nothing else get some photographs of the architecture.

My friend had a major concern that she hoped would be solved by the fortune-teller's intervention. Her older sister's home had recently been burgled, and a lot of money had been stolen. It was on her sister's behalf that we were going to the temple today to see what the monk had to say.

Sad as the loss was for her sister, I couldn't figure out quite why we were going to see a fortune-teller at this juncture. The horse had bolted, so to speak, and the thief may already have spent all the money. But I wasn't going to incur the displeasure of my friend by questioning her beliefs, so I kept my mouth shut as we set off.

When we arrived, there was a queue to see the fortune-teller, who was seated in the doorway of his *kuti* (monk's room). After a few minutes of waiting, our turn came, and I parked myself near the monk to listen to the proceedings.

My friend stated her sister's date and time of birth, and the elderly monk consulted what looked like an almanac and then made some calculations on a sheet of paper. My Thai is not brilliant, but I got the gist.

This was not a good year for the sister, and she might be in for some more misfortune. She had suffered a major loss last year, as well (true, her father had died), but things would be much better if she visited the police and told them about the theft

because ... *the criminal was living near her home.*

My friend gave a donation to the monk, and thinking we had finished, I was about to get up when he suddenly turned his attention to me and asked for my date of birth in Thai.

I understood him but pretended otherwise, since I had no desire to know my future, but my friend told him, despite her promise that she would not ask him to read my fortune. The monk chuckled at my obvious reluctance, and I could see his toothless gums stained red from chewing betel nuts. He scribbled and consulted his almanac, and then looked up with a knowing expression on his face, as if he had divined every last one of my most embarrassing secrets.

I was either a policeman or soldier, he said. That grabbed my attention since I have been both during my working life in the UK.

A lucky guess?

Before I could work that one out, he asked to look at my hand. I meekly offered the right one, and another red, toothless chuckle ensued. He said something to my friend I didn't understand, but I clearly heard the Thai word for "five." Oh my God, what was it? Five days, five months, five years? Was he looking at my lifeline?

We said our thanks and took our leave of the fortune-teller, but I hung around the temple for a while, going through the motions of shooting some photographs as I contemplated my fate. On the way home, my friend was awfully quiet, confirming my suspicion that I hadn't long to live.

I decided to take it on the chin. "What did he say?" I asked.

"I'm not saying anything," she offered, which means *I am not happy but I am going to tell you anyway.*

"Fine, have it your way," I said, knowing full well that my professed lack of interest in the subject would surely get her talking.

"Okay, I'll tell you; I'm not happy."

"Okay, why aren't you happy?"

A short pause. Then: "The monk says you have five ladies; you're a handsome man!"

So he hadn't predicted an early death for me after all. "Well, that's easy to explain," I said, feeling strangely lightheaded with this sudden dissolution of suspense. It was surprising how tense I had been ever since I had heard the monk say *five.*

The specter of an untimely death may have lifted, but there was still my friend's Spanish Inquisition to get through. "There is you, your niece, my mum, and my two daughters," I quipped, thinking fast on my feet.

"Five *ladies!*"

Clearly the monk hadn't minced his words, and none of my creative comebacks was going to throw her off the scent. "L-a-d-y!" she reiterated for good measure.

Was this Buddhist fortune-telling or divine tattling? In regard to my "five ladies," I'd never know. As events would turn out for my friend's sister, the monk's all-seeing eye was dead right about the theft. The police would eventually catch the burglar, who was a cousin and lived close to the sister's house. But for right now,

the monk's all-seeing nose was sticking firmly in my business, making very sure that there would be no peace for me that evening.

### Seeking your fortune

Many temples around Thailand have fortune-telling monks who read the future. But the convenience of going to a major temple—such as Wat Po in Bangkok, for instance—is that you can have a guide at hand to do the translating for you.

## PHUKET

### Geena Fife refuses to throw in the towel in Phuket

We arrived in Phuket the day before Songkran, the Thai New Year. We had not realized or planned for this, which on hindsight was probably a good thing: caught completely off guard by the riotous water-fight festival, we got to test our resourcefulness against the experienced Thais, who challenged us on the streets with an arsenal of water pistols, water balloons, and ice-cold water tanks.

Being tourists on a budget, we were not staying in a resort or by the beach; instead, we had laid our backpacks down in a quaint guesthouse in the heart of Phuket town, where we were among only half a dozen other Westerners. Songkran day started for us as predictably as any other. We were sitting in the open dining area downstairs, enjoying a nice breakfast, when, out of nowhere, a bucketful of water landed square on my back. I sat with my coffee cup poised in midair, dazed and drenched, while my husband led the chorus of laughter that broke out among the guests.

After the guesthouse owner was done with her laughing fit, she brought out a huge bucket of water and some smaller bowls. She set them down by the street and briefed us on a common Songkran war tactic: ambushing passersby from the sidewalk. We hid behind a strategically placed column, and for the next hour or so, we surprised would-be attackers driving past the guesthouse in pickup trucks and *songthaews* with sudden deluges of water. They were armed to the teeth with a variety of water weapons, but we half a dozen Westerners did a splendid job of beating them back before they could even point a water pistol at us. Thanks to our vigilance and marksmanship, our neighborhood, at least, was safe.

Now that we were properly involved in the water fight that was breaking out all over Thailand that day, we wanted the rest of the Songkran experience as well. Foreign

tourists in big cities often miss out on the spiritual component of the New Year festival, which goes on quietly among the locals while we are out waging battles against the good-natured Thai warriors on waterlogged streets. We hurried off to witness the Songkran religious ceremony taking place at a nearby *wat*, where there would be special prayers and food offerings for the monks.

Sadly, by the time we managed to reach the temple, weighing what felt like ten kilograms extra from the drenching we got on the way, the ceremonies were almost over. But a friendly local told us all about it: how fragranced water was poured on the Buddha in an act of cleansing to encourage good luck and prosperity in the year ahead. The Thais performed the same ritual of purifying and cleansing on their household Buddhas, and he told us to keep an eye out for it when we walked past homes.

Getting back to the guesthouse from the temple required some careful planning: we knew there was a group of twenty-something guerrilla fighters lying in wait for us near the temple, and not only did we need a safe route, we also needed fresh ammunition to defend ourselves. We bought water guns from a group of entrepreneurial teenagers at a horrendously inflated price, and stealthily made our way back to the guesthouse, near which a makeshift pool had been constructed. A Songkran parade would pass by here shortly after midday, and a crowd of kids was starting to gather, engaging in a chaotic water fight as they waited.

Our foreign faces quickly marked us as easy targets in the crowd. Not only did we get smacked with water balloons, we were slathered with mentholated talc, a wet doughlike concoction that tingled as it dried and left white streaks on our cheeks and foreheads. With the "war paint" slapped on, the last vestiges of our Western inhibitions melted away and we gave back as good as we got, whooping it up, not caring in the least that we were running amok in the middle of a street.

Then, over the top of the Asian *duf-duf* music, we heard the sound of drums and joyous singing. Heading straight down the road toward us was a heaving parade of brightly costumed locals, dancing enthusiastically to the cheers of the wet crowd. We danced along with them, feeling utterly free, as if our spirits had been unshackled for a short space of time. The kids, I noticed, had given up on their water pistols altogether and jumped straight into the temporary pool to tussle with each other underwater.

By midday, water supplies were getting low, and instead of more water, big blocks of ice were added to the large barrels placed on either side of the road. Under the hot April sun, the melted ice water was refreshing at first, but after repeated soakings it started to feel uncomfortably cold. It was a big relief when a large tanker drove up in the midafternoon to refill our large buckets with normal temperature water, and the fighting got boisterous again.

We survived five more hours of this, and then had to admit regretfully that we were knackered. After exchanging hearty goodbyes and wishing a Happy Songkran to one and all, we dragged our exhausted bodies back to the guesthouse and collapsed on our bed in a wet, happy heap.

As I lay there, trying to summon up the strength to shower and get something to eat, I marveled at how amazing this mass New Year revelry had just been. My mind played back the events of the day, and I saw myself celebrating Songkran with as much enthusiasm as any local: dancing in the street, instigating water fights with complete strangers, and screaming with laughter—rejoicing in not having to behave like an adult for just one day.

### April showers

The Songkran festival takes place each year for three days in April. Chiang Mai holds the biggest Songkran festival, which carries on for six days, at least. To find out more about the festivities in northern Thailand, visit the following website and check out the Songkran section for informative articles on everything to do with Songkran, from how to throw water to customs, history, and practical facts.

www.chiangmai-chiangrai.com

### Water warnings

During the Songkran festivities, make sure not to carry any important documents, especially your passport. If you must take documents with you—or your camera or phone—wrap them securely in something waterproof. Even if you're not joining in a water fight, you're still going to get very, very wet.

## SURAT THANI

*Colin Hinshelwood takes a silent challenge in Surat Thani*

*4 a.m.: Wake up. 9 p.m.: Bed. No reading, no writing, no smoking, no drinking, no sexual thoughts or activities … No talking at all times … for the next ten days.*

Just reading this schedule, you ought to feel nervous. By the third day, you're ready to quit. Digging deep inside yourself, you may find some scraps of forbearance that you hope will see you through. But by the end of the day, your resolution crumbles, and you're ready to quit again.

A retreat at the Suan Mokkh monastery is an emotional roller-coaster.

But if you survive it, it will cleanse your soul.

Set amidst the moist evergreen forests of the southern province of Surat Thani, Wat Suan Mokkh offers monthly retreats for foreigners who wish to learn Anapanasati (mindfulness of breathing) meditation. Accommodation is Spartan, in dormitories that house up to 120 students in tiny cells. Students are expected to emulate the daily routine of Gautama Buddha: walking barefoot, eating only in the morning, and sleeping for a minimal amount of time on a wooden pillow. In addition, everybody at the retreat must help with the chores of running the monastery.

Anapanasati meditation costs nothing and requires no equipment or preplanning. It is good for the practitioner's health and has no side effects. The instructions for a beginner are stupid-simple: feel your breath entering your nostrils; follow the breath to your navel; feel the breath going back out through your nose; think of nothing else. Yet, this is a pursuit that few mortals can claim to have mastered in one lifetime.

With sustained practice, students should be able to advance to the second stage, or the Second Tetrad: a state of rapture. More experienced meditators aim for the Third Tetrad: the ability to observe or examine the mind. The Fourth Tetrad involves contemplating the impermanence of everything, a state so advanced that only the truly "enlightened," such as the Buddha himself, can attain this.

Students are expected to stay mindful even while washing and eating. They are encouraged to observe their breathing while doing chores, which include mucking out the yard, scrubbing pots, and cleaning toilets. It all makes for a slightly surreal scene—a dozen Westerners working in the midday sun, raking leaves back and forth to the rhythm of their own breathing.

The austere daily schedule at the forest monastery is purposefully tailored to encourage mindfulness. Unable to share their emotions with each other, the volunteers are forced to work internally. This is not a bonding experience, and camaraderie is frowned upon. The rules of abstinence and the frugal vegetarian diet ensure that the body is cleansed and the breath easier to follow. Morning yoga helps loosen tense muscles and allows for greater flexibility while sitting in the same position for hours upon end. There is no TV, no radio, no cell phones ringing, no contact with the outside world. The distractions encountered are all in the mind.

A lot of people cannot complete this course. The daily sitting and walking meditations, Dhamma talks, yoga, and chanting—without any ordinary interaction with other human beings—is a tough path to stay on. But there are others who cannot get enough of it. Wat Suan Mokkh has many students who repeatedly come here. Retreat after retreat, they try to strengthen their willpower and take their ability to meditate to the next level.

When the retreat is over, students can extend their stay by moving in to the main monastery building. It's a nice halfway house, a place to assimilate and absorb the radical changes that have taken place in both mind and body. It's also a perfect oasis for those who feel the need to ease back into the outside world.

## Planning ahead

Wat Suan Mokkh's ten-day silent meditation retreat starts on the first of each month. Participants have to register in person, one day before. Visit the monastery's website and make sure to study the details before committing to this retreat.

www.suanmokkh-idh.org

## Getting to Suan Mokkh

Wat Suan Mokkh is about fifty kilometers from Surat Thani town. The monastery is on the Chumphon-Surat Thani bus route. The nearest train station is in Chaiya town, six kilometers away, and *songthaews* are available to take you from the station to the temple.

# SECRET GARDENS

*Where to hide away from the tourist crowds*

As impossible as it may sound right now, there will probably be times during your holiday in Thailand when you suddenly feel like it's all getting to be too much. When all you'll want to do is step back from so much foreignness, forget your busy travel itinerary, and *not* explore the five Buddhist temples and two night bazaars you were hoping to get through within the next twenty-four hours. Unfamiliar experiences are fun, of course, but an overload of them can be pretty exhausting, as well.

If you start feeling overwhelmed, don't do what a lot of (mostly female) travelers in Thailand tell me they do: indulge in a cathartic bout of copious tears. Be on the lookout for a "secret garden" instead—a place where you can spend a few quiet hours recovering from the stresses and strains of constant travel. Find a spot where the mind can unburden itself of all the pressure that accrues from missing buses and trains, coping with Thailand's persistently hot, humid weather, worrying about upset stomachs, and trying to keep track of where all your money is going.

This chapter shows the way with a collection of beautiful secret gardens our authors have discovered in different parts of Thailand. Their sanctuaries have served them well, providing a much-needed break from travel to recharge their weary spirits, before they hit the road again with renewed energy.

Secret gardens don't always look the same. They are a matter of individual preference, and people can find rest and relaxation at the oddest of places. A number of our authors have actually enjoyed a sense of spiritual retreat in the midst of people. Take Robert Tilley, who rejoices on the magical evening of Loi Krathong, when the glow of a thousand candles transform his small village into a fairyland, and he feels a universal bond of friendship with even the village drunk. Or Elizabeth Briel, who discovers her spiritual home in an artist's hotel located somewhere along a shabby shoemaker's alley in Bangkok,

where the air is spiked with fumes of industrial-strength glue and children play noisily outside their tenement houses with rubber soles and stiletto heels.

Others have withdrawn from human contact altogether and enjoyed their secret gardens in quiet companionship with nature. On a deserted beach washed clean by sporadic monsoon rains in Railay, we find Adam Bray savoring a sense of seclusion, even though an opportunistic male monkey has just snatched away the bagel lunch he was so looking forward to. John Henderson lives like a lotus-eating beach bum on the deserted island of Laoliang, not caring when or if or how he will ever get out of there in the midst of a raging storm. And Ian McNamara cycles off to his hideaway near Koh Chang, which, after his indiscretion of writing about it in this book, should soon be overrun with secret garden–seeking tourists from the main island.

This chapter also records a few whimsical moments of mystery, beauty, and pleasure that have become etched in the authors' minds—scenes to be revisited again and again, whenever the drudgery of everyday living seems to outweigh the delights. On a boat ride in the Amphawa District of Samut Songkram Province, Monsuda Kay Nopakun sails past stands of Lampoo trees that are glowing with swarms of fireflies desperately emitting sparks of phosphorescent light to announce their eligibility to the opposite sex. During a group tour of a Khmer temple ruin in eastern Thailand, Miranda Bruce-Mitford is startled by the extraordinary sight of countless tiny frogs spread like a large, restless, living, heaving, amphibious carpet on the green grass.

Fleeting glimpses of such miracles of nature can only be ascribed to random traveler's luck, and the rest of us may not be fortunate enough to see them, as well. We can spend days at Miranda's Khmer temple ruin and not spot a single tadpole on the grass, but it's the *knowing* that such a marvel can happen that inspires us to keep looking for a secret garden to call our own.

# BANGKOK

## *Elizabeth Briel feeds her artistic spirit in Bangkok*

I've found my home in Bangkok's Thon Buri district, the older, quieter part of the city with streets and alleyways that are rarely trampled by tourists.

To reach it, you have to stroll down quaint *sois*, passing many one-room living quarters with doors that stay open day and night. Fumes from industrial-strength glue will assail your nose as you walk through a warren of street-level workshops, where several generations of families are hard at work making the same shoes you've probably bought on the streets of Koh Samui or at the Chatuchak Market. Dodging rubber soles and stiletto heels tossed high in the air by the neighborhood kids at play, you will finally come to The Artists Place, a cozy little hotel run by my dear friend Charlee Sodprasaert.

You can't miss Charlee's front gate: tropical plants climb all over it, as colorful as fireworks. Just inside is an eclectic collection of shrines and concrete sculptures of dragons and snakes, interspersed with fresh offerings to Ganesh and the house spirits.

There's also a seating area, filled with mosquitoes, over which hang plastic toy guns and farewell notes that sound more like love letters—souvenirs left behind by hundreds of travelers.

The real reason I come to stay here is Charlee. His personality is as chaotic, informal, and welcoming as his decor. Whether I arrive at 9 a.m. or midnight, his greeting is always the same: "Good morning!"

Though the hotel is called The Artists Place, most guests are backpackers rather than professional artists. But if you've got artistic aspirations and would like to use one of the many in-house studios, all you have to do is ask. Charlee offers a free luggage-storage service too, but beware, sometimes your bags can disappear … as mine did once.

Every room here features artwork of varying quality, often donated by previous travelers who have stayed in it. Some rooms are spotless—particularly those on the roof—while others have a shabby gentility about them. If you're lucky, Charlee will take you to his favorite beef-noodle shop in Thon Buri (even if he insists on paying, don't let him!), where he's a celebrity, thanks to his radio music show. Charlee is a true Thai Renaissance man: surfer-musician à la Dick Dale, radio host, artist, poet, teacher, and traveler. His poetry is handstenciled or photocopied onto signs all around his hotel, and you'll come upon them in unexpected corners. The rhyme, you will find, is as unconventional as the man who wrote it.

You can get Internet (Wi-Fi and broadband) at a very reasonable rate of 20 baht per hour here. Check with Charlee for current Internet options. The neighborhood offers plenty of good food, a family-run convenience store, and a 7-Eleven for twenty-four-hour service. In case you're fighting a stomach bug, there's a fantastic chicken-noodle soup stall down the street from the hotel, which opens every night.

With the Skytrain route having recently been extended up to Thon Buri, a lot of tourists will now come here I guess. The quiet, Old World character of Thon Buri will inevitably change, and so will the neighborhood surrounding The Artists Place. But I know my home in Bangkok will remain the same because of Charlee. Like always, I will find him in the front yard, tossing his shock of silver hair about as he holds court with his guests, a paintbrush or a glass of Thai whiskey and water in hand.

### The Artists Place

63 Soi Tiem Boon Yang
(Via Soi Krung Thon Buri 1)
Krung Thon Buri Road
Klong San
Bangkok
(02) 862 0056
artistsplace@hotmail.com

## AMPHAWA DISTRICT

### Monsuda Kay Nopakun is dazzled by the fireflies of Amphawa

Just an hour's drive from Bangkok, Samut Songkram in the Amphawa district is a convenient weekend escape into the backwoods. A few resorts and lots of homestays have popped up here for tourists who want to do more than just a day tour of the floating market here, so it was a pretty good choice for me to take my sixty-one-year-old mum for a weekend break from the big city.

We stayed at a small resort that had only five traditional Thai houses, set a bit further away from the noisy floating market. The resort provided a boat service to go sightseeing along the canal, and that included a trip after dark to go watch the fireflies.

The fireflies are an unexpected spectacle in the midst of all the busy commercial activity that goes on in the canal after sundown. It's as if the insects hold a parallel marketplace of their own, sparkling with a greenish yellow light as they bargain enthusiastically for sexual favors with fellow fireflies clustered around trees along the shore.

At 4:30 p.m., we boarded a boat that took us on a leisurely ride past old settlements and temples before dropping us off at the floating market. We wandered among boats selling food and shophouses displaying colorful sweets, clothes, and souvenirs, until the boatman returned to pick us up again at eight thirty. The sun had disappeared by this time, and the sky was dark.

All the boats traveling in the canal alongside us had only a couple of little lights on. My mum and I sat at the back of the boat, chatting quietly in the balmy peacefulness of the night. Soon, the boatman stopped his vessel near a Lampoo tree on the shore and told us to look up.

And there they were: hundreds of fireflies flocking around the Lampoo tree, twinkling away for all they were worth. Like Christmas decorations strung up by God, a random, organic phenomenon more spectacular than ordinary electric fairy-lights, and more energy-saving too.

Unlike electric bulbs that convert energy into both light and heat, these fireflies used little or no energy to emit sparks. They saved themselves from burning to death by emitting a benign "cold light," and they could do this in synchrony with fellow insects to show off their sexual viability to the opposite sex.

As we stared for long minutes at the Lampoo tree, giving no sign to the driver that we wanted to move on, he took the initiative and started steering the boat. This was not much, he said. He was going to take us to see other Lampoo trees that had more fireflies than this.

True to his word, when we stopped at the next few Lampoo trees, there were many more flashing fireflies. The trees were ablaze with literally thousands of them, celebrating their short lifespan as if they knew they weren't long for this world.

The driver waited patiently at each Lampoo tree so we could cherish the moment. Then he turned back and headed in the direction of our resort.

My camera had failed to capture any decent photos of the fireflies, but I wasn't sorry I had only memories to take back with me. These days, we travelers have become such slaves to social networking, all we do is record everything on our digital cameras so we can upload them on our blogs and Facebook pages. Thankfully, there are still some things out there, like the fireflies of Amphawa, that travelers have to appreciate the old-fashioned way: with their own two eyes.

## Getting to Samut Songkram
Go to page 69.

## The dying light

For reasons nobody is quite sure of, the fireflies of Amphawa inhabit only the Lampoo trees. And while they're a spectacular sight for tourists, they're nothing but a nuisance for Amphawa residents who cannot get a good night's rest for the commotion created in their backyards by firefly tourism.

To deal with the problem, they are cutting down Lampoo trees on their properties along the shore. The firefly population as a result is gradually diminishing. So if you want to see the fireflies, be respectful. Keep your flashlights off and create as little disturbance as possible for the locals, who are not on holiday and have go to work the next day.

## KANCHANABURI

### Jan Polatschek goes with the flow on the River Kwai

After a brief afternoon swim in the swift, churning currents of the River Kwai, I need to rest on a chaise lounge and catch my breath. And enjoy the quiet. With the exception of an occasional motorboat taxi or the very occasional trumpeting of the elephants nearby, the only sound I hear is the murmuring and splashing of the impatient, swirling river. At this point on its journey from Myanmar to the Gulf of Siam, the narrow River Kwai slices through steep hillsides and vertical stone outcrops colored black and gold.

So, if the hills are so steep, where exactly is my hotel? It's on the river. On ... the ... river. I am spending the weekend at the aptly named River Kwai Jungle Raft Float Hotel.

My chaise lounge sits on a small bamboo raft about ten meters long by three meters wide. The raft is lashed to the side of a much larger wooden raft, about fifteen meters long. There are ten of these large rafts connected to each other by little wooden bridges. Each raft has five bedrooms. In the middle of this "train" are several larger rafts on which sit a dining area for about one hundred guests, a bar, lounge, and kitchen, and the ever-present Thai massage area. There is also a theater where we are entertained each evening with singing and dancing by a local Burmese hill tribe. The entire complex sits on steel pontoons that are anchored to the shoreline by long cables.

All the rafts are gaily decorated with a botanical garden of potted and hanging tropical plants. Just next to my chaise lounge is a small red-leafed plant with tiny ball-shaped white flowers, and a bushy green Jackson Pollock plant, liberally dribbled with bright yellow.

Our bedroom has one double bed and one single bed. The very basic bathroom has a sink, mirror, a modern toilet (except that it takes a scoop or two of water from the cistern for a proper flush), and a shower head that is just beside the sink. Hot water? Forgetaboutit. Power? Pre-Edison candles and kerosene lamps.

I am in the company of two Thai female graduate students I met several months ago. They are members of a group of Spanish students and teachers. Noi, twenty-two, and her friend Paulina, thirty, speak excellent English and Spanish. They invited me to join them on this trip. This is a "first" for me. I am sharing the facilities with Noi and Paulina. I promised to behave myself. Thai style.

So here I am, lounging in the mountain jungles of western Thailand, close to the border of Myanmar, being served by charming Burmese men and women, and practicing my Spanish. I do believe I am now an honorary member of The Bangkok Spanish Club.

This morning, my wake-up call came at 7 a.m. Through the rear window of my room, I could see two elephants walk proudly by, screeching happily as the mahouts rode them to the riverside for their daily bath.

After breakfast, Noi and I took a short hike up the hillside behind the lodge. We found some touristy gift shops, a crafts center, and a Buddha cave, complete with living quarters for the local monks and a variety of religious statuary. From the hillside were picturesque views of the wild river and the floating lodge below. The highlight of the morning, except for the elephants of course, was a kindergarten with a dozen local children dressed in the traditional attire of white shirts and colorful floor-length cloth skirts.

Back at the lodge, sweaty and dizzy from the humidity and the mountain jungle sun, I am faced with a dilemma. Do I relax on the chaise lounge at the riverside, or do I retreat a step or two to an inviting rope hammock in the shade, just outside my room? After some deliberation, I choose the hammock. It's a little early for a siesta, but hey, I left my wristwatch in Bangkok.

The food at the hotel is plentiful and surpasses excellent. American breakfast is fried eggs, toast, coffee, and fresh pineapple. Lunch and dinner are boarding house style with a table full of savory Thai specialties: sweet and sour chicken, fresh carrots and tomatoes, eggs with green vegetables, sautéed fish, steamed rice, coffee, tea, pineapple, and watermelon. All the food is delicately flavored with herbs, spices, and sauces.

The River Kwai Jungle Rafts hotel is a restful resort in a dramatic/romantic/historic setting with not much to do but ride the rapids or just relax. My energetic friends decide to don their life vests for a long float down the river. For me, one "first" was enough this weekend. I choose to observe the currents from the comfort of the chaise.

### The River Kwai Jungle Rafts

This hotel was one of the first in Thailand to offer floating accommodations on the River Kwai for guests who wanted a true eco-holiday and an escape from modern creature comforts like electricity and the Internet. The rooms are built on rafts and include private wooden terraces that look out at tropical forests on both sides of the river. The hotel offers many water activities plus an introduction to the life and culture of the ethnic Mon people who emigrated from Myanmar to Thailand many hundred years ago.

Baan Tahsao, Amphur Saiyoke
Kanchanaburi
(081) 734 0667
info@serenatahotels.com
www.riverkwaijunglerafts.com

## PATTTAYA

### David Kovanen
### runs away on the beach
### in Pattaya

It is raining—sideways—and I am in the middle of it. It is delightful.

This is Pattaya in the rainy season. People who don't think that rain and beaches go well together should come and experience Pattaya during the monsoon.

I arrived about a week ago, and every day I have visited the beach to sit under an umbrella on a chair facing the ocean. I have read my book, sipped on a split coconut, and enjoyed the vastness of the sea as I realized just how people are meant to be close to it.

If it's your first time here, the beach will seem like a sea of umbrellas and chairs, with gatekeepers demanding 30 baht to use one of them. Indeed, that is the kind of experience some people want to have. But not me.

On my first day, I walked the entire length of the beach and observed that there were many "chair stores," each operated by a family. The family tends to its thirty or forty chairs. And every store reflects the temperament of the owner. Some ignore their customers; some have a deep desire to serve. So I watched and observed, and I took note of the difference. The owners of the good stores weren't sitting and chatting, but instead paying attention. At sunset for example, when the sun is reflecting off the water and is harsh on the eye, they were placing a row of umbrellas on the sand. The umbrellas blocked the view, but stopped the sun. A good chair store owner knows how to look after his customers.

I have never been able to remember the name of my chair store owner. He is thin and works with his wife. He is probably fifty or sixty, with weathered skin and eyes that have seen life. Now when I approach, he recognizes me and smiles, and makes me welcome. It feels like home as I arrive at his store every day. And when the afternoon sun is shielded by his forward-facing umbrellas, it is like being in a tent, and literally like being a guest in his home. He offers me a coconut because he knows that is what I enjoy.

Today, it is raining and I am at my chair store, sitting on a lounge chair, under an umbrella. The Thais are out in the waters, swimming and having a good time. (Westerners don't seem to understand that the ocean is just as warm on a rainy day and the sun won't burn.) I'm safe, warm, dry, and watching the sheets of rain sweep across the waves. Today is a day of water.

Now, there is an art to choosing a chair on a rainy day. The umbrellas all overlap each other, forming a continuous canopy. The topmost umbrellas spill water onto the lower ones, and so forth, and there is always some rain leaking under the canopy. But in chairs like mine, I am dry because I have chosen one of the lowest umbrellas in the canopy. I think of it as my little bubble.

The chair store owner suggested this particular chair for me today. I wouldn't have known the difference, or why today this one was a better choice. But I have learned to trust this particular owner and so I went along with his suggestion. He recognizes me as a good customer, he knew I was going to sit for a few hours, he knew it was going to rain, and he wanted me to have a good afternoon. So he helped me choose my umbrella wisely.

The next time you visit Pattaya, you too can choose wisely—start by being people-oriented like the Thais and establishing a relationship instead of just paying for the service.

On my last day at the beach, I give the chair store owner's wife some money so she can have a manicure.

She has worked at the chair store for four years. Every day she watches her customers get manicures on the sand, but she has never gotten one. I also leave a 1,000-baht tip for the couple … and run away when they start to cry.

### Finding David's chair store

To enjoy the services of David's favorite chair store owner, turn right from the Central Festival shopping center onto Beach Road. Go half a block down until you reach the lifeguard station, where the Vegetarian Delight Indian restaurant is also located. The chair store will be across the street. None of the chair stores have names, but this one is easy to recognize because its chairs are blue, while the other stores have orange ones. The store is owned by Papa Sali and his wife, Noh. They speak very little English but are fluent in customer service.

## LAMPANG

### Robert Tilley floats his boat at a Lampang festival

The November full moon festival of Loi Krathong is a spectacular ceremony in the big cities of Thailand. But the touching simplicity with which it is celebrated in typical Thai villages, such as mine, located a few kilometers away from Lampang, makes it seem more authentic and true to tradition.

For days, the ladies of our village are busy as children in kindergarten, constructing their *krathongs,* the little boats that will be launched into the river Wang. In our household, we make the boats from the stem of a young banana tree, which we cut down from our riverside plot and bring into the yard. Saweet, the forester brother of my partner, Pan, slices up the stem into round, two-inch thick "platters," with some token help from me. With amazing skill and great attention to detail, Pan and her sister-in-law then turn those bits of banana stem into crowns that would be worthy of a monarch's head.

First, they fold green banana leaves into diamond shapes and fasten them to the outsides of the "platters" with flowers. Larger triangles of banana leaf make the points of the crowns, and those in turn are "crowned" with fresh orange and purple blooms collected from the forest.

In the center of each of these *krathongs* stands a candle and a small bunch of incense sticks—the only items to cost any money. Otherwise, not one baht is spent on creating these very beautiful objects that will light up our festivities.

As soon as the sun goes down on the day of Loi Krathong, our dusty main street transforms into an avenue of enchantment. Every housefront is lit by Chinese lanterns and candles, hundreds of them, making our little village look like a tropical fairyland. The full moon usually appears as if on command, only when the final preparations are over, to guide us with its glow to the river, two hundred yards down the road. Following a line of flickering candles, we walk in a procession until we reach the safe slipway beside the bridge where other boat builders have already gathered. In ones and twos, we add a flame to the candles inside our *krathongs* and send them off to join the others in the flotilla.

It's an extraordinarily moving sight, this modest but splendid little fleet, each carefully crafted vessel carrying a silent prayer or message of thanks. Most people in my village must be asking the Buddha for a successful rice harvest, but some I suspect are asking for the where- withal to buy a new pickup.

At my first Loi Krathong, with the black water lapping around my ankles, I was struggling to light my *krathong* when I found a 1-baht coin tucked beneath the decoration. It had clearly been put there by Pan, but I didn't want to embarrass her by questioning the motive. Instead, I pressed her to tell me what kind of unspoken messages those little boats carried off with them down the river.

"We say 'thank you' for the water we get, which washes us and which we drink," she replied.

Well, that's pretty rich, I thought. The floods had just cut off the water supply to our part of the village yet again, and I was reduced to showering in the rain. Well, my Christian religion has taught me to be thankful for small mercies, so whoever up there in the sky is turning on the taps: thank you very much, can I have some more, so I can work off the soap please?

After the *krathongs* have sailed, we usually start with the big, noisy part of the Loi Krathong celebration: the fireworks. The neighborhood kids gear up for it like commandos on maneuver. I increased my popularity no end one year by banning all bangers from the vicinity of my house. But this hasn't deterred the occasional young rogue from creeping up and letting off mortarlike devices that lift me straight off my chair and send the cats scurrying up the nearest coconut palm. All these things are Chinese, of course—the kids of my neighborhood alone must be keeping Cantonese gunpowder factories on overtime.

On the night of my first Loi Krathong, local whiskey had flowed in abundance at a party at a neighbor's street-front shanty, and I was beckoned to come over. There were a couple of rather attractive, cigar-smoking ladies there, so I didn't need much persuasion.

They were all pretty smashed, and I helped to put them further under the table by passing round a bottle of London gin. Our neighbor grabbed the tumbler that I had intended all to share and downed the contents in one gulp. Her husband took a careful nip from the refilled glass, pulled a face, and returned to his local brew.

Their battered music system blared Thai numbers from its two overworked speakers, and a sarong-clad brother-in-law weaved about, doing an unsteady, sinuous dance that kicked up dust from the gutters. Beside me, Loong (Uncle) Dam—known as the English-language expert in the village because he had worked in Saudi Arabia—mumbled two sentences repeatedly into my ear, like a temple mantra: "You good Thailand. Thailand good you." What could *the good man* mean? Pan winkled out the message from him. "He says you speak good Thai."

Well, that's a nice compliment, given that he is hardly in any condition to notice such things.

"He only speaks English when he's drunk," Pan confided.

Needless to say, Loong Dam spoke English on every Loi Krathong night thereafter. Caught up in some sort of November full moon madness, he ignored our candlelit *krathongs* in order to drink indoors while the festival was going on by the river. Afterward, he insisted on telling us many transcendental truths about ourselves … in English, of course. Sadly, Loong Dam has now passed away, and all of us will sorely miss his annual contribution to our Loi Krathong evening this year.

### Loi Krathong

On the full moon of the twelfth lunar month, Thais set sail to their ornately decorated banana leaf floats in rivers all over the country. It is believed

NORTHEAST THAILAND

that the floats, or *krathongs*, take away grief and misfortune and give hope for a happy year ahead. Lovers wish on a *krathong* for the success of their relationship. Farmers pray for a good harvest, and women invoke blessings for the families.

## Village celebrations

The grand Loi Krathong celebration in tourist hubs like Bangkok, Chiang Mai, and Phuket draw thousands of spectators every year. The same festival, however, takes place on a more modest scale in every Thai village at the same time. Loi Krathong in rural Thailand is an intimate, spiritual affair. The pomp and pageantry is absent, but the trade-off is that the villagers will welcome you to participate in whatever celebration they have managed to afford that year.

## R.S.V.P.

Interested in joining the Loi Krathong festival in Robert's village of Ban Maethot in Lampang Province? There's a decent hotel called Nakornthoen in Thoen, about twenty-five kilometers away; it has recently been renovated and now has a good multicuisine restaurant. In addition, Robert will be happy to help you with the arrangements, so feel free to send him an email.

www.nakornthoenhotel.com
robertjtilley@yahoo.com

## LOEI

### Brendan O'Reilly sees the earth move under his feet in Loei

When my travel companion suggested a day trip to see the curious rock formations in Suan Hin Pha Ngam in Loei Province, I gladly agreed to go because I knew I could return to Khon Kaen city well in time for a large Isaan dinner. Isaan food, as no guidebook will ever tell you, can be a serious impediment to certain types of people when touring in northeast Thailand. But if you're anything like me, the opposite is true, and you'll constantly worry about going too far out into the boonies, where there may not be anyone to set up a plate of tangy Isaan sausage or pound up some fresh *som tam* salad for you.

On the day of the trip, I went out to fortify myself with a simple yogurt breakfast while my resourceful friend made contact with a local who would take us to see the rock formations. Shortly after I returned, the man showed up at our fabulously Old World Saen Samran Hotel, and one look at his expensive clothes and black German-made sedan told me we had got ourselves the wrong sort of guide. What insights into northeastern folk culture could we expect to get from this obviously wealthy man?

Well, a lot as it turned out. My hasty judgment was way off mark, because not only was he an expert on the area, he proved to be a never-ending source of friendliness and good humor that made the day even more pleasurable. It's amazing how much difference it can make to the experience when your guide is enjoying himself as much as you. He happily drove the two-hour distance to the rock garden and back, refusing to entertain any discussion about monetary contributions for fuel. We didn't press the point, and we let him explain many interesting aspects of Isaan life and culture as we looked out the window. It was beautiful day to be out driving through rural northeastern landscapes, passing villages, rice fields, and farmers who stopped their ploughs to wave a cheery hello at us.

The night before, I had tried researching Suan Hin Pha Ngam on the Internet, but information had been sparse. The few travel websites that did mention the rock garden gave me the same two-line description, comparing it to the rock formations in Kunming, China. From the one or two low-resolution pictures I managed to find, I had no clue that Suan Hin Pha Ngam would turn out to be a 3,600-acre spread that required a few hours (at least) in order to explore it fully. The limestone rocks had been sculpted by wind and rain, and twisted by inexorable movements of

the earth's crust into bizarre shapes that stretched as far as my eyes could see.

I was relieved we had a guide who was familiar enough with the twisting maze of Suan Hin Pha Ngam's rock formations to keep us from getting lost. I had to bend and stretch my 1.9-meter frame to fit through so many narrow passages that left on my own, I doubt I could have remembered which way I had come.

At several spots, I stopped the tour to wander away on my own and absorb the incredible views of limestone rocks that seemed to morph and change with every step. Long ropelike tree roots, ferns, and primitive palm trees gave credence to the site's prehistoric aura, and more than once, I found myself looking over my shoulder to see if I was being followed by a Jurassic-era creature. This fancifulness, no doubt, was fostered by the fossils I found scattered around the rocks, mostly of ancient shellfish; our guide confirmed my suspicions when he explained that the entire site was under the sea 250 million years ago. Typically, limestone formations are composed of about four-fifths of organic material that come from the microscopic shell remnants of ancient sea creatures. No wonder the shapes of Suan Hin Pha Ngam looked so alive, I thought. They once were!

We covered most of the rock garden before we took a break to play the childish game every visitor must play here: identifying animals and human figures in the rock shapes. We argued over which one looked like a monkey or which one looked like an elephant until our guide put an end to our disagreements by pointing out one rock on which the opinion was unanimous: it was a well-contoured, voluptuous, and gloriously naked female body.

Laughing at our guide's guileless sense of humor, we made our way to the summit of a small hill, which afforded panoramic views of the garden. We saw the home of one monk who lives among the rocks, and a few small Buddha temples, as well. Our guide insisted we experience a local "tractor *tuk-tuk*," so we hitched a short ride on a unique, purpose-built transportation device that comprised a covered truck bed, pulled along by an old tractor. The contraption moved at a languid pace, giving me time to take many beautiful pictures of the scenery we passed.

All too soon it seemed, the day trip came to an end, and we were heading back to Khon Kaen. My friend wanted to give our wonderful new Thai friend some money for taking us out, but he explained it was impossible for him to accept any remuneration. By Isaan tradition, he was our *thaan,* he said, our respected host and elder. We must offer him respect and attention, and he must care for us.

His instinctive generosity of spirit imbued the day's sightseeing with a special warmth that will remain in my heart forever. Like the rock formations of Suan Hin Pha Ngam, this gracefulness too had its roots in ancient Isaan history. As our *thaan* is

not a professional tour guide, I took care not to reveal his identity in this essay to respect his privacy. But if he happens to read this book, he will know that his hospitality was the kind of precious souvenir every foreign traveler to the Isaan provinces dreams of taking back home.

### Getting to Suan Hin Pha Ngam

From Khon Kaen, take Highway 201 to Nong Hin. Here the road branches off to provide access to the rock garden. A twenty-kilometer paved road will then take you from Nong Hin to Suan Hin Pha Ngam.

### Saen Samran Hotel

Located on Klang Muang Road, this is the oldest guesthouse in Khon Kaen. Built of teak, the building is a storehouse of interesting memorabilia from the past, which is displayed in the hotel's public areas.

### Pit stops

While in Loei, make sure to sip Thailand's first commercially produced quality wine at the Chateau de Loei Winery. Book a tour of the vineyard, do a wine tasting, or shop at the wine store.

61 Mu 6
Tambon Rong Chik
Amphoe Phu Ruea, Loei.
www.chateaudeloei.com

# KHORAT

*Miranda Bruce-Mitford*
*encounters a sea of frogs*
*in Khorat*

It was February, and relatively cool by Thai standards. Still pretty hot to us Westerners, though. Like a mother hen, I had led my brood of aging travelers around the temples of Thailand, pointing out details that they would no doubt quickly forget, helping them climb crumbling steps, exhorting them to imagine life, here, a thousand years ago. In the evenings we would sit crammed into someone's hotel room, they listening attentively or dozing as I intoned above the drone of the air-conditioning, expounding the finer points of Thai art, history, religion.

On this particular morning we were visiting Khmer temples in eastern Thailand, on the very border with Cambodia. This arid region was controlled by the Khmer long before the arrival of the Thais in the thirteenth century. The temples built here—mostly Hindu—have the powerful rounded towers and authoritative carvings of Angkor; there could be no doubt, though, who held power in the eleventh century.

We got off the bus and approached the crumbling temple of Muang Tham. The sanctuary stood surrounded by four lakes, representing the four oceans encircling the sacred Mount Meru. The lakes looked as though they had somehow sunk into the ground, their retaining walls sagging in the middle. Each lake was surrounded by a monumental serpent-shaped balustrade with five serpent heads. These snakes were the mighty *nagas*, mythological creatures that were often found in religious buildings and served as symbols of Khmer might.

It was my first sight of Muang Tham, I remember. It was hardly visited at that time and as yet there had been no attempt at restoration. It looked lonely, brooding, magnificent. I stepped from the coach onto the green grass, and the group followed, exclaiming with a mixture of delight and relief at stretching their legs. Then the exclamations turned to anxious cries. Strangely, in this deserted place, there was movement all about us. In fact, the ground itself seemed to be moving. Looking closer, I realized that the grass was covered in tiny frogs. What appeared to be millions and millions of tiny frogs. It wasn't possible to walk without treading on them. This must have been their first day out of the water. They were exploring their new world.

Gingerly, we picked our way across the grass and entered the temple, and I keenly felt the presence of a past power. I was moved by the authority and artistry of the decoration. I pointed with delight and exclaimed about the building to the group. They wandered around, looking, commenting, photographing. After an hour or so, we made our way back to the coach. We all remembered to watch our feet, but the frogs had vanished, returning to the water from which they had emerged. It was as though they had never been there.

The group fell silent in the air-conditioned coach traveling back to Khorat. Most were asleep, but I couldn't sleep. Instead I gazed unseeing out of the window. I couldn't forget the frogs ... how strange it had been. And I thought, in religious buildings such as Muang Tham, carved creatures were often depicted spewing out other creatures and watery vegetation, as if the natural world were overflowing with fecundity. Here, in this sacred setting, and just for a moment, the uncontainable forces of nature had disgorged these tiny frogs from the sacred waters as they had done annually for a thousand years. Awed by the scale of the event, I felt as insignificant as one of those little frogs—tiny and part of a timeless mystery.

### Getting to Muang Tham

The temple is about 120 kilometers from the northeastern gateway town of Nakhon Ratchasima, also known as Khorat. Tourists mostly come here from Nakhon Ratchasima, but you can also take a bus from Buri Ram city to Ban Ta-Ko and do the rest of the journey on a *songthaew*.

Compared to Phanom Rung, the more celebrated Khmer temple ruin just eight kilometers away, the temple sanctuary of Muang Tham is less visited, so you're likely to be able to enjoy it in relative peace and quiet.

## KHO PHI PHI

*Elizabeth Cassidy finds her happy place in Koh Phi Phi*

Give holidaymakers a paradise island, and they will do as they please with it. Koh Phi Phi is full of such tourists who come to swim, snorkel, rock climb, or use the island as a picturesque backdrop for nonstop parties. Me? I disappear inside Viking Natures Resorts, a cozy little paradise within paradise, and wish I never had to emerge to go back to Chicago.

Viking Natures Resort is tucked into a cove, cut off from the busyness of Phi Phi Island by a barrier of thick forestland. Unless you want to hike through this jungle, the only way to reach the hotel is by longtail boats. The boats don't come all the way to the beach, and passengers have to jump off and wade through the last few yards in warm, knee-deep water. Knowing this, I leave off the suitcases and come to Viking with only a backpack. The first time I feel my bare feet sink into the dry, soft beach sand, I know I have reached my happy place. I don't want to put my sandals back on ever again.

As I step into the hotel's reception area, with tribal artwork displayed everywhere, I always think how the place reminds me of an artisan's workshop. Apparently, the owner, John Torsak Bumrungtrakul, is an artist, and going by his collection, it isn't hard to see that his creative inspirations come from somewhere very close to the earth. Usually, I choose to stay in a villa on top of a hill, and I'm escorted there by a fellow guest, a Frenchman, who loved the property so much he stayed back to live and work here.

The villa is quite a distance away, and I admire other accommodations we pass on our way to it, with their rustic railings made by lashing tree branches together and wide-open decks. My villa has a deck too, big enough to sit ten people at once, and a string hammock that was always occupied when I came here once with four of my friends. We also used to fight over the chair swing and compete to see who could swing right off the deck. A hand-carved staircase leads up to my room, and a barrel of water waits at the bottom. A wooden ladle is provided with the barrel, and I love the charming Thai custom of scooping water out of it to wash my feet before I step inside.

The most incredible feature in my living quarters at Viking is the tree that grows inside it. Yes, a huge, flourishing, fully grown tropical tree. Branches literally push through the floor of the villa, which is raised high off the ground with stilts, and go out again through the roof. The tree was already here before the villa was built, and John, the proprietor, simply designed the villa around it. The bathroom seems wide open with huge windows on all sides, and walking through the curtain of seashells that separates it from the rest of the living area always makes me feel like a mermaid stepping into the sea. The view of the bedroom is dominated by an enormous white mosquito net that hangs so decoratively over the bed, you wouldn't guess it has any practical use—that is, until sundown, when the mosquitoes come out in full force.

Each villa at the Viking Natures Resort is decorated differently—as you would expect when a hotel is an ongoing project for an artist trying making his creative visions come true—but I am too comfortable in this favorite villa of mine to want to stay in any of the others yet. I've lost count of the hours I have spent absorbing the atmosphere created by the handmade lanterns hanging from the rafters and other items of folk art strewn about the room. Whole mornings and afternoons of just lying in my hammock, scarcely being able to close my eyes on the marvelous view of the bay and distant islands that the deck looks out to.

Evenings at the Viking Natures Resort are a busy time for the hotel, as most guests gather to enjoy a free tasting buffet laid out at the bar-cum-restaurant. The buffet table is an old canoe, filled with ceramic statuettes and candles stuck in the crevices of boulders, corals, and other crude rock formations. Delicious Thai dishes are placed carefully inside this candlelit tableau—items from the à la carte menu chosen by the chef to showcase his skills. It is always fun to see what food the chef has put out today and enjoy a drink in the magical atmosphere of this beautifully designed restaurant.

As you may have guessed by now, I don't come to the Viking Natures Resort to do very much. After the urban demands that hometown Chicago makes on my time, I simply crave the chance to have a lot of it on my hands.

Sometimes, I go swimming in the quiet cove or walk over to Ton Sai town, just a few minutes from the hotel when the tide is out. The beach route to town floods during high tide, and I carry a flashlight, in case I have to take the only other way back to the hotel: through a jungle trail. There are taxi boats that drop people off at the hotel, but they are not always available in the late evenings, and carrying a flashlight around is a good idea.

In fact, I would suggest you carry a flashlight even when you're inside the property in the evenings. The sandy paths between the villas and the hotel's public areas are fraught with tree branches and roots that stick out in the dark, waiting to trip you if you're not looking where you're going.

Now that I have mentioned a downside, I'd better itemize a few

other negatives (to some travelers) that may influence your decision to stay here. First, there is no hot water, and the hotel pipes seawater into the bathrooms. Second, there is no air-conditioning—as of now, at least. Third, the hotel is remote, and walking around can be a strain on your calves, if you're not used to the exertion. Fourth, nights can be noisy in some of the villas because the sound of party music floats over the sea from nearby islands. And fifth, I have heard some people say that service here can be disorganized and slow, though I have never had a complaint myself.

But I don't come to Viking Natures Resort expecting splendid resort service. I come to live ordinary in an extraordinary surrounding. This place is my mental spa where I can get rid of all the psychological debris collected in the city and relax my mind with a purposeless enjoyment of nature. It is my secret garden. And it can be yours too. Just keep in mind the caveats listed above, and make sure that when you say you want to go rustic on your trip, you really mean it.

### *Viking Natures Resort*
10 Mou 7
Koh Phi Phi, Krabi
(08) 3649 9492
www.vikingnaturesresort.com
vikingroom@hotmail.com

### *Worth the hike*
Elizabeth adds: If you're willing to climb up the hill behind Viking Natures Resort, you'll find yourself in

Long Beach, famous for having the softest sand in Phi Phi. It's a steep climb—I had to use a rope at one point—but the reward on the other side was a lovely seafood restaurant at the Phi Phi Long Island Hotel. Tables were laid out on the beach, the seafood barbecues were simply delicious, and the ladyboys who ran the restaurant kept diners entertained with a steady stream of witty songs and jokes. The hotel is low budget and has nothing besides a cheap rate to recommend it, but I think its restaurant is the best place to eat in Long Beach. To find it, just walk to the middle of the beach and look out for the hotel's sign.

## KAO LAOLIANG

*John Henderson
sinks into a lazy stupor
on Koh Laoliang*

About an hour's ferry ride off the coast of Trang Province in the Andaman Sea lies a square island with sheer cliffs on all sides. The only habitable spot on Koh Laoliang is a beachlet, five hundred meters wide and one hundred meters deep. For six months a year, an entrepreneur puts

up a handful of safari-style tents on the sand here, cooks group meals under a tarp, and calls the operation a resort.

A group of friends and I were on our way to spend two nights at the entrepreneur's makeshift "resort." We planned on extending our stay if the place worked out. There were still a few minutes left before our ferry departed the mainland, and with the future uncertain, somebody went and bought two cases of Heineken.

When we landed at Koh Laoliang, we found the island to be exactly what we had dared to hope: a utopian getaway for hardcore solitude-seekers. With no restaurants, no bars, no shopping, no nightlife to inspire any sense of purpose, we passed our days in a dreamy stupor, playing cards, kayaking, snorkeling, or rock climbing. Had we been serious climbers, trying new routes on the rock faces probably could have kept us occupied for weeks. An American teenager we met there was exchanging odd jobs for free lodging and the chance to spider up the multipitch routes along the sides of the birthday cake–shaped island.

But we mostly preferred to kick back and relax at sea level. The bright corals kept us in the water for much longer than our sunblock lasted, and the snorkeling boat driver had to bribe us back on board with the promise of lunch on a small island nearby that was inhabited by fishermen. The resort had a few kayaks, and we paddled around in one, managing not to roll, even when the waves at the northern tip of the island got seriously choppy. From the kayaks, we kept an eye out for mermaids and for the mythical trail to the top of the island, but alas, no luck.

From time to time, we speculated about when we might head back to the mainland. And worked our way through the Heineken.

The weather unfortunately didn't hold steady for the entire duration of our trip. Although it was almost December and the rains should have stopped by now, we woke up some mornings to find puddles outside out tents. And the day we finally decided to leave the island, the sea turned on us and refused to cooperate.

We intended to ride out on a longtail and meet the ferry, but the choppy water made it impossible for the little boat to dock. The solution was for a boatman to wade next to a kayak and pull us away from the beach one at a time. When everyone in our group was aboard the longtail, the boatman rushed us off to the ferry before going back for the second load of passengers waiting on the island. We thought our transfer had been rather curtly handled, and it was only later that we discovered that the longtail had sustained damages when it collided with the ferry. The second group was stranded until another boat could be found. The ferry didn't wait.

As we headed for the mainland over rough seas, we heard talk of Bangkok-bound flights being canceled out of Trang. At the food center where we stopped to eat, there was more news of the Bangkok airport being closed.

All around us tourists were trying to beat the crowd and book the few seats left on overnight buses.

Should we do that too? Bus it back to Bangkok then?

Maybe. Maybe not.

Such decisions required logical thinking, and we had only just got off Koh Laoliang. The inertia induced by the lazy little island hadn't worn off yet, so at this time, frankly, none of us much cared.

### Getting to Koh Laoliang

The island is located twenty kilometers away from mainland Trang. Boats bound for Koh Laoliang and other nearby islands leave from Trang's Hat Yao Pier.

### Staying at Koh Laoliang

To book the tented cabins, visit the resort's website.

www.laoliangresort.com

### Passing time

Besides lazing around, the island also offers some energetic activities like snorkeling, fishing, rock climbing, island hopping, and superb photography opportunities. Since there are no permanent residents on Koh Laoliang except the resort guests, you always have the sense of really having gotten away from it all.

### When to go

Nobody stays on Koh Laoliang during the rainy season because the waves are too rough to land a boat. The island's lone permanent structure is a tall metal pole supporting four large speakers, an early warning system paid for out of international donations following the 2004 tsunami.

## Koh Mak

*Ian McNamara spends his alone time pedaling Koh Mak*

When I moved to Koh Chang seven years ago, it was just as well that I chose a quiet spot to live in, hidden away from the congested main road and a short walk from one of the island's most isolated beaches.

For outside my secluded little kingdom, Koh Chang was busily metamorphosing into yet another popular sea resort. The unsightly concrete buildings, meant to house tourist-driven businesses, were coming up so fast, I rarely had a sense of being close to the sea anymore when I went into town.

Fortunately for me, while my "tropical paradise" of Koh Chang was under siege, I still had a few quiet, scenic locations around the island I could escape to—places like Koh Mak, approximately thirty kilometers south of Koh Chang. In terms of traveling time, Koh Mak is a two-hour slow boat ride or forty minutes

by speedboat. In terms of development, I'm glad to say it is still a lifetime away.

The island has been spared the onslaught of tourism by the foresight of five clans of longtime inhabitants who own most of the land here. When travelers discovered the beautiful beaches of Koh Chang, these families swore to prevent large package tour resorts from taking over Koh Mak as well. Of course, you can find accommodation on Koh Mak, but it is in the form of simple beach huts and luxury villas, meant for couples and families. Very private, very small-scale. Not to everybody's taste I know, but it's still nice to come here and do nothing once in a while.

Koh Mak's cross-shaped appearance means that although it is only sixteen square kilometers in area, it has more than twenty-seven kilometers of coastline. The local community on Koh Mak has recently established a network of cycling trails, and the best way to see the entire island is on a bike.

An enjoyable day for me is to follow any of the three marked trails on Koh Mak, simply known as A, B, and C. Distinctive concrete route markers guide the way, and signs in English and Thai posted at each point of interest provide details on their significance to the islanders.

Route C is the easiest one. It mostly keeps me on paved roads and takes me past a ninety-year-old teak mansion, the island's temple and an interesting erotic art garden called The Kingdom of Somchai's Affection.

But to my mind, the best routes are those that take me to places I would normally never see or find on my own. I often combine routes A and B to make a loop around the north and east of the island, where there's an interesting sight waiting for me at every turn. One moment I'm riding through a coconut field, the next I feel the air getting noticeably cooler as I pass through regimented rows of rubber trees. Exiting the plantations, I keep stumbling into a small no-name hamlet by the sea, one of the original settlements on Koh Mak. Tourism still hasn't impacted the inhabitants' lives here, and I always seem to attract shy, curious smiles as I pass by.

Like any island, Koh Mak's reputation is built on the quality of its beaches. And although long swathes of white sand are only found on the northwest and southwest shores, there are a couple of gems elsewhere. My favorite is Ao Tao Kai (Turtle Egg Beach, named after the hawksbill turtles that laid their eggs here in the past), located at the northernmost point of the island and only accessible by following cycle route A. This beach is a two-hundred-meter-long, picture-perfect scene of sand and sea, with no development other than a small wooden shrine where fishermen pay their respects and pray for a good catch. Standing by the sea here, I can see the islands of Koh Wai, Koh Mai See Yai, Koh Klum, and in the far distance, the peaks of Koh Chang laid out before me.

And the best thing? Even in high season, I have my favorite beach on Koh Mak all to myself.

### Renting bicycles

To rent bicycles on Koh Mak or take a half/full-day guided

cycling tour on the island's bike routes, contact "Ball" at Koh Mak Tourist Office, located by the pier at Koh Mak Resort. You can also find information by visiting the following website.

www.koh-mak.com

### Island history

There are two excellent reasons why you must visit the Koh Mak Seafood Restaurant in Ao Nid Bay during your tour of the island. Obviously, food is one. The other is a neighboring house, one of the original teak homes on the island, which has been turned into a small museum. Here you will see old photographs that give fascinating insight into life on the island throughout the past century. The owner of the restaurant enjoys giving visitors a free fifteen-minute tour in English, and explaining the stories behind the photos.

## KOH LANTA

### *Roberta Sotonoff savors the art of pampering on Koh Lanta*

Work is a hassle, and the kids are giving us grief. My husband and I long to escape from Chicago to some idyllic place where we will be spoiled rotten.

We find it. But the problem is that Pimalai Resort & Spa is on Lanta Island in southern Thailand—halfway around the world.

You *really* have to want to get there. It takes many in-flight movies to reach Bangkok, plus another flight after that to reach Krabi. Then there is the white-knuckle taxi ride with a driver who thinks he's training for the Indy 500, and an hour-long boat ride into the roiling night waves of the Andaman Sea. Finally—and this is the toughest part—a roller-coaster walk, aided by the resort staff, down a long slithering pier.

But it's all worth it.

Once we reach Pimalai, we are whisked away to luxurious, Thai-style accommodations which are scattered around an undulating patch of rainforest. Everything is so delightfully secluded. The trail to the dining room is hidden in blooms and greenery. Our only companions when we walk on the resort's pristine beach are some scurrying sand crabs. Yes, we have truly escaped.

Pampering at Pimalai is honed to a fine art. Just let me share one of my spa experiences with you. A cool towel and a cool drink greet me at the reception hut. My therapist leads me past a fountain in a tropical garden to a gated hideaway. She eases me into an outdoor, sunken Jacuzzi tub. It is covered with flower petals. A Japanese garden and soft ambient music surround me. Pouring from a wooden trough is warm water that flows over my body. Thirty minutes

pass. My therapist appears and helps me out of the tub.

"No wipe. I'll do it," she says as she gently pats my body with a thick terry towel. I am led to the massage table in the indoor part of the treatment area where fresh flower petals are piled in a bowl on the floor. A soft breeze brushes past the open French windows. Holding her fragrant hands over my nose, she repeats one of her few English phrases: "Inhale, please."

So begins my aroma massage, and after that, an Ultimate Aromatic Facial. My face is drenched in a creamy blend of plants that contain proteins and Vitamin E. The treatment is supposed to take away my wrinkles. Funny, I think. It ought to take a lot more than just one facial to do that. But my face does feel great when it's done. Two and a half hours later, I am brought back to the reception hut and given a cup of ginger tea. My brain is blank, and my body is limp. I hardly have enough energy to make it back to my room. The cost for this bit of heaven? About $162.

Next, my husband and I opt for a hike in Mu Ko Lanta National Park. The drive down the winding road is strewn with rocks and ruts that are more like fissures. Where is a Jeep when you need it? The driver finally stops and points to a hiking path, promising to return in a couple of hours.

There's a path somewhere. Oh yeah, it's the little trail that curves along the beach past a lighthouse, over a small bridge. A red-brick walk leads into the lush tropical forest and becomes a series of stairs—big and little, wide and narrow. Humid air vibrates with the sounds of cicadas. The path twists and turns. Every now and then, there is a soft breeze. Sweaty and tired, we reach the shoreline and trudge back to the parking lot, where I think, When we get back to the resort, I'll have my foot and leg massage. How much better does it get than that?

The next time we venture off the property, it is to kayak around Talabeng Island. Caves and rock formations hug the isle's shoreline. In some places, sea urchins and coral are plainly visible. We paddle to a small beach on a nearby island. While we laze on the beach, two cooks magically appear to prepare a barbecue lunch for us. During the last leg of the kayak tour, I tell myself that this exercise earns me an Ageless Thai Herbal Scrub at the spa. Oh, if only a few years could be successfully scrubbed away, as well.

That doesn't happen. But I get over it and go elephant trekking. The elephant plods noiselessly through a patch of virgin forest. Except for the squawks and squeaks of birds and monkeys, it is utterly silent. After about forty-five minutes, we dismount at the elephant disembarking stop. We walk the rest of the way to a waterfall. The thick jungle hides much of the sunlight. We pass eerie caves that have giant tree roots sprouting through them. The rocks are slippery in the shallow stream we ford. The cool water feels good on our feet. At the cascade, trickling water drops from a thirty-foot embankment. Then it

is back to our trunked transport and our last night at Pimalai.

Over a romantic candlelit dinner, we sup on sumptuous, omelet-wrapped *pad thai*. We do not want to return home. But we will—our return to reality fortified by our escape to the Pimalai resort.

*Pimalai Resort & Spa*
99 Moo 5, Ba Kan Tiang Beach
Koh Lanta, Krabi
(075) 607 999
www.pimalai.com

## KOH LIPE

*Elizabeth Cassidy marvels at the customs of Koh Lipe*

I remember reading somewhere that Koh Lipe is an island available only to those who are worthy of the journey. This made me wonder if our attempt at a reasonably quick and uncomplicated route from a neighboring country made us any less worthy of holidaying there. Instead of sticking with our original plan of approaching Koh Lipe from Krabi, my friend Maureen and I had decided at the last moment to get to Koh Lipe via Langkawi Island in Malaysia—doing a merry three-suntan-lotion-bottles' worth of hopping through ten other islands in the process.

The ferry we boarded from Langkawi reached Koh Lipe in only about two hours, and after dropping us off, went farther north, making pit stops at several islands along the way. Since Koh Lipe has no docks, colorful longtail boats had to come far out from shore to pick up passengers arriving on the ferry. Hoisting my trusty backpack, I climbed nimbly down the ferry ladder and took a seat in the nearest longtail, which then whisked us off to Koh Lipe's Pattaya beach, where the most exciting immigration procedure in my experience was about to unfold.

Pattaya beach, not to be confused with the famous one of the same name in, well, Pattaya, is the most developed that you will find in Koh Lipe. The immigration office here consists of several fold-up tables set down along a shady stretch of sand, and the officers greeted us in bikinis and swimming trunks. Never in my entire career as a flight attendant had I passed through an airport where the immigration staff wore beach clothes as uniform and said things like, "Go have a beer or something, and come back for your papers in fifteen minutes."

There was a restaurant a few yards away, and I—never one to challenge security protocol—went off to swing in a hammock strung up in its trees while the officers put an approval stamp on my passport and I drank a banana shake. "Wow! USA!"

a Thai officer in Bermuda shorts exclaimed as he pulled out the only dark blue United States passports in the pile and waved them around in the air. Evidently, Americans rarely show up on Koh Lipe from a foreign country, as Maureen and I had.

When our turn came, we passed through the easiest customs in the world, and officially stepped into Koh Lipe—the most pristine and beautiful island I ever had the luck to lay my beach towel on. There were no high-rises in sight, no cars, no Starbucks, no McDonald's or ATMs, not even Thailand's ubiquitous 7-Eleven convenience store. As far as I could see, the only places to spend my money were a handful of hut restaurants and some shacks selling sarongs and seashell necklaces.

Another longtail boat was waiting to take us on to our next pleasant discovery in Koh Lipe: Mountain Resort, our hotel on the northernmost tip of the island. The comfortable bungalow we were renting for $22 a day, less than the price of an omelet at our last hotel in Langkawi, was perched high on a hill with an endless view of the Andaman Sea. From this vantage point, the water appeared in every marine color I could imagine, turning from a soft tourmaline blue where the water was shallow to the smokiest purple that looked ominous and thrilling at the same time. On and on the sea stretched, barely disturbed by the craggy green mound of Adang Island that broke through its surface in the near horizon.

We settled in quickly, as we had only five days on the island. Koh Lipe is so compact, we could have covered all of it on foot in less than three hours, but we chose to break up the tour and enjoy a little of it every day. Besides four beaches, the island also has a quaint little village at its center, named after the Chao Ley (sea gypsy) people who live here in shacks and eke a living out of the sea. Of Malaysian descent, the sea gypsies had reluctantly been given refuge on the island by the Thai government, and politics involving long-term territorial rights lurk under the serene existence of these nomadic people. An unpaved footpath runs through the village. and tourists came here to buy necessities like shampoo, water, and hammocks and to eat great home-style food.

We soon discovered our own favorite hangout in Chao Ley: a place we christened "Thai-Hop" for its delicious pancakes. Officially, the restaurant goes by the name of Pancake Lady, and it's a worthy, if somewhat faraway, competitor to the American IHOP chain, with thirty different kinds of specialty pancakes. I always went for the traditional banana pancake, while Maureen never stopped raving about the papaya version. The calories we packed on at the Pancake Lady were worked off later in the afternoon at Karma Beach, the prettiest stretch of sea in Koh Lipe, located right in front of our hotel. Karma Beach was scattered with seashells that nobody gathered, and the sand was so fine-grained, I wanted to bury not just my feet, but my whole body in its soft, powdery warmth. I would have, too, if a sharp pinch from an indignant little white crab hadn't warned me that I was digging right into his sandy home.

The sea was so shallow at Karma Beach, I could tread water until I came within touching distance of the Tarutao Marine Park Island nearby. An inquisitive shoal of multicolored fish followed me all the way, and wading through open sea with these friendly creatures for company, I often pretended I wasn't a Chicago-based flight attendant for United Airlines but a carefree mermaid.

How idyllic life would be if I really could exchange my airline uniform for swimwear, eat pancakes all day long, and spend my time frolicking in the Andaman Sea, safe in my paradise hideout of Koh Lipe where no phone calls from the mortgage company would ever reach me.

### Getting to Koh Lipe from Langkawi

During peak season (November to May) Tiger Line runs several shuttle ferries a day from the Langkawi Islands in Malaysia. For routes, bookings, and timetables, visit the following website.

www.tigerlinetravel.com

### Mountain Resort

Elizabeth adds: In all truthfulness, the service at Mountain Resort, especially in its restaurant, was slightly iffy, but for such a stunning view, I was more than ready to serve myself.

www.mountainresortkohlipe.com

## When not to go

From May to November, most tourist facilities close down on Koh Lipe because of torrential monsoon rains and storms, and not many ferries make the crossing. For some thrill seekers, though, the low season is a perfect time to enjoy deserted, windswept beaches and drastically reduced rack rates at the few hotels that do stay open. If you're one of those thrill seekers, confirm all transport arrangements beforehand, and keep your schedule flexible since bad weather could keep you off—or on   the island longer than expected.

## Sea gypsies

To learn more about the history and lifestyle of the Chao Ley, read Amit Gilboa's wonderfully in-depth article at the following website.

www.offtherails.com/chaoleh.html

## RAILAY BEACH

*Adam Bray*
*loses his lunch at*
*Railay Beach*

The forty-five-minute boat ride to Railay/Railey/Rai Leh—the name was spelled differently in every guidebook, map, website, and sign that I consulted—might have seemed shorter if not for the rain that started as soon as we set out across the bay from Krabi. I counted the seconds under my breath as I shivered and clutched my bags underneath me like a mother hen protecting her babies.

The boat finally pulled into East Railay, a silty stretch of sand invaded by tall mangrove trees. Fiddler crab minions scuttled about like tiny goblins amid their roots. I could see the wooden decks of restaurants, bars, and guesthouses set back behind the mangroves, under some stands of palm trees. The atmosphere was dark and cozy, yet rustic and lively, with a group of backpackers enjoying a round of beers at several wooden picnic tables. I imagined the setting would make a perfect secret hideaway for a classic pirate movie.

I quickly checked into my rather stark but spacious room on the third floor of the wooden-planked Yaya "Resort" (more accurately: a backpacker guesthouse), bought a picnic lunch, and headed for West Railay Beach, on the other side of the peninsula.

Railay Beach is really a whole collection of several beaches harbored between clumps of tall karst peaks. Railay is only reachable by boat, as it is cut off from the mainland by these soaring limestone formations. The karsts are crowned with lush vegetation and pierced by countless caverns. They offer some of the best rock climbing opportunities in the country, and create one of the most stunning landscapes too.

I plopped down on West Railay's white sands to eat my lunch. Unwrapping a bagel sandwich, lathered in cream cheese and bacon, I held it in my lap as I looked around. West Railay was quite different from the east side. The restaurants and boutique resorts along the beach here were rather classy, and of course a lot more pricey. A number of longtail boats waited at the shore to ferry guests to surrounding islands, while snorkelers paddled around the colorful coral reefs just offshore.

A karst peak shot a few hundred feet up out of the water at the end of the beach, and I was watching the vivid reflection it cast on the calm emerald sea, when I felt a vigorous tug on my sandwich. I turned to face a large, male macaque. His hair bristled as he nodded and gave a toothy grin just inches from my face. This was a beggar with an overwhelming sense of entitlement, who expected I should give up my bagel without a fight. I momentarily weighed my options. I had spent the last four months in remote China, and this was the first bagel I'd seen in a long time. I was sure I wanted it a whole lot more than he did. I'd been dreaming of having bagels, Dunkin' Donuts, and Dairy Queen in Thailand for weeks.

I looked down and saw his grubby little hands wrapped tightly around the sandwich and asked myself, "Do I really want to eat something handled by a dirty monkey?"

Maybe I could just pinch off the part with monkey cooties and eat the good part.

The monkey curled his lips, and his long, yellow incisors popped out into view. I knew my chances of getting bitten were getting more and more likely. With a sigh of regret, I surrendered my precious bagel and watched the monkey spirit it up a tree and disappear into the canopy above. Apparently, though, he didn't like raisins in his bagels, as I was showered with them a few moments later.

After finishing what was left of my lunch, I wandered south through the jungle to Phra Nang Beach, past Princes Cave (or Tham Phra Nang Nok, a shrine dedicated to an ancient fertility goddess) and went for a swim under primeval stalactites at the mouth of another cavern. Colorful reef fish darted around the piles of fallen rock formations on the sandy cave floor. The water was so soothingly warm and clear that I could have contentedly remained there for the entire afternoon, but curiosity propelled me further north into the caverns to explore the winding tunnels.

My waterproof flashlight came in handy as I squeezed my way through the limestone passages, away from the sunny beaches outside. Eventually I came to a dead end and found a hidden treasure. It wasn't the pirate's chest of gold that I had fantasized about. Instead, it was a pair of giant Tokay geckos, their powder blue scales studded with red, blue, and white spots, like tiny rubies, sapphires, and pearls. They clung to the cavern walls, where they guarded a small hatchery of milky white eggs. I marveled at them until the parents suddenly noticed me and croaked in alarm.

I backed up and followed a set of monkey hand- and footprints out of the cave. They led me to a natural staircase through the forested karsts. As I paused to catch my breath I noticed a small conch shell lumbering through the leaves on the jungle floor. Cautiously, I picked it up and turned it over. A rather startled, giant blue hermit crab dangled from the barnacled shell. He was as big as my fist. I fumbled for my camera—I'd never even seen a land hermit crab before, let alone such a behemoth as this one—but before I could snap a picture, he dropped to the ground, abandoned his shell, and skedaddled through the underbrush. Apparently he was as impressed with my immensity as I was with his.

At this point it began to rain again. It was monsoon season, and the showers came several times a day. As I headed back for dinner, I realized there were more natural wonders here than I could explore in a single day, or even two or three. Then I relished the fact that I wasn't traveling on a schedule.

## Railay Beach

This small peninsula is located between the towns of Krabi and Ao Nang in southern Thailand, and its limestone cliffs attract rock climbers from all over the world. Soaring peaks, tranquil beaches, jungle valleys, caves, caverns, and lagoons make this beach an extraordinarily beautiful holiday spot for hikers and nature lovers.

## Getting to Railay

The town of Krabi is the most sensible jumping-off point for Railay. Boats depart from Ao Nammao pier in from 8 a.m. until late. Keep in mind that they wait until there are eight passengers on board. This isn't usually a problem during the day, but if you are in a hurry, you can charter the entire boat at a pretty reasonable price. Boats also depart from Chao Fa and Ao Nang piers, also in Krabi.

## Railay Princess Budget

At this popular, seventy-room guest-house for backpackers (formerly known as the Yaya Resort), accommodations are in wooden, multistory buildings. They come with private baths and are comfortable and spacious, though noise carries through the thin walls. Mind the stairs, which are always slick after the rains.

www.yaya-resort.com

## Natural wonders

One of the area attractions is karst, an eroded limestone landscape characterized by cliffs, sinkholes, caves, and underground streams that create spectacularly scenic settings. Make sure to set aside enough time to explore at your leisure. And remember to bring your camera, as photo ops are plentiful.

# RETAIL THERAPY

*Discovering local markets, boutiques, and artisans*

During a shopping expedition in Bangkok's Chatuchak Market, I fell in love with some beautifully embroidered "tubes." Impulsively, I bought half a dozen pieces and distributed them among my friends, who all said, "They're gorgeous, really, but what *are* they?" From the sales pitch delivered in fluent Thai by the Chatuchak stall owner, I had gathered that the silk tubes were outdoor lampshades, meant to be hung on decks and patios, but once they had been unwrapped from their packaging, I wasn't so sure anymore.

Over the years, several shopping faux pas like this one have led me to conclude that tourists with an acquiring bent of mind are not being very well served by travel websites, guidebooks, and magazines. Why is that? I mean, a quick Google search throws up a whopping 151,000,000 web pages full of information about shopping destinations in this country. Surely, that adds up to enough markets and malls to satiate even the most discerning of buyers?

Well ... not really.

As any frequent visitor to Thailand will tell you, buying things is no difficult task here. Tourists don't need special assistance to find places to shop in any city or town; after all, Thailand *is* the shopping mecca of Southeast Asia. What's more, there is so much good stuff for sale on the streets alone—T-shirts, shoes, jewelry, bags, etc.—that you can easily fill two suitcases with your pavement purchases if you choose, without having to step inside a single market.

My problem is that I rarely ever get *specific* recommendations from travel resources, to help me streamline my shopping experiences. I want names and addresses of the most interesting shops; I want descriptions of unusual local products that I would otherwise not notice. I want to know the cultural context of particular pieces of folk art and craft. And sometimes I need help in choosing the right gifts for certain people.

As much as I love strolling through marketplaces bargaining like a fishwife and staring hungrily at the irresistible medley of handloom and handicraft on display, I often wish I had a secret shopping genie by my side who speaks Thai, knows the uses of every interesting-looking ethnic product, and leads me to the best purchases.

This chapter, as a consequence, is skewed heavily in favor of acquisition-minded tourists like me, who are tired of reading market overviews. (After a while, they all start to look, smell, and sound exactly the same.) Our authors are your private shopping genies who guide you to some really extraordinary purchases that you may not have found on your own.

I love the essay Eric Petersen has written on indigo Lanna-style shirts, for I did not know they were a symbol of the proud, independent spirit of hardworking Lanna farmers of northern Thailand. I do recall seeing a lot of locals wearing that signature indigo color when I was in Chiang Mai and Chiang Rai, but I did not stop to appreciate the stark, beautiful garments then, or consider buying one. Same thing with the traditional, triangular-shaped "axe" cushions. I had to read Asha Mallya's essay in this chapter to realize what a practical piece of furnishing they are, or how marvelously ornate they would look in most Western homes.

Helene Shapiro introduces us to one of Thailand's most desirable handicraft products in the luxury range: Yan Lipao bags. On my last trip to Bangkok, I made a point of going to Narai Phand, Bangkok's premier handicraft store in Ploenchit, to see if the Yan Lipao bags were really as special as Helene made them out to be. The shop assistant at Narai Phand extracted a few samples from a glass display case—unlike most of the other items selling in the store, the Yan Lipao bags were kept under lock and key—and placed them reverently on the counter. The woven reed bags with gold clasps and handles were a little smaller in size than I had expected, but they were so delicate and classy looking, it wasn't hard to see why they were considered suitable only for the Thai royal family several centuries ago.

At the other end of the shopping spectrum, far removed from ethnic handmade goods, is a gamut of trendy Thai-made lifestyle products that appeal to modern, Western tastes. Ananya Basu gives us the lowdown on jeans, with a selection of well-cut, well-constructed local Thai brands that can be such a unique style statement when worn overseas. I have contributed an essay on a small fragrance boutique in Phuket that creates complex, sophisticated scents out of ordinary Thai ingredients like basil, galangal, and kaffir lime. And Michael Roberts explains why men love to wear silk ties with the country's distinctive elephant motif imprinted on them.

The recommendations in this chapter are not exhaustive, of course, but they do highlight some excellent local items that our authors have handpicked for you to consider. Mostly handmade, they reflect the best artistic traditions of a unique culture, and you'll treasure them for a long time afterward as worthy souvenirs of your time in Thailand.

## BANGKOK

*Oindrila Sen
helps preserve a floral
tradition in Bangkok*

I am the sort of shopper who is easily overwhelmed by too many choices. I've never relished playing the "this-one-or-that-one" game that most women seem to enjoy, so the biggest plus point of Thai markets—their mind-boggling variety of goods—is a big minus point for me. A few attempts at trying to shop like an average tourist had resulted in too many wrong items bought in the heat of the moment, and forced the realization that I had to change tack. Instead of considering everything on sale as a potential purchase, I had to zero in on only one thing.

I found this strategy worked very well for me. On a Chiang Mai trip for example, I only went to celadon factories and bought a teapot, coasters, and glazed bowls with delicate sea green veins on them. At the night bazaar in Chiang Rai, I only looked for a woven hill tribe jacket and pleated skirt set in my size. At the Siam Square market in Bangkok, I restricted my shopping to a pair of exquisite, if somewhat impractical, pencil-heeled party shoes.

But how to apply this one-item-at-a-time strategy to my gift list? I had many people to buy presents for, all in different budget categories. I planned to spend no more than $5 on each of my office colleagues. But for my mother-in-law and a cousin, I wanted something really special. And my three closest girlfriends fell somewhere in between.

The answer came while I was having a foot reflexology massage in Bangkok's Ploenchit neighborhood. As the masseur pressed on my left big toe, sending fresh energy impulses to the cerebrum part of my forebrain, I suddenly knew it had to be orchids.

Not fresh orchids, of course—even if they did survive the twenty-one-hour journey back to the United States, I'd have to rush around delivering them like a florist the moment I got off the plane. What I had in mind was preserved orchids. Perfect purple symbols of Thailand embedded in acrylic resin or Perspex.

I scoured the markets and found some beautiful photo frames, bedside clocks, and tiny bud vases with a real purple orchid preserved inside each. I fell in love with some rough Perspex "rocks" that looked like ice cubes with delicate orchids nestling within. The cheaper varieties had the word *Thailand* emblazoned on them—too tacky and souvenirish for my tastes—but after visiting a few market stalls, I was able to collect seven or eight really good quality pieces without any lettering.

For my mother-in-law and cousin, I decided to go for jewelry, which was a little more expensive. While browsing at the Narai Phand store near that inspiring massage parlor in Ploenchit, I stumbled upon a collection of twenty-four-karat-gold-plated orchid necklaces, brooches, and earrings made by the famous Siam Royal Orchid company. They looked like miniature works of art.

Individual orchids had been electroplated to preserve their natural shapes, and then set into gold, silver, or copper-plated jewelry. And since no two orchids were exactly alike, none of these handmade pieces looked exactly the same either. The workmanship was exquisite, and the pieces looked so fragile, I was almost afraid to touch them.

After changing my mind a few times, I settled on an Ascocenda orchid pendant for my mother-in-law. The petals were a vignette, flowing from yellow to purple, with a trim of gold plating around the edges. For my cousin, I picked earrings that had purple Dorites orchids with speckled petals hanging from gold-plated hoops. There were orchids in other colors too, but I deliberately selected purple ones, so the recognition of the flower would be instantaneous. Neither item cost over $50. I got these two treasures at a price that was well under my budget.

A lot of people I know find Asian handicraft a little too exotic for their tastes, but the appeal of orchids is universal. After all, who doesn't like flowers, especially when they are preserved and packaged in such artistic ways? I was pretty certain that everybody would simply adore the orchid gifts I had chosen so carefully for them … especially my cousin, who had only recently got her ears pierced and was constantly borrowing my danglers.

### Siam Royal Orchid

The natural orchid jewelry collection crafted by this company is sold at Narai Phand in Bangkok. In Chiang Mai, the company has its own showroom at the Central Plaza near the airport, in the Northern Village section of the shopping complex.

### President Tower

973 Ploenchit Road
Bangkok
www.naraiphand.com

## Helen Shapiro bags a stylish souvenir in Bangkok

I had arrived in Thailand with my sister's repeated instructions about Yan Lipao purses still ringing in my ears. I wasn't to scrimp on the price or mistake any old handmade bag for Yan Lipao. I was to window-shop as much as I could to familiarize myself with various styles and shapes, and if possible, email her a photo of the one I picked before buying it.

Her enthusiasm for Yan Lipao wasn't misplaced, since hundreds of years ago, Thai royalty and aristocracy had revered the bag and treated it as a symbol of their special status in society. Yan Lipao was back in fashion in Thailand, and Linda had read somewhere that it was only a matter of time before it became a very desirable fashion must-have in the United States, as well.

Her biggest fear was that I would be duped into buying a second-grade Yan Lipao handbag, because traditional handicraft isn't something that interests me greatly. As I'm not fond of shopping, I tend to get satisfied easily, but top-quality Yan Lipao bags are collectors' items, and Linda is a serious bag collector. If I hadn't been the only person she knew who was likely to go to Thailand in the near future, the task of buying a Yan Lipao for her would never have fallen on me.

Her mistrust of my shopper's judgment ate away at my small reserve of shopper's confidence, and the prospect of buying a Yan Lipao bag was beginning to cast a shadow on my trip. I decided that the best thing would be to finish this assignment as quickly as possible, and for a couple of days, I stopped to check at every bag store I passed in Bangkok. But none of them sold Yan Lipao bags.

As it turned out, Linda had forgotten to tell me about the bag's most unique attribute: they were not made of leather, but of some special kind of vine that grows in the forests of southern Thailand. A Thai local, who knew what a Yan Lipao bag was, finally told me to stop hunting for them in leather stores and try the big handicraft emporiums instead. She recommended that I start my search with traditional craft stores such as Chitralada, and that is where I found this elusive commodity.

Their shapes were fascinating. While some Yan Lipao bags resembled round, squat pots, others were square, oblong, or hexagonal with elegant planes and curves. Almost all of them had a lid, and slim metal handles with delicate curlicues at the base. But the most interesting features that immediately caught my eye were the elaborately carved metal clasps, studs, and edges. The metal used to embellish the top-quality bags was usually *naak*, an alloy of gold and copper. The polished surfaces of the bags were either black or shades of brown that would not become brittle or lose their luster even after decades of continuous use. They looked so grand and old, and exuded so much character, I could well see them taking the Western fashion world by storm.

The lady at the shop told me that most of the designs were ancient, and Her Majesty Queen Sirikit had personally helped the weavers revive the Yan Lipao craft by showing them examples from her own collection of well-preserved royal heirlooms. Under the Queen's patronage, the production of Yan Lipao had resumed after languishing for many years, and it was not just foreign tourists, but the people of Thailand too, who were growing to appreciate this amazing piece of their own heritage.

I had a most difficult time trying to decide on which to buy. One option was to ask for the shop lady's help in choosing one that was the best representative of the Yan Lipao style. The other was to go with something that I thought would suit Linda's tastes. Finally, after carefully weighing the pros and cons of what I was about to do, I went ahead and bought the one that I personally liked best. It was beautifully shaped, with a squarish base that rounded out at the top. The lid was more prominent than on all the others, giving the bag a double-tiered look, and the clasp was a large golden leaf.

Twice, I went back to the shop to study this piece with fresh eyes, and each time, it charmed me with its unusually graceful, three-dimensional structure more than all the others. My description probably makes it sound too fussy, but in spite of the gilt detailing and elaborate styling, the bag was truly a masterpiece of understated sophistication. It was a heritage product of Thailand, after all, and if there's something you can never accuse the Thai artistic sensibility of being, it's unrefined, tacky, or loud.

## Yan Lipao

Making these handbags requires a high level of expertise, and the artisans who are engaged in the craft come mostly from the southern province of Nakhon Si Thammarat. Workers carefully select individual

Yan Lipao vines by hand, as only the most supple can be used to make the best-quality products. The vines are stripped down, and the delicate strands inside are extracted and tightly woven to make the bags. But before that can happen, the strands have to be treated to make them flexible and durable. A fair amount of softening and polishing goes on before the product acquires the marvelously rich luster that Yan Lipao bags are so valued for. Starting out at around $100, these bags can sell for as high as $800, and sometimes even more, depending on quality. But the price is fair, given the time and artistry that goes into them.

### Where to shop

It is advisable to buy an expensive product like a Yan Lipao purse at established handicraft stores such as Narayan Phand (see previous fact file) or a Chitralada outlet (the most convenient outlet is in the Grand Palace in Bangkok).

## Michael Roberts gets tied up in Bangkok's silk shops

Once you've been in Thailand for a few days, it isn't hard to work out that the local people love wearing uniforms. From hairstylists and massage professionals to shop girls in polyester skirt suits, everybody is dressing to a code to fit in and be identified as member of a certain social group.

This observation would be nothing more than an interesting cultural comparison with the more individual-minded, aggressive West, where we hate uniforms because we're all striving to be different. But it did happen to draw my attention to Thai silk ties—something I noticed that all male office workers wore, despite the temperature being stationary at a three-digit Fahrenheit, not to mention the humidity.

Though nothing says "Thai" as much as silk, I wouldn't have known much more about this fabric beyond its association with the name of Thai Airways' business class, had I not seen these ties. It was love at first sight with the tiny, repetitive motifs, so like the busy, signature prints designed by Hermès. The most popular motif is the elephant—there is no end to how many different sorts of pachyderms you can find. You start with classical, artistic renditions and then run the whole gamut down to really silly jumbo cartoons. I love them all.

I bought a few at local markets for about 100-150 baht each, but I suspect they were imitation stuff. Then I discovered two meccas of top-class silk products—Jim Thompson and Anita Silk—and was willing to pay their fancy prices for ties that were absolutely the thing.

Jim Thompson, to give you a bit of history, was a Delaware man who realized the potential of Thai silk way back in the 1950s, when it was still a small cottage industry. Thompson became so famous as the patron and savior of Thai silk that, according to a biography I read, a letter once arrived from overseas addressed simply to "Jim Thompson, Thailand," and he still received it. Thompson's story had a movie-script ending with him getting lost in the jungles of Malaysia, never to be found again, but his legacy survives in the form of The Thai Silk Company. (And the Jim Thompson House, which is a marvelous example of a traditional Thai home that has been transported from elsewhere and reassembled "inside out.")

Anita Silk is another old name from the fifties. It may not have had such an illustrious founder, but it has built up a solid reputation nonetheless, as producers of superb quality silk. Both companies carry a wide range of elephant-motif ties, mostly with a smooth fabric texture. (There's a rough kind of Thai silk, as well, that looks raw and knotty, but I've only ever found stripes and solids in that.)

One more type of Thai silk tie I want to recommend is the iridescent one. The fibers in these have light-reflecting properties, and apparently some protein to make them glossy. The iridescence makes the fabric look light and dark at the same time, creating an illusion of motion. I remember buying one for a friend in Syracuse, who opened the package and said, "My God, it shivers!"

As a male who isn't much of a shopper, I can't guide you in regard to the rest of the range at Jim Thompson and Anita Silk, but their shops do sell some really attractive clothes, cushions, curtains, and such. One tip I have to share about Thai silk is this: if you're not constrained by a budget, go for the Jim Thompson label. It's always a good one to impress people with. Especially if you have read about Thompson's fascinating life and experiences in Thailand, and can incorporate this amazing background story into your gift-giving.

### The Thai Silk Company

The flagship Jim Thompson store is located on Surawong Road in Bangkok, with additional outposts throughout the city and in Hua Hin, Pattaya, Phuket, and Koh Samui.

9 Surawong Road
Suriyawong, Bangrak
Bangkok
www.jimthompson.com

### Background research

To learn more about Jim Thompson, visit his former home in Bangkok and read *Jim Thompson: The Unsolved Mystery*, by William Warren.

www.jimthompsonhouse.com

### Anita Silk

Anita Silk items can be found in some of the major department stores in Bangkok, such as Siam Paragon, The Emporium, and Central Chidlom. The original outlet is located at 298/2 Silom Road.

www.anitasilk.com

### Ananya Basu traces her Thai jean-eology in Bangkok

High-end fashion in Thailand may be all about labels from the West, but when it comes to jeans, I think Thai people consider their homegrown brands to be cutting-edge stuff. Whenever I have visited Sirocco, Q Bar, or some other swish nightclub in Bangkok, I have noticed the city's trendy crowd wearing local labels on the back of their jeans. Labels that you have probably never heard of.

This relative anonymity of Thai jeans outside Thailand is precisely the reason why I think it's a great idea to buy a pair. If you cannot afford a pair of $700 classic Roberto Cavalli jeans, you can manipulate the perception of snobbery and flaunt your eclectic tastes in denim wear instead.

Here are a few excellent Thai labels you can look out for when you go shopping. Some of them are available in the denim section of department stores, and for others, I have provided addresses in the fact file below.

### Hara

The first pair of jeans I ever possessed was from Hara, so this Thai brand has a special significance for me. Western labels were not so easily available in Asia in the seventies, and Hara enjoyed a cult following among young people at the time. All my friends dreamed of wearing Hara. I remember buying a pair when I was fourteen, excited and nervous at the same time because my mom had drilled into my head that girls from "respectable" Indian families didn't wear pants. On a recent visit to Thailand, I was surprised to see that Hara is still in the market. Instead of the unisex jeans they used to make in those days, Hara is now well-known as a niche brand for women. The jeans are cut to suit the Thai female figure, so if you are slim-hipped, Hara is a good label to try out.

### IndigoSkin

Nothing says "Thailand" as unequivocally—or as subtly—as a pair of IndigoSkin jeans. By co-opting the country's artistic legacy into the pattern of his jeans, designer Tuchawee Sonthirati has enhanced an ordinary item of clothing with a touch of national pride. The hallmark of his jeans is the bits of traditional Thai textile he uses as detailing in the waistbands, pockets, and inseams. These fabrics, handpicked by Tuchawee, represent important milestones in Thailand's textile history, such as Jim Thompson classics or Khomapastr hand-printed cotton from Hua Hin. But the neatest thing about IndigoSkin jeans in my opinion is the label. Instead of "Made in Thailand," it says "Made in Siam."

### Mc Jeans

The sturdy, no-nonsense Mc Jeans brand is a Thai staple, and unbelievably affordable. Last time I checked, you could buy a pair for less than 400 baht at hypermarkets like Big C. I love the Mc Jeans range in black, a color that is becoming increasingly hard to find these days. Because of its affordable pricing, Mc Jeans used to have a fuddy-duddy image, but the company's spectacular success with a series of ad campaigns targeting youth has changed all that. Thai teens, and not just their parents, are now wearing Mc Jeans.

### CPS Chaps

This is a hip, up-to-the-minute street clothing brand that has a huge male following in Thailand. For several years now, I have noticed how Bangkok's trendy, young-adult crowd hangs around the CPS Chaps store at the Siam Center mall, especially during their big sales. CPS Chaps has more than twenty retail outlets all over the country, and their jeans have come to represent the bold, borderline-egotistic style statement that modern Thai men and women embody so well.

*CPS Chaps*
Siam Center
Rama 1 Road
Pathumwan, Bangkok
www.chapsclothing.com

*Hara*
www.hara.co.th

*IndigoSkin*
The Esplanade
Ratchada
99 Ratchadapisek Road
Din Daeng, Bangkok
www.indigoskinjeans.com

*Mc Jeans*
www.mcjeans.com

## Nabanita Dutt falls for Thai pantaloons in Bangkok

I was in Bangkok's famous MBK Center, searching for a particular shop that sold funky T-shirts with bold religious symbols. Without a shop number, I had to look into dozens of little stalls until I finally recognized the one I wanted by the winking Jesus Christ staring out the front of a full-sleeved T-shirt hanging right above the entrance door.

The shop had stacks of printed tees with attractive hand-stitched details, but my mind was distracted by the sight of something even more interesting: a young Japanese-looking salesman wearing stylish purple pantaloons. The legs were so wide, I first thought he was wearing a long skirt, but when he moved, they turned

out to be pants that swung most elegantly with each footstep.

As I paid for the shirt I had chosen—with a gigantic, all-seeing eye that spread from the front to the back—I chatted with the salesman, who told me the pants were not Japanese but a Thai style known as *kaang keng ley*. They were working clothes for fishermen once upon a time, but now they were treated as unisex casual wear, and women were wearing them as much as men.

I kept an eye out for a pair of *kaang keng ley* in shops after that, and they proved to be quite easy to find. I bought one at the Chatuchak Market a few days later and took it back to the hotel to try on. Though the label said small, the garment looked really enormous when I opened it up. There were two strings hanging from the front, and I tried putting the pantaloons on like regular pajamas, but it didn't work. I had an armful of extra fabric in front I didn't know what to do with, and no matter how I tried to bunch it up, I looked fat and distended in the middle.

Naturally, I was disappointed, but I didn't give up. The guy at the store wasn't much thinner than I, so my body shape was clearly not the problem. All I had to do was learn how to wear the curiously shaped pants the correct way. And so I went back to the T-shirt shop at the MBK Center, to the only *kaang keng ley*–wearing person I knew.

The salesman was delighted to be able to help me with my problem. It was lunchtime, and with no customers about, he could take me to a corner

...shop and ask me to step into ...ntaloon over my jeans. My first mistake, as it turned out, was that I had tried to wear the garment like a pajama with the strings in front. The right way to start was with the strings at the back. Then, instead of trying to bunch the extra fabric, I had to fold one pleat so the waistband sat snugly against my stomach. Once that was accomplished, the strings had to be brought forward and tied up in a single bow. The last step was to pull down the fabric that now lay above the string and arrange it to fall neatly over the hips.

I glanced at the narrow mirror hanging by the cash register and saw that the *kaang keng ley* looked perfect now. When I moved my legs about, the wide ends swung just above my ankles, drawing attention to my tiny, size 5 feet. I made a mental note to buy some dainty, open sandals to wear with these pants, and, of course, a couple more *kaang keng leys* in cotton and silk for every occasion. Given how cheap they were I could buy half a dozen and not spend more than $50.

## Where to shop

You can find *kaang keng leys* in any major market in Thailand in the traditional fabric and clothes shops or stalls. Prices begin at around 200 baht and go up depending on fabric quality.

## MBK Center

444 Phayathai Road
Patumwan, Bangkok
Skytrain station: National Stadium

## The perfect fit

Don't believe shopkeepers when they tell you one size fits all. Well, it does—technically—but the pants look bulky instead of überchic if they're too big for you. Look for *kaang keng leys* that come in small, medium, and large sizes, and buy a pair closest to your own size for a far better fit.

## Great expectations

If you're pregnant, *kaang keng leys* are a great thing to wear that don't scream maternity. They're roomy and comfortable, making them ideal for plus-size people too.

## Asha Mallya is inclined to shop for cushions in Bangkok

I had been resting my back on *mon kwan* (known as axe cushions) for years in Thai restaurants before I turned around one day and really looked at them.

You know the triangular-shaped cushions I'm talking about? Built like pyramids with individual triangles of long, narrow cushions stitched together? If you have sat against one of them, you must know how super comfortable they are. Or, like me, you may have taken the axe cushion for granted, until you leaned back one day and marveled at how the cushion did not move one bit with the pressure of your weight.

Axe cushions are a prominent feature in most traditional households in Thailand, and there's some science involved, I believe, in the way they are made. The triangular design was purposely created to withstand pressure, as well as offer a soothing incline for the upper back to rest on. If you want a firm support, you have to sit straight up against the axe cushion. If you want to lie back and relax, just slide down a little and find an angle that feels most comfortable.

Whether you're watching TV, reading a book, or lounging around with friends, these multipurpose cushions can soon become indispensable once you start using them. And the lovely Thai silk panels used to make the covers, usually with gold woven borders with elephants and other motifs, look great in whichever room you put them.

The first time I bought some axe cushions was at the Suvarnabhumi International Airport. The thought that I could actually buy a few to take home occurred not in the markets of Bangkok where choices were plenty, but in front of a duty-free store where the price no doubt was three times more. But I'm an impulsive shopper, and went in anyway to see what the duty-free shop had. Alas, there were no axe cushions in a practical size. The ones they had were twelve-inch miniatures, for decoration purposes only. I bought two anyway, and carried them as hand luggage into the plane. I enjoyed the miniatures for

the splash of color they added to my living room, but resolved to buy full-size ones I could actually use the next time I went to Bangkok.

Maybe a year or so later, when I was spending a weekend in the City of Angels, I picked up an axe cushion from a handicraft stall at the Suan Lum Night Bazaar. This one was green and had the added feature of a folding mat attached to it. The mat had three folds that opened out to make a sort of bed. The mat could be folded over once for sitting, and when not in use, the mat could be placed neatly under the cushion. My son and I now fight over who gets to lie on the cushion-mat combo when we watch TV in the evenings, so maybe I should buy another.

But there's a limit to how many axes one can keep in the house without overdoing it, and I have already set my heart on a twin-seater axe cushion that can work like a floor-level loveseat. The only problem is the size. One resourceful saleswoman at Suan Lum had offered to take all the stuffing out for me, so I could pack just the cushion cover in my suitcase. I thought she was simply trying to make a sale, but later I found out that you can buy just the cushion covers and fill them up with batting or cotton when you get home.

The loveseat should finish my complement of axe cushions for the time being. It's my favorite home accessory at the moment, because it goes so well with my jute rugs and rattan furniture. As well, when taken out of their Thai context and placed in a contemporary living room, axe cushions take on an especially striking look. They also become a talking point with friends and family who have never seen anything like them before.

### Suan Lum Night Bazaar

This market is located at the intersection of Wireless Road and Rama IV Road in Bangkok.

### It takes a village

Located in Yasothon Province in northeast Thailand, Ban Sri Than village specializes in making axe cushions. You can watch the villagers as they work on these triangular cushions and even buy directly from them instead of at a handicraft store in the cities.

## CHIANG RAI

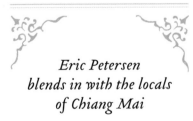

### Eric Petersen blends in with the locals of Chiang Mai

When I'm on the road in Southeast Asia, I love buying local clothes. Specifically, the shirts worn by men. They make great souvenirs from my travels, and I'm reminded of their country of origin whenever I wear them.

My fascination with ethnic shirts must have something to do with the fact that I had spent eight years of my early professional life in retail. The habit of noticing little design details and style innovations has now become ingrained in me. But the real reason why I buy so many of them is that they help me blend in. As a tour operator, I often travel deep into remote parts of a country to find offbeat destinations for my passengers. During these visits, the similarity in clothing takes some of the foreignness out of my appearance and makes the local people feel more comfortable around me. It's my way of showing respect for their culture, and when language becomes a barrier, I have found that a locally made shirt can speak a thousand words on my behalf.

After many trips to Thailand, my wardrobe is quite full of different made-in-Thailand shirts. I enjoy the selection of colors I get in vibrant purples, reds, and greens. Fun colors that are quite acceptable in Asia. Back at home in the United States, they frequently open conversations about travel at weddings and dinner parties, so I like to wear silk Thai shirts with subtle embellishments for any special occasion.

But among all the rich silk and fancy cotton shirts I have bought over the years, my favorite is the most humble one of them: a *mor hom* shirt from Chiang Mai. This is the indigo blue garment that the Lanna people of northern Thailand wear to do their daily work in.

*Mor hom* shirts are made in Phrae Province, a short distance away from

Chiang Mai. I remember seeing hundreds of these shirts drying on the clotheslines of village homes when I drove through there once. Their signature indigo color comes from boiling the leaves of the *hom* tree (a species that is abundant in this part of the country) with lime and the alkaline ash of burnt banana trees.

On my very first visit to the north, I noticed how the local people wore the *mor hom* in combination with matching indigo tie-up pantaloons, giving them a strikingly smart, monochromatic look. Naturally, I had to have one as well. At the time, I didn't know that these round-necked, buttoned-up shirts with half sleeves were a symbol of the hardworking people of the north. They wear the hardy shirt with great pride; to celebrate their Lanna heritage, highly paid government officials and executives often wear them to work on Fridays.

I also learned that Westerners referred to the *mor hom* as "Thai rice-farmer's shirt"—a description that my Thai friends in Chiang Mai had some reservations about. It robs the garment of its dignity, they said, and I couldn't agree with them more. The descriptive name, though not meant as an insult, failed to communicate the *mor hom*'s relevance in the northern Thai culture.

After that, I wore my *mor hom* with great pride, as well.

The *mor hom* is made of a rough cotton that softens gradually and becomes more and more comfortable with each wash. As the material breathes easily and allows perspiration to evaporate, the *mor hom* is perfectly suited to Thailand's hot, humid climate, unlike many of the Western summer clothes I first brought with me. Large sizes are not a problem either, as the shirts are designed to be worn loose, and you'll easily find a true Western XL size. Expect to pay between 150 and 190 baht a shirt—not bad at all, when you consider the many years of wearing you'll get out of one *mor hom*.

### *Where to shop*

In Chiang Mai city, the best place to find *mor hom* shirts is the night market on Chang Klan Road. And if you're traveling through nearby Phrae Province, visit the Koew Wanna on Route 101 in Nan Chak village. The shop specializes in not just indigo-dyed shirts, but also contemporary accessories and gift items from the traditional indigo fabric. In addition, the residents of Tung Hong village make most of the *mor hom* shirts you will see in the markets; if you're interested, you can visit the village and watch the entire manufacturing process in a Thai home.

### *Handle with care*

The *mor hom* shirt's all-natural indigo dye may bleed in the washing machine, so it is advisable to hand wash your items every time. Normally, the shirts are starched when sold, but the cotton fabric becomes soft and pliable after several washes. You can soak yours in water overnight to get rid of the starch more quickly.

NORTHERN THAILAND

## SUKHOTHAI

### *Laura Bartlett*
### *Jurica just says*
### *"no thanks" in Sukhothai*

Instead of renting bikes, my husband, Cory, and I used the tram to go from site to site in Sukhothai's Historical Park. We thought we could enjoy the ruins of the ancient Siam capital and take photographs at a more leisurely pace if we didn't have to pedal around the seventy-square-kilometer park.

As it turned out, we could save time on shopping too—the tram proved to be a moving marketplace, with probably one vendor for every passenger on board. And they were selling all sorts of locally made goods, making it unnecessary for short-stay visitors to squeeze in a shopping trip to To-Rung, Sukhothai's night market.

A lady sitting across the aisle from me bought a crocheted tank top with a scalloped neckline, even before the tram had started to move. The hasty transaction made me wonder if the tram salesmen were giving better deals than the shops in town. While I was mulling this over, a gentleman sitting in front started bargaining over a beautiful carved-wood elephant.

I leaned forward to hear what price was being quoted, but my attention was caught by a vendor who whizzed by us on a moped. I stuck my neck out the window to see that he was in the midst of a negotiation over a Buddha statue. The prospective client, sitting several rows ahead of me, wouldn't pay the asking price, and the seller was chasing our tram to find out if he'd take the Buddha at a 10 percent discount on the last and final amount.

"I hope the man is buying the Buddha as a gift for somebody," the lady next to me commented. "Did you know the Thais believe buying Buddha statues for yourself brings bad luck?" I didn't, and couldn't help asking what happened if they liked a Buddha statue so much they wanted to keep it for themselves. "I guess they'd have to get somebody else to gift it to them," the lady reckoned.

We started chatting about Thai handicraft, and I discovered she was buying locally made knick-knacks from every village and town she visited. Her purchases were mementos of their places of origin, and she got a much better price when she bought directly from the artisans.

A young boy broke into our conversation to show us a collection of ceramic bowls, trays, and other small decorative items. "Original antique, original antique," he assured us, which obviously couldn't be true because the artwork on the pottery had no sign of wear and tear. The lady noticed the disbelieving look on my face and explained that the potters of Sukhothai had mastered the art of copying the ancient designs and styles that had made Sukhothai ceramics so famous in the olden days. She encouraged me to buy a piece, but I had no idea what the going rate on items like these were, so I admired a bowl with a pool of glistening jade green accumulated at the bottom, and sent the young boy on his way. He immediately turned his attention on the lady and harangued her to buy something until he was pushed out of the way by a fried-peanut seller.

"You must try some of this," the lady said. "They're a Sukhothai specialty that was invented by a family of sisters who mixed eggs, flour, and seasonings and came up with this delicious snack " I wasn't hungry, and neither was Cory, so we passed on it, but I made a mental note to try some in the evening when we went to the To-Rung night market for dinner.

Just before the tram reached our next destination, a tube skirt seller stopped near us with his arms laden with long, straight Thai skirts with vivid panels of fabric picked out in golden thread. These were *phasins*, I learnt from my new shopping guide, who tapped the twelve-inch thick border of a plum-colored skirt and explained that the geometric border design was a unique weaving tradition of the craftsmen of Sukhothai. The skirts were extremely attractive, and I was tempted to buy the plum one. The vendor, sensing my indecision, stepped up his sales pitch, but then I remembered my Western proportions. It was too risky to buy a skirt without trying it on first to see how it sat on my hips.

When the seller rushed off to catch another customer before the tram stopped, the lady asked me curiously, "How is it that these vendors are leaving you alone each time you say you're not interested?"

From the corner of my eye, I saw Cory smiling in amusement, knowing I was going to enjoy this. The nice lady had told me so much about Sukhothai art and craft, and now, it was my turn to tell her something that would save her from harassment during the rest of her Thailand trip. "Just say '*mai ow*,'" I suggested. "If you say 'no, thank you' in English, the shopkeepers interpret that as a conversation starter. But if you say '*mai ow*' instead, they will immediately stop trying to bargain with you."

The lady pulled out a small notebook from her bag and wrote the phrase down. "Where did you learn that?" she asked, admiringly.

"You learned so much about Thai products because you love to shop," I replied, as I waved a goodbye and made my way down the short aisle. "I learnt *mai ow* because I'm traveling light and don't want to add extra pounds to my luggage."

When I jumped off the tram, Cory playfully pinched my arm. He had overheard my parting shot, and I knew I was in for some good-humored razzing for this harmless bit of showing off.

### To-Rung night market
This market is located near the bus station in the center of new Sukhothai town.

## Local delicacy

If you eat only one meal at the night market, make sure it's the local noodle dish served in a *tom yum*–style soup with lots of boiled green beans. This dish can also be found in Bangkok at the Nara chain, which does a remarkably good version of it.

www.naracuisine.com

## Sukhothai fabric

We recommend shopping for Sukhothai fabric from the quality collection at the Sathon Golden Textile Museum in the Sawank-alok-Srisajchanalai highway.

477 Mu 2
Tambon Hat Siao
Sri Satchalai

# PHUKET

## Nabanita Dutt surrenders to sensory overload in Phuket

I have come to the conclusion that Bobby Duchowny can coax a perfume out of simply anything. I mean, would you dare doubt the imagination of a perfumer who can make a scent out of *bacon*? Yes, he really did that once—to lure customers to a hotel breakfast buffet—but the fragrances he sells in his shop in Phuket are considerably less outlandish, designed to appeal to the olfactory bulb rather than the taste buds.

Lemongrass House, located across from Surin Beach in Phuket, is a shop you must visit if you're into aromatherapy bath-and-body products. An impressive range of naturally scented soaps, creams, candles, etc., with at least ninety different essential oils at their core, are available to be tried and tested, and even mixed and matched to your own specifications. Bobby loves to experiment, and when he's not having fun making body wraps out of Godiva chocolate, he's at the shop, encouraging his customers to do the same.

Now, I have recently become a bit of a perfume snob: I buy artisanal perfumes instead of duty-free brands, because that's what perfume snobs do. I can keep myself happily occupied for hours comparing different vanillas or bergamots to see which interpretation I like best, so I have a natural affinity for people like Bobby, who loves to talk about his products, and educate his customers about perfumes in the process.

Hoping to catch him off guard in the midst of our conversation, I asked the perfumer to name three favorite items at Lemongrass House that he uses himself. Wicked, I know, like asking a father to choose among his kids, but instead of politely dodging the question, he came right out and named the three of his own creations that he loves best.

I am noting them down here, in the hope that this little piece of "insider" information will help you narrow down your choices when you're shopping at the Lemongrass House.

### Royal Lotus & Pomelo Massage Oil

Whenever Bobby and his wife Palita go out for massages, they take a bottle of this oil with them. Usually, spas don't mind if you bring your own, and therapists are enchanted by the unusual scent of lotus, which most have never smelled before.

### Blue Chamomile Aloe Vera Gel

Living in Phuket means the beach is a big part of Bobby's life. He has very fair skin that burns easily, so he originally created this product to relieve his own discomfort. Soon, all his sunburned friends started asking him for it, so he took the production mainstream. Once you rub this gel on, the redness decreases and the pain of sunburn is instantly minimized.

### Lemongrass Room Spray

This is Bobby's personal favorite. He sprays his house, his car, his office, and his hotel room with lemongrass and never gets bored of it. Wherever he is in the world, it always reminds him of Thailand.

To add my own two pennies to Bobby's list, I must suggest the wonderfully effective insect repellents. Not those vile-smelling coils that the hotel staff thoughtfully put under your table when you were dining in the open, but incense, candles, and sprays with soothing citronella and lavender scents that insects don't seem to like for some reason.

The decor of Lemongrass House has a preponderance of bamboo that reiterates its all-natural, organic theme. Though the shop is not large, the counters are set well apart from each other, so you have all the space you need to roam around and sample different products. The highlight is of course the central display of Bobby's ninety-odd essential oils, where you can test them on your skin (the scents can vary from person to person, depending on how the essential oils react with each individual's natural body oils). Try a few scents from the native Thai range such as galangal, kaffir lime, anchan flower extract, and pandan extract, as they'll be something unique to take back from Thailand.

And if you're feeling adventurous, go crazy and mix them up and see what you get. A warm, lemony scent maybe, with a touch of lotus-inspired oomph, a splash of spicy nutmeg overlaid with the dark, mysterious notes of pure sandalwood; something exotic, playful, and blatantly sexy that grabs people by the nose and makes them think of—you!

Yes, it could well be that your very own "signature" perfume is waiting to be mixed up and created in those glass vials at Lemongrass House.

### Lemongrass House

106/14 moo 3, Surin Beach Road
Cherngtalay, Thalang, Phuket
(076) 271 233
www.lemongrasshouse.com

# Into the Wild

*Tales of trekking and beyond for adventurous travelers*

The phenomenon of "Unseen Thailand," it seems, has exploded upon us. "New" destinations have sprung up all over the country, stretching the old tourist trail of Bangkok–Chiang Mai–Phuket to such an extent that it really does seem as if a whole new Thailand is out there.

My passport records more than sixty visits to the country in the past eighteen years, and on fifty of them at least, I have to confess that I've had no serious desire to step outside Bangkok. For me, and for numerous other foreign tourists who cannot resist the siren call of this city, Bangkok *is* Thailand. With so much good food, great shopping, 200 baht/hour massages, etc. here, what could the rest of Thailand possibly have to offer that topped this kind of marvelously self-indulgent, sybaritic holiday experience?

My reluctance to acknowledge the great tourism possibilities in other parts of the country finally broke in 2006, when I had to ask somebody the stupid question: "What's Krabi?" It seemed that an extended circuit of exotic beach destinations, mountain tours, and wildlife adventures had opened up, and thousands of smart tourists had already discovered them, while I stayed holed up in beloved Bangkok with two index fingers stuck firmly in my ears.

The humiliation didn't end with Krabi. There was Koh Samui, Koh Lanta, Koh Lipe, and scores of other Kohs (islands) in the south with pristine beaches, endless stretches of ultramarine waters, local peoples, arts, crafts, and histories I had no clue about. To the north, there were spectacular mountains and jungles, which were home to tribes like Akha, Lisu, and Padaung, each unique in their traditional garments, languages, looks, and past. To the northeast, there were marvelous Isaan food and hardworking Isaan people who added yet more interesting variety to the diverse cultural melting pot.

As a result, editing this chapter has been quite a learning experience for me because our authors have shared a nice, big

slice of Unseen Thailand with us. Alice Driver travels far south to the Surin Islands, for example, where the ancient Moken people are desperately trying to cling to their rootless, sea gypsy existence, and to the traditional boats that have been their lifeline for centuries. And Stu Lloyd stops his motorbike at a village near the Laos border, where pomelo farmers give him a taste of rustic northern hospitality: a midday hotpot meal washed down with copious amounts of local whiskey and no charge afterward because "Thailand-Australia friends, number one ...!"

While some of these essays reveal the hidden heart of Thailand not visible from downtown Bangkok, there are others that take us on adrenaline-pumping adventures into the country's wilderness. We have Andrew C. Godlewski out on a conquest of the Mae Tang valley, hurtling through its mysterious forest trails on an ATV. Elizabeth Cassidy makes a panic-stricken pass through a submerged cave on Koh Mook, desperately swimming in pitch dark until she comes out on the other side to find a secret paradise accessible only during low tide. Ryan Humphreys goes off to climb Koh Phangan's highest peak, braving snake-infested hill trails where trekkers are known to get lost. And Dee Shapland undertakes a precarious excursion to the top of Phu Chi Fa Mountain, and while I'm fascinated by his descriptions of a landscape submerged in a sea of swirling fog, what really attracts me to his essay is the cozy picture he draws of contented family life in a village with his hill tribe girlfriend and her father, who is perpetually intoxicated on moonshine whiskey.

A few authors sought their thrills in more unusual ways—Nicholas Towers embarks on a cave excursion to help kill a bagful of bats, which will be cooked later by his village hosts for dinner—and also in more controlled environments. Kristina Wegscheider becomes part of an aquarium exhibit as she swims with sharks at Bangkok's Siam Paragon Center, and David Kovanen makes a mad dash down a zipline like Tarzan in Pattaya.

The experiences you read about in this chapter don't follow any recognizable pattern. Each of these authors has stepped out of his or her individual comfort zone and into the unpredictable arms of Thailand's captivating outback, taking leaps of faith, facing up to challenges, and pushing boundaries to see just how exciting their passage through Thailand could possibly be.

## BANGKOK

### Kristina Wegscheider swims with the sharks in Bangkok

Tucked inside Siam Paragon, Bangkok's hippest shopping center, is a serene world of sea creatures known as Siam Ocean World. To the ordinary visitor, it may appear to be a regular aquarium, albeit of humungous proportions, but Siam Ocean World actually allows you to cross the line between just looking at the displays and becoming part of the exhibit.

My little adventure at Siam Ocean World started like any normal aquarium visit. I spent more than an hour admiring various creatures, especially the penguins that were receiving one of their meals during that time. Then I was called to the rear of the aquarium to begin preparing for my dive. Yes, I was actually going to enter the Open Ocean exhibit that housed the resident sharks.

Suiting up in scuba diving gear, I could feel the excitement building as I glanced into the 2.8-million-liter tank I was about to dive into. I pulled on a mask, hitched an oxygen tank to my back, and gingerly wet my toes on the first step leading into the water. It was unexpectedly cold. I went in deeper, and as soon as my accompanying dive master gave me the command, I submersed myself, dropping into a bluish gray underwater world with silhouettes of huge sharks casting dark shadows around me. I could feel the synthesized current, and hear the sounds of the eagle rays crunching on shells as they snacked.

I descended to the tank floor, where a school of iridescent yellow fish came up to greet me. There were many other sea creatures residing in the underwater rock formations, but my attention was squarely focused on the sharks. A reef shark passed by me, and right after that I almost brushed against a lemon shark. I glided through the water, trying to stay parallel to the creatures so I could see the intricate details on their streamlined bodies. The sharks ignored my presence, giving me enough opportunity to study them at close range.

Outside of the tank, tourists and Thai locals captured photos and videos of me and my new aquatic friends. For those who prefer to stay dry and watch the sea creatures from outside, there's a clear tube running through the tank that allows you to see all the excitement going on underwater.

While I sat on the tank floor, I discovered there was a third way of exploring the aquarium. When I happened to look up, I saw a glass-bottomed boat drift by above me, with people peering through the glass to catch a close glimpse of the sea creatures.

In too short a time it seemed, my oxygen began to run low, and I had to signal the dive master to start instructing me on my ascent to the surface. The artificial light was bright as I emerged from the water, and for a moment I was confused to find myself in a modern aquarium instead of in the open ocean.

As an experienced scuba diver, I have stepped into the underwater world countless times, but never has it happened in such an unlikely location as a plush shopping center. But the sharks were as real as they get, and the experience was just as exciting as a dive off one of Thailand's southern coastal islands.

### Siam Ocean World

Siam Paragon Center
Level B1-B2
991/1 Rama I Road, Pathumwan
Bangkok
www.siamoceanworld.co.th

### Diving details

You don't have to be a certified scuba diver to take part in this adventure, but you should be aware of some basic precautions. For example, even though the dive is relatively shallow, it is advisable to avoid flying for twenty-four hours after the dive. Siam Ocean World will provide all of the equipment. You just need to bring a swimsuit to wear under your wetsuit. We also recommend bringing your camera and a nondiving friend to take pictures of you swimming in the Open Ocean exhibit with sharks. And if you're not comfortable with scuba diving, there's an Ocean Walker program. Wearing a special helmet, you can go into the tank without even getting your hair wet.

## PATTAYA

### David Kovanen has a change of heart near Pattaya

I admit that when I first heard about the Flight of the Gibbon, the idea of being suspended in the air by a rope across a kilometer-wide canyon frankly terrified me. If you have traveled at all in Thailand, the first thought that should come to mind is how well the rope is tied to the trees and how many previous uses the rope may have served before being bought at some surplus market. At least, those were my thoughts. The experience I'd just had, of riding a *tuk-tuk* going the wrong way down Lang Suan, a one-way road in Bangkok, didn't endear me to the Thai view on personal safety.

But some perverse impulse compelled me to sign up for the zipline adventure. I paid 4,000 baht for two tickets—for my girlfriend, Aya, and me—and arranged for a pickup at the hotel the following morning. I didn't sleep well that night, worried that I'd have a terrible accident or make a fool of myself. I even sent an email home, so my remains could be claimed.

At 7 a.m. sharp, a minivan came to pick us up in Pattaya. (There are also pickups in Bangkok, as the zipline site is halfway in between.) After an uneventful ninety-minute drive, we arrived at what looked like a zoo, and the minivan drove up a dirt road. When it stopped, at an arbitrary spot in the wilderness, my girlfriend casually said to me, "The trees are beautiful. Are there wild animals here?"

I felt like making an audible rendition of a chicken, which was how I was feeling right about then. What had I got myself into?

We arrived at the base camp and were told to put on our gear: basically, harnesses that we were strapped into, with two ropes with clips. It was reassuring to see that the equipment looked new and in perfect condition. Meanwhile, our guide gave his name in

Thai (a mumble that passed me by) and then said to just call him Jackie Chan.

The first fifteen minutes were spent on training and safety. Rather than giving a lecture, we were started off by being hitched up and sent down a twenty-foot rope that was just a foot off the ground. We were shown how *not* to do certain things. One customer unclipped from the demo rope by himself and Jackie Chan immediately stopped and said, "If any of you even touch your clips, the tour is over." The *only* thing that could ever hurt us was if we removed a clip ourselves.

It was great to know that safety was no joke here. After the training, I felt pretty confident. Silly me.

We went up a spiral staircase that wound up and up and up and up a large tree. I mean, so high that I felt very close to God. At the top of the stairs was the first of what turned out to be a dozen and a half platforms.

The platforms were without hand rails, and it was disconcerting to be looking down at treetops from a shelf. My knees buckled, my palms went sweaty, and my girlfriend requested, "You die first, okay?"

The guide said, "Do nothing but enjoy the ride."

With those two opposing instructions ringing in my ears, I stepped off the platform, into the arms of the unknown.

Zzzzzzzzzzz ... Down the cable I slid, reeling from the speed, the views, and the terror. Life has never passed me by so fast. Colors were more intense at that moment. I clearly remember the smell of the forest and the sounds of birds talking about watching people fly.

And then, before I knew it, I was standing on the next platform where another guide was waiting to pull me in. From there, I went again until I landed safely on the platform after that. And so on. Like a gibbon, swinging from tree to tree.

My girlfriend came behind me, zipping down the line. She normally smiles a lot, but I didn't know she could smile like that, from ear to ear. I got an unexpected hug upon her arrival. When I asked if she was okay, she responded, "Not okay. Not *only* okay."

We proceeded through a series of yet more challenges and platforms, and the guides told us we were doing very well. I don't know where they found these guides, or how they trained them, but they were a delight. They went slow with the people who needed encouragement and added some spice for the adventurous ones. But always they watched for safety. Polite, funny, and safe.

(Spoiler warning! Skip to the last paragraph if you want to preserve the element of surprise of this experience.)

My normally shy girlfriend was starting to get self-confident by about the tenth run. She was splaying her arms out as if she were an angel and sort of showing off. The guides must have noticed, because they maneuvered to send her last on a rather scary-looking stretch. She zipped down the cable, came within ten feet of the destination platform—and then started going backward. The rest of us watched in horror as Aya finally came to a stop near the center of the cable and hung helplessly in the air. Everyone started having various visions of how to rescue her, mine involving a helicopter. But Aya, with her wonderful personality,

decided there was nothing she could do, so she smiled and signaled that the view was beautiful!

When the guides decided we had had enough excitement, they revealed it was a trick they had played on Aya—by a simple twitch of the rope! Of course, they brought her safely in right after that. Aya had never been in any danger at all, and she was quite amused at having been set up like this. Apparently, the guides can tell which customers will get a thrill out of a mock "accident," and on this tour, Aya was it.

Looking back, I guess I hadn't been really that worried. The guides were trained professionals I would trust my life to—mostly because trust had nothing to do with it. The inherent safety of the Flight of the Gibbon operation was no accident.

Earlier on, I suggested the ropes might be secondhand surplus. As it turned out, all of the equipment was top-grade stuff. I talked with the owner, who told me it was the best quality in the world, and I had to agree. I am an engineer and recognize solid design. On top of this, the folks who operate the Flight of the Gibbon were obviously experienced and professional, making the whole zipline adventure as failsafe as any piece of engineering could ever be—and this is being said by a chicken at heart! I will never ever bungee jump. But I cannot more strongly recommend the Flight of the Gibbon as a life experience you absolutely mustn't miss.

## Flight of the Gibbon

This adventure tour can be taken from three cities: Bangkok, Pattaya, or Chiang Mai. This is an all-inclusive experience, as Flight of the Gibbon will arrange your transport, meals, and itinerary. To book a tour or for more information, visit the company's website.

www.treetopasia.com

## KANCHANABURI

### Martyn Bartlett tells tiger tales from Kanchanaburi

I did a web search on the Tiger Temple at Kanchanaburi and read arguments both for and against visiting the temple's captive tigers, which some claim are heavily sedated to make them less threatening to tourists. To explore this issue for ourselves, my girlfriend, Wonderful Wi, and I booked a tour to the temple, also known as the Wat Pa Luangta Bua Yannasampanno sanctuary, some thirty kilometers outside Kanchanaburi town.

During the previous three days of our stay in Kanchanaburi, the weather had followed a familiar pattern. Daytimes were baking hot, while at night the heavens opened and rain lashed the near-empty streets. The day of our trip to the Tiger Temple had started out warm and sunny, but minutes before the afternoon pickup arrived, the skies darkened and rainfall looked imminent.

At just after two, a *songthaew* share taxi vehicle pulled up with its side rain flaps raised. Sitting inside were two young European ladies wearing waterproof jackets that suggested they had seen the afternoon weather report. Wonderful Wi and I were both clad in T-shirts and shorts. By the time we reached the Tiger Temple, we were absolutely drenched.

The entrance fee for the temple sanctuary was 500 baht for foreigners and 300 baht for Thai nationals, both of which included a decent, well-written brochure with a good background history of the place. Apparently, the sanctuary had started when an injured jungle wildfowl was given to the temple's monks by local villagers. Soon after, a motley bunch of various other animals moved in, and we could see these refugees-turned-residents roaming freely around the sanctuary grounds.

Then, in 1999, an abandoned tiger cub found near the Thai-Burmese border was given to the monastery. But the cub died within days. Weeks later, two healthy male cubs were brought to the grounds, having been retrieved from border poachers who had shot the cubs' mother. In this way, the Tiger Temple was born. The border police kept handing over more rescued cubs, and years later, the fully grown tigers started to produce cubs of their own.

The gates opened to let us and 150 other tourists into the temple grounds, and we walked a short distance to Tiger Canyon, the place where the tigers are taken for their afternoon exercise and photo shoot. "Exercise" was a loose description in this case, because around their necks, the tigers wore short, two-meter chains that were fixed to the ground. Maybe the camera flashbulbs helped them work up a sweat. In any case, they all looked lively enough to me—not drugged, just a little bit snoozy.

The entrance fee allowed us to enter the cordoned-off area where the tigers were "exercising" and have our photo taken by one of the Thai workers using our own camera. But a couple of foreign volunteers were standing outside of the ropes and letting everyone know in very good English that group photographs of between two and five people could be taken for a charge of 1,000 baht.

A large queue immediately formed of people willing to spend that much for a photo. Only the downright scared would walk away from the Tiger Canyon with their baht still intact, I thought, as I watched one couple stroll away looking thoroughly terrified.

The photo shoot ended all of a sudden when one of the English-speaking volunteers declared there would be no more pictures as the tigers had to be walked back through the canyon to their resting area. Perhaps the protein, vitamins, and iron from the tigers' morning red meat brunch was starting to wear off. Like a flock of sheep (bad word choice with tigers about) we obediently trudged off on the half-kilometer trek to our next port of call: The Three Tiger Falls.

The Three Tiger Falls was a manmade quarried pit, where three tigers lived with a semblance of their natural habitat. What struck me as odd was that these three tigers spent the whole time sleeping and were the least active beasts we had seen all afternoon. The Tiger Temple brochure tried to explain this:

*Why are the tigers so calm? Are they drugged?*

*All of our tigers have been hand-raised and imprinted to humans and therefore have no fear of people. The "fierce" behavior often associated with captive tigers is caused by placing wild animals in stressful conditions of the captive environment. Our tigers have been regularly handled from a very early age and thus have become desensitized to being touched by people. This is why they are able to sleep while people sit next to them for photos ...*

From here, we moved on to a location for another tiger photo shoot, this time conducted in a relaxed and commercialism-free manner. Buddhist monks led out some of the younger tigers (not cubs), and we could pose for pictures with the magnificent beasts if we dared, free of charge. Plenty, including myself, took the chance to get up close and personal with the tigers. The best part of the afternoon for me was seeing one of the monks bottle-feed milk to a very alert and appreciative tiger.

This was where our two-hour tour ended. Wonderful Wi bid the tigers a fond goodbye, and then we headed for the exit gate, passing the Meditation Training Center on the way. At the center, the forest monastery offered accommodation for those wishing to learn meditation techniques.

Having dried out from our earlier drenching, Wonderful Wi and I boarded the *songthaew* for our return trip to Kanchanaburi. Wonderful Wi talked about how impressed she was by the way the monks casually handled the beasts. And concluding that the tigers seemed to be well treated at the temple, we chatted about tigers pretending to be dogs, until we hit the Kanchanaburi highway, when the skies opened and we were soaked all over again.

### Getting to the Tiger Temple

The Tiger Temple is located on Kanchanaburi-Sai Yok Road. If you're coming on a day trip from Bangkok, the most convenient way is to book a tour. From the nearby town of Kanchanaburi, you can hire a *songthaew*, which will take you to the temple and bring you back to town afterward for a prearranged price.

### Color me safe

The Tiger Temple will refuse entrance to anyone wearing red, pink, and/or orange, as these colors ap-

parently disturb the tigers. So make sure to dress in neutral tiger-friendly shades to avoid having to buy expensive clothes at the temple shop.

### Unsavage beasts

Tigers are conditioned to rest during most of the day, as it's their way of conserving energy for a big hunt. Because of this, the Tiger Temple is not a place where you're going to get "action" photographs, so don't get your hopes up on that score. The excitement to be had here is in getting close enough to these human-friendly tigers to be able to touch them— under supervision, of course.

## CHIANG RAI

### Nicholas Towers is batty for dinner in Chiang Rai

As I banged my head on the sudden narrowing of an already narrow tunnel, I wondered if my impulsive decision to come on this cave exploration adventure was a serious mistake.

The confidence with which I had set out, not half an hour ago, to collect bats with a Thai family in Chiang Rai, had started to evaporate the moment

**NORTHERN THAILAND**

I realized that this anonymous cave was nothing like the numerous, officially surveyed caverns I had explored in the past in Thailand and Malaysia.

During the first fifteen meters of crawling through a pitch dark tunnel slick with mud and slime, I kept reminding myself that I was in the safe hands of an adult and six young boys who were all seasoned locals. I was a guest in their house, and Thais are so careful about how they treat their guests; it was impossible that they would deliberately put me in the way of danger.

When the tunnel widened out at last, I found myself inside a fairly large cavern, but when we flashed our torches on the rock walls, there were no bats hanging off them. We pressed on further, with me slipping and sliding in flip-flops that seemed Teflon-coated, until I finally took off the inappropriate footwear and placed them carefully on a protruding rock. Who knew, the flip-flops might have to act as breadcrumbs and guide me out of the cave if I got separated from the others in the darkness.

After a number of twists and turns, I gathered from the shouts of the boys that we had—thank heavens!—found the elusive bats, and there was no need to go any further. I couldn't see very much by the light of my torch, but the boys took out their catapults and started firing rocks at the bats with amazing accuracy. Maybe it wasn't so much their good aim as the stupidity of the poor blind bats trying to intercept what they mistook to be insects, but the boys were taking out one bat after another at a reassuringly steady pace.

Their success had a calming effect on my nerves, and other than a terrifying glimpse or two of something pink and glistening at the far end of the long tunnel, I think I managed my claustrophobia and fear of being hit any moment by a rock missile very well.

When the sack we had brought along was filled with enough dead bats to make our dinner that night, we began to crawl back the way we had come. Usually, I have top-class spatial awareness, but on this occasion, my disorientation was such that I was startled to find my flip-flops much sooner than I had expected. Going in, my mounting worries had made the journey seem longer; coming out, I was shrugging them off, so the distance to the mouth of the cave seemed to take less than half the time.

But who can predict the precise time and location for misfortune to strike? Just when I thought I had emerged unscathed from the experience, the accident happened. And the nature of it was so embarrassing, I wanted to slink back inside the cave, even if that meant being gnawed on by the pink and glistening thing, just to preserve my self-respect.

It was bits of broken glass, you see, that proved to be my downfall. Someone had decided the ideal place to dispose of their glass waste was outside the entrance to the cave, and before I could slip my flip-flops back on, I had big shards of broken glass buried deep in my bare right heel.

Standing in a growing puddle of my own blood, I drew air painfully into my lungs and asked to be taken home.

But back at the house, it became clear that two plasters weren't going to be sufficient. I had to go to the hospital.

My host family rushed me off to Chiang Rai's Overbrook Hospital, where I was immediately seen by a doctor, but when the time came to stitch my foot back together, the anesthetic failed to kick in. I explained this, but the doctor was insistent. "Your toes will go numb," he assured me.

"I don't care about my toes," I replied, not sure what he meant.

We argued in the same strain for some time, but weakened by the loss of blood I finally let him do what he liked.

Several minutes of truly awful pain followed. I had to bite down on a towel while the nurse held my leg still. Naturally, once the procedure was complete, the anesthetic started working and my foot was completely numb. The doctor seemed surprised to see me hop off the bed and calmly hobble away. "Because the anesthetic is working *now*!" I shot back at him before I left.

Even though they were not at fault, my host family felt terrible about the incident and bought me a pizza. But I also wanted to try the bat, and after a couple of mouthfuls I had to say that the taste of bat meat was fairly indistinguishable from beef. The wings were tricky to eat, but the spicy dish made with chest muscles was surprisingly tasty. I sat happily in the kitchen, chewing on pizza and bat and thinking that overall, I'd had a fun, action-packed day. And with the exception of the incident with the glass bottle, it had contained just the right amount of abject fear mixed in with raw excitement and sharp relief to make it a memorable twenty-four hours spent in the wilderness of rural Thailand.

## Finding the bat cave

From Chiang Rai city, cross the Mae Fah Luang Bridge, and stay on the road for about one kilometer until you see signs showing the left turn for the Buddha Caves. Take this left turn, and continue past a small village with a church until you see a mountain on the left-hand side. A slope here leads down from the road to a structure that looks like a deserted shrine. This is the entrance to the cave.

## Bats on parade

Twenty kilometers north of Ratchaburi town, you will find the Tham Khang Khao Cave, which is home to millions of bats. At dusk, when they all fly out together to feed, they blanket the sky in an amazing display of flapping black wings. Near this cave is the Buddhist temple of Wat Khao Chong Pran. Its floor gets heaped with so much bat guano that the monks make a decent income for the temple by mucking it out and selling tons of it every year.

## Bat salad

Kalasin Province in northeastern Thailand is famous for its woven *phrae wa* fabric, dinosaur fossils from the Jurassic era, and classical *pong lang* instrumental music. Less known to tourists is the fact that you can enjoy delicious bat meals in the village of Baan Toom, where locals net little mouse bats from trees and cook them into a deliciously spicy salad that you can enjoy with locally grown sticky rice.

## Insurance policy

Nicholas hadn't considered the hospital bill until he was bleeding, but as it turned out, he needed have worried at all. The total amount for fixing him up came to 1,500 baht—not even enough to make a claim on his travel insurance.

# WIANG KAEN

## *Stu Lloyd recommends taking a wrong turn into Wiang Kaen*

Every now and again in a traveler's life, there comes a day that stands out as a "real" travel experience because it is completely spontaneous and utterly authentic. About halfway through a 2,500-kilometer motorcycle odyssey around northern Thailand—covering Chiang Mai, Mae Hong Son, Doi Inthanon (Thailand's highest peak), the Golden Triangle, Sukhothai, and Lampang—I was about to have one of those days ...

After a photo opportunity at the huge golden Buddha that sits serenely on the Thai side of the Golden Triangle, Phil and I fired up our motorcycles. The plan was now to follow the mighty Mekong River as we tracked east on Highway 4007, keeping the river on our left.

Before too long, we were passing through Chiang Khong, the border town where backpackers and "visa runners" hop on ferries across to Laos. Every now and again the road would rise up, affording wondrous views of the river and the jungles of Laos on the other side, holding tightly onto whatever secrets it keeps.

We picked up Highway 1155 and tracked the Mekong a little more, until we came to a T-junction near Wiang Kaen (the easternmost district of Chiang Rai Province). We turned right. But after a hundred meters, we pulled over. Something didn't feel right. Should we have gone left? The signage in Thai offered no clue ... one squiggle pretty much looks like another to foreigners.

We U-turned then and found the road growing smaller and smaller until we reached a typically soporific Thai village. No, this was definitely not the right road either.

I pulled up outside a house/shed to consult my GT Rider map. No sooner had I switched off the ignition than there was a beaming Thai face right next to me, proffering a glass of whiskey filled to the rim. I beamed and declined with thanks. It was not quite 11 a.m. By the time Phil had pulled up, this guy was pointing across to a shaded carportlike shed, where I could see about half a dozen of his friends sitting in a circle, with several bottles of SangSom whiskey in front of them.

They motioned us to join them. We exchanged greetings. With sign language and my sketchy Thai, I tried to signal where we were headed. They laughed. Have a drink, they said. Phil is a teetotaler, so I felt obliged to take one for the team. I can't stand bloody whiskey. Not even at night. Aaargh! NASA would be interested in this stuff as an alternative fuel source. Have another, they insisted. I was drinking for two.

These likable chaps were local pomelo farmers, who had just finished their morning shift. Sitting around on the dirt floor, they were slicing, dicing, cubing, and julienning vegetables, all to go into a huge pot for lunch. I hadn't even noticed till then, but all their womenfolk were sitting off to the side, gossiping, while the men prepared the food. Quite typical in northern Thailand, apparently.

Have another drink. Hahaha. There was no taking "no" for an answer because they didn't even ask the question, just topped up the glass. And topped it up, and topped it up.

They started handing around some spicy minced pork while the main dish was boiling on the little wood fire nearby. One of the guys lifted the lid, and—*eeeek!*—a *Lord of the Flies* flashback. A pig's head smiled at me from the bottom of the pot. I mean a whole damn head: ears, snout, and all. And I swear, it winked at me.

Stay for lunch, they demanded. Well, yeah okay, why not? After all, the sun was beating down and this was so pleasant, sitting around with the farmers, trying to negotiate across cultures with uproarious results.

Then these outwardly hardened young men did something truly touching. A couple of them went out, grabbed some cardboard sheets, and covered our bikes with them so they wouldn't get too hot. A deeply considerate gesture. Soon after, a 4WD pulled up, and a most glamorous, leggy lass sidled out. She was one of the guys' sisters, who runs a flower market in Chiang Mai. Suddenly it was Phil, and not the pig in the pot, who was all ears! Within a few minutes, he was announcing that they would be getting married. Riotous laughter from the gang.

Lunch was served soon after, and the pork, vegetables, rice, and soup went down like a five-star gourmet feast. "Drink more whiss-a-key, Khun Stu." One more for the team. Aaargh! As the heat of the day pounded on the roof, and the humidity reached triple if not quadruple figures, I could feel my energy sapping. Phil was doing fine with the ladies, still fine-tuning the wedding details in his inimitable, gregarious style.

In a moment of clarity, I recalled that we had many kilometers yet to go. We had to get out of here while I was still able. I went to slip some money to our gracious host—a nominal sum, just to cover the whiss-a-key and the food. Not a big showy *farang* amount. It was summarily declined. No, they would not hear of it. This was not about money, it was about friendship. "Thailand-Australia friends, number one." We said our thanks and goodbyes and left, to a big farewell of waves and laughs.

I'm ashamed to say the whiskey wiped the names of these guys from my memory, but Phil, I'm sure, still dreams about what's-her-name. While the details of that day are not so clear, thanks to the Sang Som, I know I will always remember it. It was one of those "real" travel experiences, completely spontaneous and authentic.

I took a wrong turn—and discovered the real heart of Thailand.

## The Golden Triangle

The Golden Triangle is the three-country meeting point reached by way of the Chiang Rai province of northern Thailand, from where you can see Myanmar, Laos, and Thailand all at once, separated only by a thin sliver of the Mekong and the Ruak rivers. The Golden Triangle zone was notorious for opium smuggling until the Thai authorities clamped down on this illicit trade. There are two casinos here, in Laos and Myanmar territory, that travelers can visit with special permission.

## Bargain hunting

From the Golden Triangle, a five-minute boat ride will take you to Laos, where you can shop at a "duty-free" market without needing any travel paperwork. The goods here are similar to the handicraft and knock-off items you get on the

Thai side, but they are significantly cheaper. A lot of local and Chinese whiskey sells at this market too, in massive glass jars with large snakes, scorpions, and fake "tiger penis" floating at the bottom.

## Getting your bearings

For motorcycle touring information and maps for Thailand and the Golden Triangle area, check out The Golden Triangle Rider website.

www.gt-rider.com

# MAE TANG VALLEY

*Andrew C. Godlewski steels his nerves in Mae Taeng valley*

The day began without a cup of coffee, when a tour bus arrived at 7 a.m. to take me adventuring in the Mae Taeng Valley. Along with the bus came my enthusiastic guide, whom I mentally code-named X. Since my life and safety would be in his hands while we were out in the wild, a bond had to be established. Once he was code-named, I felt I could lay my trust in him.

X and I joined my fellow adventurers who were waiting for us in the

Chiang Mai Adventure Company's tour bus, and after stopping for a quick breakfast in the market, we set off for the Mae Tang valley camp, located two hours north of Chiang Mai city.

The plan was this: we would ride through the spectacular Mae Tang valley, traversing through forests, ponds, and streams on all-terrain vehicles (ATVs), and then we would go whitewater rafting in the Mae Taeng River. Mind you, this wasn't one of those "soft" adventures, meant for timid, feeble-hearted tourists. In Chiang Mai adventure jargon, this was a full-blown "moderate"-level adventure. Naturally, I was nervous.

Once we reached the camp, we were introduced to our ATVs—mammoth scooters with oversized wheels meant for off-road travel—and given lessons on how to ride them. We practiced backing up, doing figure eights, etc., until X was confident we had mastered our giant vehicles. Then we set off in a cavalcade down a dirt road that led into the tropical rainforests.

Our ATVs hurtled through forest trails with tall trees, shrubs, and hanging creepers looking dark and ominous on both sides. Who knew what creatures lay waiting in the deep vegetation, and I was glad my fellow adventurers were there to divide up the risk with me in case anything chose to attack. We darted around sharp hairpin bends, climbed steep slopes, and kicked up enough dust to conceal ourselves from the black bears and other wild animals I imagined lurking behind every tree. It was truly a venture into the unknown,

with no safety nets other than an old ATV and a few bottles of water.

X gave us one break in the three-hour ATV tour to catch our breath and look around a bit. I had grown tired from concentrating on the route and gripping tightly onto the handlebars, so I took a brisk walk to exercise my muscles and see things I'd missed while speeding along the dirt paths. X had chosen a beautiful spot near a small pond filled with fish, and I stood near the water, soaking in the silence and thinking how this pond had to be a watering hole for all the wild animals in the area. Then, of course, I had to hotfoot it back to my group before I accidentally ran into a thirsty, hungry beast.

Back on our ATVs again, we resumed the tour, going up and down the muddy roads before we finally exited the jungle trail and headed back to the camp. A delicious lunch was waiting for us, and we ate while we were prepped for the next leg of the journey: rafting in the Mae Taeng River.

Originating high in the mountains, near the Burmese border, the Mae Taeng winds its way through valleys and canyons until it empties into the Gulf of Thailand. The fast-flowing river offers about ten kilometers of superb whitewater rafting, with rapids classified up to grade 5.

We bid goodbye to X and said hello to Kip, who would be our captain on this tour. I would have code-named him Captain Hook perhaps, or Jack Sparrow, but the river looked pretty frightening from the bank, and I was concentrating on trying to remember all the safety instructions we had just been given. My

NORTHERN THAILAND

life jacket and helmet were on, and I scrambled onto my raft feeling decidedly underprepared for whatever lay ahead.

We started nice and easy with a fairly smooth stretch, and I had to admit that the feeling of being carried swiftly through the current was quite enervating. Then our raft hit a grade 3 rapid and lunged down a trough while I hung on to the sides for dear life, hoping the whole time that Kip would hold us together. On more than one occasion after that, we got stuck sideways in the middle of a rapid, with Kip shouting "lean left, lean left" as if our lives depended on it. Maybe it did, so I worked really hard to do my bit to keep us all alive.

It was embarrassing when we got stuck like this in full view of a village where people were preparing to eat lunch. Our raft was caught between some rocks, and I'm sure we looked really cool in our smart rafting gear, sitting motionless, providing lunchtime entertainment for the villagers. To make matters worse, the village kids got into the water and started splashing at us and laughing in our faces. Not one to tolerate this kind of ridicule, I rose to the occasion on behalf of all the others stranded in my raft and splashed them right back.

As it turned out, Captain Kip was not above having some fun at our expense either. He'd wait for a smooth patch of river, and then he'd point to the trees and cry, "Oh, look!" Naturally, we'd look—unhitch ourselves from the raft, in fact, so we could look better. Then Kip would reach out with his paddle and smack us off the side of the raft and into the water. That

wasn't all. He devised a game called helicopter, which made the raft spin wildly around in circles, practically causing us to vomit everywhere. Great guy, that Kip. He really knew how to take it easy and keep us in the boat.

One good thing that came out of his pranks, though, was that my nerves finally calmed down, and I started feeling safe. If there was any prospect of danger, Kip wouldn't be fooling around trying to dunk us in the water. At last, I could sit back, let down my guard, and enjoy the rest of the trip. I was able to appreciate the stunning scenes of forests, hills, and waterfalls we were passing through. Even the rapids didn't frighten me as much as they had earlier because I knew our worthy Captain Kip was fully in control.

### Chiang Mai Adventure Company
184/1, 3rd floor D Town Inn Tunghotel Road Amphur Muang, Chiang Mai www.chiangmaiadventure.co.th

### Bamboo rafting
If whitewater rafting seems too adventurous, head out of Chiang Mai city for the day and try bamboo rafting on the Mae Wang River instead. This river is shallow and calm, and the bamboo rafts float quite safely here. Two to four people can get onto one raft at a time, while a "pole" man situates himself at the helm with a long stick of bamboo for rowing. This is a fun soft adventure option for those who want to

enjoy views of the rainforests in a more leisurely fashion. Be warned, though, that water will flood into the raft now and then, and your feet (at least) are going to get wet.

# Phu Chi Fa

*Dee Shapland doesn't have the foggiest idea in Phu Chi Fa*

Early one November, my girlfriend, Poy, and I traveled to her Akha village high in the mountains to the northeast of Chiang Rai. She wanted to show me around the area and said we would visit Phu Chi Fa the next morning. I had no idea what, who, or where this Phu Chi Fa was, even though she had vaguely pointed out a mountain range in the distance.

Perhaps I should mention here that Poy's native language is Akha, and her English is very limited. My Thai too could certainly do with improving. But armed with my little phrasebook, we somehow manage to communicate. In any case, my traveling maxim has always been to go with the flow; in my experience that is usually when interesting things start to happen, so I didn't press her for more information.

When Poy woke me at 5 a.m. the next morning, I was still groggy from the copious amount of local whiskey I had drunk with her extended family the night before. And I was extremely cold. I put on as many layers of clothing as I had in my kit bag, and we set off as dawn was breaking. Poy had asked to borrow her brother's motorcycle, a 100-cc step-through that climbed almost-vertical hillsides, slowly but surely. We rode along beautiful hill roads with Poy's *"Don pi! Don pi!"* (Straight on! Straight on!) and *"Leo si! Leo si!"* (Turn left! Turn left!) guiding us up a route that seemed to be getting progressively steeper and steeper, slower and slower, and colder and colder until twenty kilometers and forty minutes later we arrived at our destination.

It was a car park, full of little shops selling snacks and knick-knacks, and more importantly, vendors with steaming hot coffee. After I quickly drank one cup, and bought another to take with me, I followed Poy up a steep track. It was light by now, and worryingly, everyone else seemed to be coming down.

Bravely I battled on against the flow, huffing and puffing until I came to a full stop at an incredible sight. Coming down the mountain was my old friend Kim—fellow Harley rider, ex-Dubai resident, and erstwhile traveling companion—accompanied by his girlfriend, Bee. We had parted company in Chiang Mai some three weeks earlier, and I had no idea he was heading this way. We stopped to chat and made plans to meet the following week, before setting off again.

After a mile or so of this arduous climb, we finally reached the top. A carved wooden sign showed the elevation: 1,628 meters. We were perched on the wide, grassy summit of a perpendicular cliff that rose arrogantly up toward the sky. To the east, I knew, was the neighboring country of Laos and a big swathe of the Mekong Valley. Below us … my heart lurched when I looked over the edge of the cliff and saw nothing at all. Phu Chi Fa seemed precariously suspended in space.

A thick veil of fog blanketed whatever lay a long way below, and only when I spied a few mountain tips poking through the fog did I start to get my bearings. Phu Chi Fa wasn't going to take us crashing down after all. It was standing quite straight and solid, hundreds of meters above everything else around it. The misty fog cover had disoriented me for a moment there, but now that I felt safe again, I could fully appreciate my surroundings. The view, with the sun rising in the distance, wasn't just beautiful. It was stunning and completely uplifting. The feeling that my feet had lost contact with Mother Earth gave wings to my spirit, and the clean, cold air seemed to expand my mind. I couldn't thank Poy enough for bringing me here.Sadly, we were rather late, and the sun was already above eye-level. I hated to think I had missed the sunrise, and resolved to come back another day.

And that we did, three months later. The weather was warmer, and we were accompanied by Poy's two boys and *adah* (father). This time we arrived an hour earlier, in good time to catch the sunrise. Another big plus during this February trip was that the mountainside was covered with small white flowers called *dok siao*. Poy's *adah* informed me that there was a festival nearby to celebrate this blooming.

We stayed long enough for the fog to dissipate, revealing the mighty Mekong River snaking through a bright green jungle in the distance. We could see picturesque little villages and a Lao army camp at the base of the mountain. This area has traditionally been a smuggling route between Thailand and Laos, and even today it is a popular exit for the indigenous Mien and White Hmong people who run away from Laos to escape persecution.

On my previous visit, there were no foreigners at the Phu Chi Fa except Kim and me. This time, too, mine was the only white face in the small crowd of locals who had come to watch the sunrise and picnic.

Afterward, Poy's *adah* was thirsting for some prelunch moonshine, so he went off to buy *lao khao* (rice whiskey) while the rest of us went back to Poy's Akha village. In this place, recycling is the name of the game. Nothing is wasted, and I saw Poy's *adah* coming back from his shopping expedition with booze tied all over the motorcycle. Gallon-sized plastic bags sealed off with rubber bands held the clear liquid. What a good idea, and environmentally friendly, too.

I helped him decant some of the whiskey into old and well-used plastic Coke bottles. Then we raised a toast to

Phu Chi Fa and proceeded to seriously imbibe yet again. It was the "man" thing to do in this village. Not to mention that Poy would have no reason to wake me up at five again tomorrow morning.

### Getting to Phu Chi Fa

Phu Chi Fa is located in the Amphoe Thoeng District in Chiang Rai Province. The distance from Chiang Rai town is approximately 108 kilometers. The easiest way to get from Chiang Rai town to Phu Chi Fa is by hiring a private taxi with a driver for the entire day for about 1,000 baht. After watching the sunrise at Phu Chi Fa, you can continue on northward, passing several Akha and Hmong villages until you reach the old riverside trading town of Chiang Khong. A word to the wise: don't pay your driver until the very end of the journey, to make sure he doesn't disappear at some point along the way.

## KHAO YAI NATIONAL PARK

### Brendan O'Reilly follows his nose in Khao Yai National Park

The greatest thing about traveling alone with no itinerary is that my mind is wide open to strangers and new experiences. With the agility of an eel, I can slip in and out of situations and make on-the-spot travel decisions without having to consult my to-do list that had started to look predictable and boring anyway, from the moment I landed in Thailand.

I was thinking about this when I met a Hungarian-German in Ayutthaya, who was also journeying solo. We quickly became travel buddies in that single meeting and decided to go trekking in the Khao Yai National Park together. We fixed up to meet at a guesthouse called the Greenleaf in the nearby town of Pak Chong the next day. On my way there, I met a tall Finn on the train, and we also fixed up to stay at the same guesthouse and take the same tour.

Of course, once I got there, my Hungarian friend was nowhere to be found, but as a lone traveler, I have to respect flexibility—mine and also his. So I put him out of my mind and happily joined a tour group with the tall Finn, plus seven other people of different nationalities, ranging from Peruvian and Israeli to Brazilian, German, and Italian. We sat down on covered seats in the tour guide's pickup truck and quickly established a group camaraderie by trying to share stories, laughter, and half-understood jokes. It was exciting to know that we were about to drive into Thailand's oldest national park, and all of us were dying for the adventure to begin.

The Khao Yai National Park, a mix of clear grasslands, tropical evergreens, and dry deciduous forests, is apparently one of the few monsoon forests in Asia that is still intact. It is home to a large number of animal and plant species, and I hoped we would fit in as many sightings of Asiatic black bears, barking deer, wild pigs, and other Khao Yai inhabitants as possible in the two-hour period this tour was going to last.

On the drive up to the hiking trail, I was fairly startled when our Thai guide quickly spotted a multitude of birds all at once, perched on a canopy of trees hanging low over our heads. The Israeli raised an enthusiastic cheer for our guide, in response to which the man said, "They are plastic. I put them up there last night." After a moment, we realized he was making a joke, and we laughed, allowing him to take pleasure in his own sense of humor.

Then the jungle hike began. Our group got off the pickup truck and was immediately engulfed by huge moss-laden trees. The air was fragrant with dirt, leaves, and moisture. In certain places, I could put my ears close to the ground and actually *hear* the incessant commute of thousands of ants. Being a resident of Washington State in the United States, I am fairly well acquaint-ed with wandering in forests, but I have to say that the abundance of life in Khao Yai was well beyond my experience.

We had trekked for about an hour when the guide suddenly motioned for us to cease all conversation. Our decibel level was so high, we were drowning out the conversation of the gibbons! Looking up, we saw a couple of young gibbons lounging on a treetop and chatting with each other. Their own

conversation must have been pretty interesting, because neither of them had noticed us either. This was my very first sighting of wild apes, and I was thrilled.

The next big moment on the trail came when our guide sensed the presence of an elephant pack nearby. Even though they are the largest land animals on earth, elephants are sur-prisingly difficult to track in the jungle. I suppose it might be in part because elephants can walk *over* bushes, while puny humans such as myself must walk *around* such obstacles. Much of our last hour in the forest was spent in futile pursuit of these elusive animals. We found fresh feces, heard branches cracking, and smelled the distinct scent of elephants in the air. But no sighting. A dog might have been satis-fied, but unfortunately for us humans, we have a strong need for the visual.

We stopped to swallow lunch along with our disappointment. To cheer us up, our guide said he would show us a very famous waterfall instead—Haew Suwat Waterfall, which had served as a location for the Hollywood block-buster *The Beach*. As we approached Haew Suwat, the march of the forest was stopped abruptly by huge boulders that cradled a small pool in its midst. The cataract poured over a high rock face into this pool in three frothing columns, like milk boiling over the lip of a saucepan. It was an incredibly beautiful scene, and as I captured some outstanding shots of it on my digital camera, a sweet little butterfly came and sat on my arm, mistaking it perhaps for a swaying branch of a tree.

With that, our two-hour trek was over. We prepared to return to our lodgings feeling generally satisfied. We'd had some good laughs, made new friends and, got plenty of exercise.

Then, when we were least expecting it, the elephants arrived! It was the same pack we had been chasing through the forest. Thinking we had got tired of the hide-and-seek game, the family of four had finally come out to let us view them right on the road!

Here was proof, I thought, that we had hadn't even begun to understand the mysteries of the forest in the short time we had just spent trekking. It had teased us and played with us, and then—in a fit of kindness—rewarded us with a parting gift that clearly reinforced its superiority in the power game between man and nature.

## Getting to Khao Yai National Park

The gateway to Khao Yai National Park, the small town of Pak Chong is located approximately two hundred kilometers northeast of Bangkok. The town is easily reached via bus and train from Bangkok, Ayutthaya, and the northeastern Isaan provinces.

## Greenleaf Guesthouse

This guesthouse is about eight kilometers away from the Pak Chong train station on the main road to Khao Yai National Park. If you let the guesthouse know the time of your arrival, someone will pick you up from the bus or train station. The guesthouse has clean, functional rooms, and the food is exceptional. It also has a tour company that offers various guided tours around the park.

www.greenleaftour.com

## Song of the gibbons

Gibbons are not monkeys, but apes, like gorillas, orangutans, and chimpanzees. They are the opera singers of the primate family. They love singing, and their territorial cries can carry over a distance of almost a kilometer, even in dense jungles. Each pair of the Lar gibbon species has a mating and territory-defending song that is completely unique to its family unit. These gibbons spend almost their entire lives in the forest canopy, and eat fruit, leaves, and some insects.

# PHUKET

*Jamie Monk recons in a Phuket mangrove forest*

Northeast on Phuket is Bang Rong, where a small Muslim fishing community lives amidst wild mangrove forests, far away from all the tourist hoopla that has overrun the island's western beaches. The fishermen here have started a floating restaurant near the Bang Rong pier to supplement their income, and we often visit this eatery to enjoy fresh seafood and undisturbed views of a picturesque coastline fringed with oddly stunted mangrove trees.

The day's catch is held in large nets at the back of the restaurant, and it is an exciting treat for the whole family to choose what they like from it. The *klong* on which the restaurant floats is alive with fish as well, and to my daughter's endless delight, they constantly come up to the surface to entice her into giving them a large portion of our meal.

If anything could improve the experience of eating freshly caught fish at the floating restaurant, cooked in tasty southern Thai style, it is a glass of chilled Singha beer. But that isn't to be—drinking goes against the community's Muslim faith, and a large, red "No Alcohol" signboard hangs prominently outside the restaurant. In a way, though, this rigid adherence to Bang Rong's Muslim way of life is reassuring. I'm always fearful of the day when the community might see profit in tourism and exchange its boats and fishing nets for neon-lit bars, massage parlors, and cheap clothing stalls.

One weekend afternoon, I was at the restaurant having yet another leisurely lunch, when I noticed something I had never seen before: four or five orange kayaks bobbing in the water. Some people were being taken in them on an excursion to the mangrove forests. As I watched, the kayaks floated out into the sea until they disappeared from my view, and then returned not long after, with the kayakers looking all flushed and excited. Naturally, that made me want to get into a kayak and see the mangroves up close too.

Since the whole family was up for the adventure, we returned to Bang Rong a few days later and hired the orange kayaks for 150 baht each. We also hired two rowers for an additional fee of 100 baht. My daughter would need someone to row her kayak, and I would too, as I needed my hands free to take photographs. Once everybody had slid in and secured their safety jackets, the rowers picked up their paddles and we were off.

The restaurant was already in the forest, with a view of open sea, but within fifty meters, we rounded a bend and the water tapered into a creek with the mangroves rushing in at us from both sides.

The trees stood with thick layers of sky-facing prop roots and aerial stems billowing out at the bottom, creating a continuous, randomly woven barrier between land and water. These roots in fact save the mangroves from the impact of shifting soil and currents, and like snorkelers, they breathe in air through little pores at the tip to avoid suffocation in the saline water and oxygen-deprived mud. It is incredible to think how sophisticated a survival plan these strangely shaped trees have come

SOUTHERN THAILAND

up with, their leaves, roots, and bark working constantly to store oxygen and purify themselves.

It was low tide, and the water's edge was teeming with activity as creatures hosted by the mangrove-protected ecosystem went busily about their business. Our rowers guided the kayaks closer to the shore, so we could get a better look at all of them. I spotted crabs of several sorts— from ordinary hermits to the curious-looking fiddler crabs with just one oversized claw. Lazy, bug-eyed mudskippers, or *pla teen* as they're called in Thailand, preferred to forage in the muddy mangrove soil than go out in the open water and try to swim like most other fish. A large water lizard jumped up as soon as it spotted us, thrashed its tail once, and disappeared into the forest. My rower also pointed out several cones of mud on the bank, inside which mud lobsters had built their many-tunneled homes.

At my daughter's insistence, we stopped at a sandbank so she could dig for seashells. We pulled our kayaks in, feeling like the first humans ever to set foot in this silent mangrove world. The trees and shrubs leaning into the water seemed slightly creepy, now that we were on solid ground, their network of tangled roots looking as if they might rise up any minute and wrap their tentacles around us in a cannibal death grip. A couple of crab-eating monkeys eyed us curiously from their perch on a high branch, and I wondered if they expected we would supplement their seafood diet

with fruits and other goodies humans usually had around them.

My daughter, meanwhile, had enlisted the help of our rowers, and the three of them were digging furiously in the sand. We were all so caught up in playing or taking pictures, nobody noticed when one of our kayaks came untied and started floating away.

We stood on the sandbank and cheered as a rower jumped into the water and chased it some ways down the creek. When the kayak had finally been recovered, my wife noticed the time and wondered if we should be heading back. Our empty stomachs were also telling us it was way past lunchtime, so we started for the restaurant, rowing downstream with the tide.

Checking on Google Earth later, I discovered we had traveled about one kilometer up the creek. During high tide however, it was possible to row up to two kilometers, and there were many little side streams that could be explored as well. We definitely had to come back and do this trip all over again, when the water level was high. The mangroves would look very different with their nether regions flooded.

All in all, our first short kayaking trip into the mangroves proved to be a great success, and we added it to our list of favorite family outings. The trip had provided many *National Geographic* moments for my daughter and made her feel like a "big girl" because she didn't have to share a kayak with Mom and Dad. We could come exploring here whenever we liked without any advance planning or preparation, and there was always a hearty meal waiting for us afterward at the Bang Rong floating restaurant.

## Bang Rong floating restaurant

To reach Bang Rong, head east from Phuket's Heroines Monument on Highway 4027 and travel for about ten kilometers. Look out for a large mosque, and then turn right to reach the pier and the floating restaurant.

## All-terrain vehicles

For information about touring Phuket by ATV, go to the Phuket ATV Tour Co. website.

www.atvphuket.com

# KOH MOOK

## Elizabeth Cassidy triumphs over a dark hour in Koh Mook

The entrance to the Emerald Cave is little more than a small opening on a craggy rock face. Hanging low over the water, it looks dark and mysterious, as if it's hiding some diabolical secret inside. During low tide, there is just enough space between the roof of the cave and the sea for people to pass through an eighty-meter tunnel and come out on the other side, where a piece of paradise awaits.

But that paradise is to come later for me. Right now, all I can think about is that once I swim into the bowels of this spooky cave, it will swallow me up and I'll never come out again.

Along with a boatful of tourists, my friend Marita and I are in front of the Emerald Cave, located on the western side of a rocky mountainous island called Koh Mook. We had set out from Koh Lanta on a full day's trip and hit several snorkeling spots on the way. The tour included a nice lunch too, on a private beach where Marita, with her enormous respect for the sea, had astonished everybody by diving into the water to remove bottle caps and other plastic waste carelessly thrown out by the picnickers. Now that the tide had ebbed, we were finally going to make the much-anticipated pass through the Emerald Cave.

The man who steers our boat is acting as our guide as well. He instructs us to put on life vests over our swimsuits and get off the boat one by one. Everybody has to stay close together, because a human chain has to be formed to make the crossing through the cave safely.

As the others get into a single file and hold on to the back of each other's life vests, Marita and I join the chain near the end and bob along toward the entrance of the cave. The water around me has a stillness that suggests great depth, and I feel better knowing I have Marita going ahead of me. The deeper we drift into the cave, the less I can see around me. The emerald green sea turns murkier in stages, until it disappears completely in the pitch darkness of the cave, leaving me feeling completely disoriented.

Our guide turns on a battery-operated light bulb he has attached to his headband and creates a weak pool of visibility around himself at the very head of the human chain. "Follow Closely! Hang on to each other!" His voice ricochets off the walls, sounding distant and urgent at the same time, as if he is guiding us through a microphone from a ship anchored safely out in the open sea. At the tail end of the twenty-person chain, we are too far from his light, and I realize I have to make the journey with only the strings on the back of Marita's vest to guide me forward.

But it is difficult trying to hold on to a life vest with one hand while paddling with the other to keep up with the rest of the group. I reach out to steady myself against the rocky wall, and pull my hand back quickly, stung by the sharp, jagged edges of the stone. "Don't touch the sides of the cave! They are very sharp!" our guide yells from the front, too late because I have done it already—and lost my grip on Marita's vest in the process.

I can see nothing, and for a moment, I give in to sheer panic. The water feels oppressively cold, and I have no idea how far I have drifted from the others. "Marita?" I shout, drawing large gulps of air into my lungs so I can get that one word out. "Marita!"

A deep voice of a man answers back. He is the very last person in the chain, and I grab hold of him, thanking God that I was within his reach before he too moved away. The man senses the fright I took at being separated from the others, and keeps an eye out for me until we see a glow of daylight in the far distance. The cave is coming to an end, and as each member of the chain passes out onto the other side, we hear cheers, whistles, and shouts of amazement and delight.

At last, it is my turn to emerge from the cave, and I tread shallow water as I stop to see the small beach laid out in a semicircle a short distance away. Impossibly steep cliffs rise immediately behind the narrow belt of white sand, overgrown with lush tropical trees. The cliffs create a secluded arbor, as if shielding the tiny lagoon from the eyes of the world. Standing in waist-deep water and staring at this scene, I find I cannot echo the others and scream out my surprise. I am struck dumb by my unexpected encounter with paradise. This is the coziest face of nature I have ever seen, and I can't believe I am, at this very moment, a part of it.

I look around for Marita, and her eyes tell me she too is asking herself the same question: "What have I ever done to be worthy of this?"

We spend an hour in the lagoon, absorbing and internalizing its beauty. We hardly speak; there will be time enough for that once we reach our hotel room in Koh Lanta.

When our time is up, the guide blows his whistle to get us to re-

SOUTHERN THAILAND

group. We return the way we came, and that means forming another human chain. Breaking out of my reverie, I rush to take up a position close to the guide. Having made the journey through the Emerald Cave once, I'm not afraid to go inside it again. But no way am I tagging along at the back this time. I'll stay right next to the guide and take full advantage of his headband light to guide me all the way.

Our chain starts moving, and I look back at the lagoon for the last time. I don't feel bad having to say goodbye. The fact that nature denies constant access to this spot by flooding the cave entrance during high tide can only mean one thing: no human is allowed to demand endless time here. This is paradise after all, and I feel lucky that I was allowed to enter it, even if it was only for an hour.

### Getting to Koh Mook

Traveling to Koh Mook is an easy process, as longtail boats connect it to Trang, Koh Lanta, Krabi, and other major tourist islands in southern Thailand.

### Play it safe

If you visit the Emerald Cave in a private boat, respect the tide and leave the lagoon as soon as your boatman asks you to. The cave can flood quickly, and if you delay for even a few minutes, you might find yourself stranded.

### Fishy business

If something brushes against you in the dark as you pass through the Emerald Cave, don't panic—it's just a fish, and it's probably as startled by you as you are by it.

## KOH PHANGAN

### Ryan Humphreys climbs to the very top of Koh Phangan

It was an odd thing to ask on Koh Phangan—Thailand's infamous all-night Moon Party island—but surely there was something interesting for people to do here during the day? Scanning my guidebook, I found Khao Ra, the island's highest peak. At 630 meters, it seemed scalable, and a safe distance away from the postparty drunks and dopes still dancing in the waves or lying wasted on the main beach.

The guidebook suggested that I go to the island village of Ban Madua Wan and hire a guide at the Phaeng Waterfall Park to take me climbing. Once I got there, however, I found the information booth was boarded up. I wandered into the park's office nearby and almost ran into a tall bald man, who I realized after a moment wasn't a skinhead reveler spilled over from the Full Moon Party, but a Buddhist monk, attending a religious festival here with scores of his orange-robed brothers. I pushed my way through the throng and asked an old lady seated behind a desk for a guide to take me up the mountain.

She made a phone call, and I could hear the excited voice of a man on the other end saying he would certainly take me up for 500 baht. That was the same price mentioned in the guidebook, so I agreed. About ten minutes later, a middle-aged guy arrived and we set off to climb Khao Ra peak.

The trail was poorly marked, and I was very relieved to have someone showing me the way. As we walked up the long winding, barely discernible path, my guide told me about many tourists who had lost the trail and needed to be rescued. My Thai was more advanced than his English, and he chatted happily with me about the island, showing me various flora and fauna along the way.

At one point, he pivoted suddenly and pointed into the distance. "Cobra!" he shouted, as if in warning. I froze with fear. My brain recalled having read something about snakes, pigs, and deer being common on this trail, and I crouched low, feverishly scanning the ground around my feet for cobras.

The guide looked at me quizzically. "Khao Ra," he repeated, pointing at the misty peak in the distance.

"Oh yes, Khao Ra, of course," I muttered, continuing to act a little strangely to dilute some of the strangeness from my behavior of a few seconds ago.

We carried on with the climb, which was pretty treacherous at many points, until we safely reached the top about midafternoon. Drenched in sweat and covered in scratches from thorny bushes and sharp overhanging branches, I sat quietly on a rock, letting the stunning panoramic views of a glittering turquoise ocean wash over me. I could see Koh Tao to the north and Koh Samui to the south, laid out like two jade pendants on blue chamois-satin cloth in a jewelry store. The bone white beaches were directly below me, and foamy waves were breaking almost noiselessly and in slow motion on the shallow coral.

My guide waited patiently while I took a few pictures, and then we started the climb down. Near the bottom, we stopped at a cool, natural plunge pool surrounded by rocks. Two elderly Italian men were lounging naked in the pool. I paid off my guide, stripped down to my boxers, and joined the men. They asked me if I had climbed to the top of the mountain, and when I told them I had, we exchanged high fives, feeling that we had all earned this marvelously relaxing soak in the pool.

After the men put on their clothes and left, I floated on my back for a long time, thinking about nothing in particular, just enjoying perfect solitude on a perfect day in paradise.

## The trail not taken

There are several trails that lead up to Koh Phangan's Khao Ra peak, and they have many confusing subtrails where you can lose your bearings if you're not watchful. It is very easy to get lost on this climb, and the safest way to stay on course is to hike with an experienced guide. But if you still want to strike out on your own, make sure to carry a torch, guidebook, and map. Also give yourself plenty of time to come back down while there is daylight, and let others know where you are going, so they can raise an alarm if you don't return within a stated time period. Lastly, wear sturdy hiking shoes and not flip-flops.

## KOH BON

*Chris Mitchell
swims with a manta ray
in the waters of Koh Bon*

I glanced to my right. Then I did a cartoon double take. Directly parallel to me, not more than ten feet away, glided a manta ray, effortlessly keeping pace with me and my dive guide.

The manta continued alongside us for another minute or so, wholly unfazed by our presence or the noise and bubbles of our scuba gear. It was huge, equal to my height in its wing span, and it was simply mesmerizing to look at. Never had I seen a creature seem so wholly at home in its habitat. Then, with a single flick of its massive black wings, the manta banked away and disappeared into the blue. I looked at my dive guide, and my dive guide looked at me. We high-fived each other as we hovered at fifteen meters below the surface—I'd just seen my first manta ray! Later, my dive guide told me I was hugging myself with glee.

I had been hoping to come face-to-face with a manta ever since joining a scuba diving liveaboard boat going to the Similan Islands, a remote, uninhabited archipelago off the west coast of Thailand renowned for world-class diving. For four days, we explored the underwater world of the Similans, and went to three even more remote islands beyond them. One of these islands was Koh Bon—the Island Of Hope—which is a hotspot for adventurers chasing manta rays.

My own hope of seeing a manta ray near Koh Bon was high, even though the dive guides warned me there were no guarantees that the mantas would be there. As we dropped in on the dive site, which was a quite dramatic near-vertical wall plunging from the surface to around fifteen meters before leveling out into a coral reef, I tried to push all thoughts of the manta out of my mind and just enjoy the dive for what it was. And then I happened to glance to my right …

Since that first time I saw a manta ray, I have dived in Koh Bon every year, continually drawn back to the spot by the spectacular underwater conditions and profusion of marine creatures there. But the manta rays remain for me the star attraction of diving in the Similans, and I've been incredibly lucky with the sightings. Every time I have dived at Koh Bon I've seen them—sometimes just a solitary manta, sometimes whole squadrons of them wheeling in and out of the blue, coming to investigate the strange bubble-creature by the reef. And the exhilaration is always the same as the very first time.

### Getting to Koh Bon

Koh Bon is located about twenty kilometers north of Island #9 (Koh Bangu) in the Similan archipelago. The main dive site that Chris explores is off the southwestern corner and consists of a thirty-three-meter wall facing a small cove laden with colorful brain and mountain corals.

### Diving the Similan Islands

Liveaboards offer scuba divers an opportunity to live on a boat, eat on a boat, and dive straight off the boat into top diving sites in Similan Islands. Typically, a liveaboard tour spends four days out in the Similans, as well as visits Koh Bon, Koh Tachai, and Richelieu Rock. If you've never dived before, you can learn to scuba dive on a Similan Islands' liveaboard by doing a PADI Open Water Diver course.

Departing from Phuket and Khao Lak, many liveaboards operate on the Similan route, and you can choose one depending on your budget. The most basic amenities—no

matter what your price category— will include air-conditioned cabins, on-board catering, and nonalcoholic drinks and beverages.

The Similan dive season runs from October to May each year— the monsoon season (June to September) creates conditions that are too rough for safe diving.

### Manta rays

Mantas are the largest species of rays in the world and can weigh as much as three thousand pounds. They have no stinging spine or teeth (they eat by sieving their food) and pose no threat to humans. In fact, they are curious about people and often surface near boats or swim alongside divers. In spite of their enormous size, mantas are extremely graceful creatures, and their acrobatics are delightful to watch underwater.

## SURIN ISLANDS

### Alice Driver
### sets sail with the gypsies
### of the Surin Islands

Tourists can visit the Surin Islands only between mid-November and May, and my husband, Isaac, and I were on the first boat that reached the islands when they opened one year. Isaac was working on a project documenting the unique boat-building techniques of the Moken people who lived there. Fascinated by the four thousand years of history of this nomadic sea gypsy community, I too had come along, hoping to learn more about the Moken way of life.

At one time, the Moken traveled among the islands of Thailand, Myanmar, and Malaysia, living on their boats. The influences of the modern world slowly pushed them to live on land, but they still maintain a strong connection with the sea and regard their *kabang* boats as a symbol of their identity.

We stayed in Koh Surin Tai, a small island with a fishing village built by two hundred Moken people. The village atmosphere was peaceful. Friendly stray dogs and cats roamed the unpaved paths of the settlement, looking for food and affection, while nut-brown, naked children played boisterously around us in the ocean. I noticed that the kids wore their hair very short on the sides and long on top, its blackness bleached to a burnt red from life in the sun. Groups of women in bright sarongs played cards, wove baskets of pandanus leaves, or watched over sleeping babies in the shade beneath houses on stilts. The faint sound of music floated out from radios, and the occasional hum of popular soap operas could be heard on the few televisions on the island.

At low tide, we saw twenty-five boats sitting in muddy tidal flats; most of them were wooden longtails, a

post-Tsunami gift from local NGOs that must have come after many Moken lost their homes and boats in the 2004 tsunami. Of the unique *kabangs*—the anthropomorphic boats that my husband had come here to study—there were just a few. Most of the *kabangs* on the island had been destroyed, and it was sad to see modern, motor-operated vessels replacing what had been at the heart of Moken culture for thousands of years. There were just four boat builders now left on the island. Salama, the leader of the village, was building his own *kabang,* which he hoped would last him until he died.

During our stay, we became friends with Khun Taht, one of the four boat builders, who invited us to go spear fishing with his family in a *kabang.* We were joined by Khun Taht's wife, two kids, and a friend. The men carried three harpoons onboard, and we set off to enjoy a *kabang* ride in the Andaman Sea and watch the Moken men fish.

Traditionally, the *kabangs* were made with wood and Salacca, a fibrous plant that swells when wet. The boats were extremely light and required no caulking. When built with Salacca, a *kabang* was so buoyant it was almost impossible to sink. However, Salacca had to be replaced every six months, so the Moken began making their boats entirely of wood. The heavier boat requires a large motor rather than the traditional pandanus palm frond sails. I looked closely at the bifurcated bow of the *kabang* and remembered a piece of Moken oral history that compared parts of this boat to parts of the human body: the split bow represented the *kabang*'s mouth and the stern, its anus.

Our *kabang* anchored at a point where a wall of coral dropped steeply to about fifteen feet, and we watched Khun Taht and his friend jump into the water. They swam with their spears until they reached the coral floor, and then stood up, their muscular, T-shaped bodies glistening with droplets of water. The Moken men wore no shoes despite the sharp coral, and I was amazed that even after hours of walking, their tough feet were not bloody. They waded toward the shore and disappeared into the jungle to wait for the tide to recede and leave fish trapped in the coral.

I sat cross-legged in the *kabang* while Kun Taht's wife rested with her two young boys, aged four and five. All of us were waiting patiently for the men to return. After an hour or so, I saw Khun Taht and his friend come back to the corals. The water now only came up to their ankles. Khun Taht unstrung a blue and orange parrotfish from his line and called to his older son to come and collect it. The parrotfish passed from the large brown palm of the father to the tiny, eager fingers of his son. However, the fish slipped from the boy's grasp and began to float away. When it had been rescued, Khun Taht showed the boy how to hold the fish by putting an index finger through its gills and a thumb through its mouth. With the fish safely on board, we motored back toward the Moken island amidst a purple sunset.

I sat back in my seat, enjoying the cool wind and the peacefulness of the passing scenery. Looking at the tired faces of Khun Taht and his friend, my thoughts went back to their ancestors. How resolutely they had clung to their nomadic lifestyle for thousands of years, forever wandering the sea, as the Moken people like to say, eating and excreting, choosing never to save or store.

Even now that they have been compelled to abandon their sea adventures and make home on solid land, the Moken show little interest in assimilating with mainstream culture. "This is my land," Khun Taht told me, about Koh Surin Tai. "I want to stay here. And I hope my children will stay here and marry people from the village."

### Getting to the Surin Islands

The Surin archipelago lies about sixty kilometers off the west coast of Phang Nga Province. It can be reached from Kuraburi Pier in Phang Nga. The ferry crossing from Kuraburi is about three hours and is only open during the tourist season. Boats can also be chartered from the Kapoe Pier in Ranong Province, and the journey will take about seven hours. Some diving boats from Phuket also offer trips to the Surin Islands.

### Word of advice

As the Moken struggle with alcohol and other addictions, please don't bring gifts of alcohol, instant noodles, and other junk food to the islands.

# WHEN IN ROME

*Lessons on living local and making yourself at home*

Sinking into a foreign culture has never been so easy. Ask the thousands of expats who have chosen to make Thailand their home, and they'll tell you how instinctive it is to adopt the Thai way of life. Many of the authors in this book live in different parts of the country with Thai wives, kids, and extended Thai families, and they seem so well integrated with the local society, it's hard to think of them as Americans, Europeans, or Australians anymore.

"When my folks in Michigan want to know why I live here, I always confess to a deep, abiding love for the favorable currency in Thailand," one of them told me. "But the real reason I bought property, married locally, and stayed back is the strong attachment I feel to the country and its people. A three-month teaching assignment in an Isaan village exposed me to such a unique, friendly culture that at the end of it I saw no reason to leave."

The rest of us are not so lucky that we can call Thailand home, but as tourists, we can still participate in many of the joys that expats get to experience on a regular basis. The Thai people have devised many interesting ways to entertain and occupy themselves, for instance, and they are always delighted to have us join them for an energetic bout of, say, Muay Thai.

Muay Thai, or kick-boxing, is a sporting event that Thais are crazy about, and Charles Benimoff knows of a bar in Koh Phi Phi where you actually get a chance to kick box yourself. The bar offers a "bucket" of free drinks as prize to whichever customer is still left standing in the ring, and Charles fervently hopes that some Americans among you readers will disabuse the bar owner of his notion that—unlike Europeans, who are at the top of the game—American tourists make lousy Muay Thai fighters.

Steven McCall hits the greens in Koh Samui, expecting to play a regular round of golf, but he soon realizes this is going to be a Thai version of the game when a *girl* arrives in a hot pink outfit to be

his caddie and help choose his shots. Andrew C. Godlewski works alongside rice farmers in a Suphanburi village with two bullocks harnessed to his plough to appreciate the sweat and toil that go into producing a handful of the precious grain. And Mike Rose buys into the national obsession with the lottery, but narrowly misses a payout because he is too blinded by logic to see the secret lucky number that is clearly visible on his house lizard's tail.

We foreigners may be a little slow on the uptake when it comes to Thai "signs" and "omens" like that, but something we understand very well is the pleasure of a good Thai massage. Our authors broaden the scope of our Thai spa experience by introducing treatments you have probably never heard of— blood vine steam baths, the Hammer massage, and even an organic pedicure given by schools of little fish, who hungrily nibble away at the dead skin on your feet.

This chapter contains many other essays that suggest more ways to enjoy living the Thai life, but I'm afraid you cannot say you've totally immersed yourself in the culture unless you have tried the local transport. I earned my shirt by jumping onto a motorcycle taxi once—it took me on the most frightening ride of my life down the main drag in Bangkok's Sukhumvit area. Between the two lanes on the road, the driver seemed to see an imaginary one, and we rode on it for a full fifteen minutes to Pratunam Plaza, squeezing past vans, buses, and cars. I screeched all the way, much to the annoyance of the driver, who thankfully ignored the number of times I fell against his back and tried to wrap my arms around his waist. These motorcycle taxis are not something tourists typically use, or even know about, but Dà wèi is quite sold on this local mode of transport, and gives great tips on how to ride them with more decorum and self-control than I exhibited on my maiden journey.

Much like Dà wèi is Lot Schuringa, who is a fan of an unconventional public transport that locals seem to favor: buses.

Don't ask what's unconventional about buses in Bangkok. Just ride one, carefully following Lot's instructions, and you'll be a hero among your fellow travelers who are too afraid to try ... just because the buses have no timetables, no proper stoppages, and no route maps, not to mention that the driver may park and wander off whenever he pleases.

To keep a perspective on this experience, just consider the upside: according to Lot, even *you* can stop the bus and get off wherever you please. Do your efficient bus systems at home offer such personalized service? And what's the worst that can happen anyway? You'll end up getting lost. And isn't that one of the best ways to make new discoveries and possibly even find yourself when you're on the road?

## BANGKOK

*Lot Schuringa decodes the mystery of Bangkok buses*

Take bus 56 on the right side of the roundabout at the end of that road with all the yellow flags. Pay 8 baht. If you're charged anything else, you're on the wrong bus. It will go straight ahead for quite a long while, so only start paying attention once the bus turns. You will see a building in front of you that from a distance looks a lot like the Colosseum. There the vehicle will turn left and immediately cross a bridge. Big chances it will get caught in a traffic jam there. Get off if it takes too long. Otherwise stand up and press the red button as soon as it turns again—to the right this time—and then get off. From there, take a left, and walk to the highest building in Chinatown—the one with the striped red and white hat on top.

These were precisely the directions I received for my first ride on a Bangkok bus. I had a job interview that morning, and my friend and soon-to-be colleague assured me it was dead easy. Turned out she was perfectly right. Unlikely as it may sound, I got there without any problems.

Ever since that first time, I've been hooked. Now my bus map and I are inseparable.

The Skytrain may be convenient, but the bus is really great for getting to know Bangkok. But to fully appreciate this mode of transport, you have to forget whatever bus services you have ever encountered in other parts of the world. There are no rules here—and that is the beauty of Bangkok's bus system. So if you're ready to make your own choices, and not be troubled by small inconveniences, you'll love Bangkok buses as much as I do.

Here's a short introduction to the apparent chaos that is Bangkok's local bus network. Once you consider all the advantages and try it for yourself, you may also admit it's actually the best—and cheapest—way to get around the capital.

### You're in charge

Bus stops in Bangkok are rarely indicated by anything more than a small blue sign, which, more often than not, is hidden behind a tree or a food stall. Even if you do manage to spot that sign from inside the bus, the driver will have passed it by the time you've pressed the stop button. So, to get off the bus, do what I find works best for me: study your bus map. Count the number of bridges you'll be crossing or keep track of how often the bus turns and in which direction. Then just stand up whenever you think you're close enough. The bus will actually stop, just for you.

It's true. Bangkok buses stop wherever and whenever they like.

But it's quid pro quo. You better not make a fuss when the driver stops for reasons of his own.

Bus drivers think nothing of stopping for fuel at a gas station with passengers on board. Or, for example, last week, when my friend got on bus 2, it came to a halt unexpectedly and stood there for a good ten minutes. Nobody asked why. One by one, passengers started getting off after the driver had obligingly opened the doors. Calculating the cost of a taxi, my friend decided not to follow them but go and ask the driver what the problem was instead. Turned out the conductor had gone to find a toilet—she had diarrhea.

### Decisions, decisions

Just consider the many options this bus system gives you. You can choose between air-conditioning or open windows. You can choose minibuses, average buses, or huge buses. You can either go the expressway route or stick to ordinary roads. You can jump off a moving bus or wait until it comes to a complete halt. It's all up to you, how you use this flexible transport system to your best advantage.

### What's your color?

Bangkok has red, white, yellow, pink, blue, and green buses, but they're not meant to be just a treat for your eyes. Each color indicates a different ticket price. So if you're cheap, you take the small green bus and pay 6.50 baht. If you're a big spender, you jump into a pink and white one and pay 25 baht.

## Government versus private

A mix of government and private-owned buses ply the roads of Bangkok. And it's dead easy to tell the difference between the two. On a government bus, you often travel for free because the conductor has more pressing things to do than collect your ticket money. Not so in a private bus. A private bus conductor will never once forget to collect fare because that's what keeps his company in business. But there is one convenience in going private: the door is always open. If the traffic jams get too bad, you can just get up and leave.

## Premium seating

Upholstery on Bangkok buses is always plastic, so you have sweaty pant seats no matter how short a distance you travel. But this discomfort is balanced out by the fact that Thais usually give fellow passengers a lot of bench space, so you're unlikely to be crowded in your seat.

Talking of crowds, if you think you have spotted the only empty seat during peak hour, that "seat" next to the driver is actually a trunk lid. Nobody is going to stop you from sitting on it, if you don't mind burning your bum.

So, to cut a long story short, I strongly advise you to head for the 7-Eleven convenience store nearest you and get your hands on that bus map. Then hop onto the very first bus you see and jump off whenever you feel like it. Once you're done eating, shopping, and strolling, walk to the other

side of the road and take the same bus back. The bus system in Bangkok is all you could ever want from public transport: cheap, quick, and never once dull. I'm sure you'll agree—it's an experience not to be missed.

### Bangkok Mass Transit Authority

www.bmta.co.th/en

The Bangkok Mass Transit Authority website offers information about government-operated buses. There is no downloadable bus map available, but the site does publish bus routes. There is also a Travel Guide section that explains which buses go directly to the popular tourist sites in the city.

### Dà wèi uncovers the purpose of Bangkok's biker gangs

I like to walk, and would often walk from my hotel on Sukhumvit Soi 24 to the nearest Skytrain station. It was a nice twenty-minute stroll. I did this day after day, and each time, I noticed there were groups of semi-tough-looking men, huddling around the street corners on motorcycles. There might be three or twenty of them in one spot, wearing what I assumed were "gang vests." Like the gangs in America, they were color-coded: orange or red or green or blue. I steered clear of them, not knowing who they might be on the lookout for.

Soon, though, I began to notice something else: local Thais (often, conservatively dressed women) would walk up to a gang member, and then they would ride off together. There was never any conversation or discussion. It was very curious. Where were they going?

There was something uniquely Thai happening right under all of our tourists' noses, and yet I had never heard of it. I asked other tourists, but none of them knew either. Many hadn't even noticed the motorcycle gangs.

One day, I decided there was only one way to solve this mystery. I sent my friends an email explaining what I was going to do, so if I ended up dead, they would know what had happened.

The next day, I walked confidently up to one of the motorcycle gang members and made a hand gesture as if to indicate "take me to your leader." The biker pulled out his bike, and I got on the back. Luckily, I had enough common sense to grab the handle behind me. We took off.

The ride wasn't at all what I expected. First of all, we drove on the wrong side of the yellow line, toward oncoming cars. Then we drove through a private parking lot to get around a traffic blockage. We weaved back and forth between cars. And, in about five minutes, we had reached the Skytrain station. The driver stopped, looked at me as if I was supposed to know what to do, and muttered, "*Sipihsbh baht.*" At least I caught the baht part. I reached

into my pocket and pulled out a handful of coins. He picked through them and took 20 baht.

Aha! Finally, I saw the light. They weren't gangsters at all, but the motorcycle version of a taxi service! They weren't skulking around the *sois* to do gangster-type things as I had suspected. They were merely waiting for passengers!

I took the Skytrain to wherever I was going that day, but on my return trip I walked down the Skytrain stairs and headed straight for the motorcycle gang waiting nearby. One of the guys pulled out his bike, and I got on. We took off. But where to? I hadn't been asked for an address. The bike drove on with me on the backseat. We just went and went, and after a while, we passed my hotel. Now what? I tapped the driver on the shoulder, and—presto!—he stopped. I got off, reached into my pocket, and grabbed a handful of coins. He took 15 baht from it.

For the next few days, I took the motorcycle taxis up and down every *soi* in the neighborhood. The fare seemed to average between 15 and 20 baht.

An expat I met soon after explained whatever I hadn't already discovered about motorcycle taxis on my own:

Each *soi* or road has a group of motorcycles, and they only go up and down that one road. The drivers don't usually do point-to-point service, but sometimes they will if you ask and they are not busy. The rate is usually 15 baht for Thais and 20 baht if a foreigner wants a ride. They mostly run only during daylight hours. The color-coded vests identify them as taxis and which road they are licensed to serve. The codes also help to keep pirate motorcycles from encroaching on sanctioned drivers' territories.

It was interesting to learn that the motorcycle gangs informally serve an additional function as well: to make Bangkok safe for all women. Because most of their customers are women, they protect them. If a woman is being hassled by any guy, the bikers will apparently beat the heck out of the abuser. (Note to female travelers: if you are in trouble, look for the colored vests of a motorcycle gang.)

As I have ridden on motorcycle taxis regularly ever since, I have learned that they are the most polite, courteous drivers you can ever imagine. They are aware of every bump on the road, and of everything that might make your ride uncomfortable or unsafe. They are really good at what they do.

Now, you should understand that if you get on a motorcycle taxi, you will go against the flow of traffic, drive on the wrong side of the road, travel onto sidewalks ("pedestrian bowling" is what I call it), and go very, very fast. It is Thailand after all, and not your hometown, where you get tickets for going five miles over the speed limit.

Few tourists in Bangkok take the motorbike taxis, but I highly recommend them. Try one, even if you don't need to go down the *soi* for any particular purpose. The rides are always thrilling—the best rush you can get for 20 baht. And definitely not recommended for travelers over the age of ninety-five or those who shop at Prada.

## Practical travel

Motorcycle taxis, or *motosai* as they are called, are a blessing when roads are jammed and you need to be somewhere in a hurry. The drivers may ignore the traffic rulebook, but they are certainly your best bet in an emergency situation. Another plus point, from a tourist's point of view, is that the drivers don't try to scam you. They may have a higher rate for foreign passengers, but they won't quote outlandish fares like the savvy *tuk-tuk* operators in Bangkok.

## Motorbike safety

*Motosais* are awkward at first, but after a few minutes of riding pillion, you do get the hang of it. To make the experience a safe one, avoid wearing a skirt on motorcycle taxis, so that you can sit astride. Thai women typically ride side-saddle for modesty, but you'll feel a lot more stable if there's no danger of slipping off the seat. Technically, you're supposed to wear a helmet, but the reality is that few do. That said, ask to wear a helmet if the driver is carrying one. In addition, there is a handle on the back to hold on to for balance. If you find you are frightened, you may put your hands lightly on the sides of the driver, and he will slow down. Finally, keep your arms and legs close to you at all times, because the driver might squeeze through narrow spaces without taking your outstretched limbs into account.

## Natalie Magann fishes for a foot massage in Bangkok

I had an appointment with a tankful of fish "dermatologists" in Bangkok's Khao San Road. They were going to nibble all the scabs and dead skin off my feet, leaving them softer and smoother than they had ever been.

The present condition of my feet wasn't worrying me in the least, but the service was described as a "massage" at all the fish pedicure parlors I looked into. And for a massage junkie like me, an hour of being nibbled at by the toothless gums of hundreds of Garra Rufa fish sounded like a pleasurable, if unorthodox, experience indeed.

I chose a parlor on Khao San Road for a number of reasons: It was across the street from my accommodations, and it was a little cheaper than the other places. Also, the parlor offered "unlimited time." The rate card read something like 150 baht for fifteen minutes, 180 baht for thirty minutes, and 200 baht for unlimited time. I figured I could last for thirty minutes, and given the small difference in price, I opted for the unlimited time. Unlike others, I didn't "test" the fish massage first.

The lady who ran the parlor led me to a square Plexiglas pool filled with live fish, ranging in size from one to two inches. As soon as I dipped my feet into this pool, she said, the fish would start feeding on the dead skin on the bottom and sides of my feet. It was around noontime, and there were no other customers whose facial expressions I could read for signs of pain or pleasure. So I had to go it alone. Sitting down on a wooden ledge, I took off my shoes and wiped my feet with the wet washcloth I had been given. It wasn't meant to clean my feet, but it would remove any traces of lotion or cream I had on them.

As soon as I swung my legs over the edge of the pool, an army of fish raced toward them from all directions in a first wave of attack. All I could feel right then was their slippery bodies brushing against my skin as they darted under my feet and between my toes. They seemed to be jockeying for a good position, because soon each settled down to a particular toe or curve on my feet and remained there. It was at this point that I actually felt some tiny bites. Yes, the larger fish were definitely nipping at the calluses I had developed from walking around Bangkok in open sandals. The sensation grew on me, and I soon got used to the feeling of tiny currents in the water gently massaging my feet.

As I was sitting there, a Japanese couple entered the parlor and came over to ask me how it felt. As I began to tell them, the lady at the shop encouraged the couple to dip their finger in the water. Fingers are more sensitive than feet, and when a fish nibbled at the woman's hand she jerked back, saying it felt weird. I assured her that once you got used to the sensation, it was actually quite enjoyable.

They both opted to join me, and they pulled their feet out of the water several times before finally settling down. The man asked if all the fish got to eat was our dead skin. I told him yes, as far as I knew. Then he asked if I knew what kind of fish they were. At the time, I didn't know they were Garra Rufa, but I suspected that as they grew bigger in size, they had to be removed from the tank. The man's question made me wonder what this fish ate in its natural habitat, and I resolved to look it up later.

After the Japanese people left, a man from Germany sat down with me, and we started chatting about our experiences of various tourist attractions in Bangkok. When the German had finished and I had seen him off as well, I finally glanced at the clock. Having come to spend thirty minutes in the fish tank, I couldn't believe I had actually been here for two whole hours!

I pulled my legs up and rubbed them down with a towel before inspecting the job the fish had done. Certainly, my feet felt much softer, and the few cracks of dead skin I detected earlier had disappeared entirely. Happy with the pedicure as well as the massage, I slipped my sandals on, thinking that the next time my feet got all dirty and dry from too much walking, I'd come right back here and offer the fish another tasty snack.

## Spa afishionados

There are many fish spas along Bangkok's Khao San Road with rate cards displayed prominently on the shopfronts. Since the price differences are marginal, choose one that is clean, comfortable, and uncrowded. Other tourist spots in the city, like the Suan Lum Night Bazaar, Siam Square shopping area, and Chatuchak weekend market also have plenty of fish spas. For a more upmarket experience, try the Happy Fish, Happy Feet Pool at Siam Ocean World in the Siam Paragon shopping center.

## More about Garra Rufa

Garra Rufa is a freshwater fish that has been used to give pedicures in Turkey since the early 1800s. It is believed that these harmless, toothless creatures are beneficial for people suffering from eczema and psoriasis, though the claim hasn't been scientifically proven. In their natural habitat, in the coastal river basins of southern Turkey and northern Syria, the Garra Rufa feeds on algae, phytoplankton, and zooplankton.

## Tom Crowley cues up in the pool halls of Bangkok

One casualty of the so-called Tom Yum Goong (or Shrimp Soup) Financial Crisis that hit Thailand in 1997 was the local night scene. Many bars, nightclubs, and karaoke parlors went out of

This was my way of assimilating with the culture of the country I was traveling in. I never dreamed then that I would be a farmer for a day, and actually cultivate rice myself. But the opportunity came along during a visit to Baan Kwai village in the central province of Suphanburi, a three-hour drive northwest of Bangkok. And when it did, I tightened my belt, rolled up my sleeves, and grabbed on with both hands.

Baan Kwai, also known as Buffalo Village, is the place to go for a daylong visit with buffaloes. For more than a thousand years, these docile creatures carried the responsibility of feeding Thailand on their strong, dependable shoulders. But modern technology has retired them from the farmlands and made them largely irrelevant today. The residents of Baan Kwai, however, still use buffaloes to cultivate rice the old-fashioned way, and to generate extra income, they allow their animals to interact with visitors, take them on rides, and put on shows where they turn tricks and do a *sawatdee*.

I spent the first half of my day in Baan Kwai enjoying many nonbuffalo activities, like sailing on the Tha Chin River and exploring a *wat* and a quaint, hundred-year-old market. The highlight of the tour was a visit to a traditional Thai village home, located deep in the forest with no modern amenities. The farmer who owned the house had four wives but no television, and I wondered how the women got along with nothing to do but talk to each other all day. I walked around the farmer's house and ate coconuts and watermelons before making my way back to the village fields, where I was scheduled to do a few hours of serious rice farming.

With the hot sun beating down on my back and temperatures soaring as high as 110 degrees Fahrenheit, I started out with great enthusiasm, pushing an old wooden plow behind two massive buffaloes. Grabbing the reins in each hand while tightly grasping the plow at the same time, I urged the beasts to move forward, so I could have a small tract of ploughed land at least to my credit.

Let me tell you this: the job is a whole lot tougher than you'd suspect from looking at postcards of rice farmers at work. The buffaloes I had been given were lazy guys, constantly needing course corrections, and the heavy plow proved to be just as recalcitrant, getting stuck in the soil and trying to topple me over with every step. As if to further test my staying power, the bad buffaloes constantly relieved themselves, forcing me to stagger through steaming piles of their smelly dung without so much as a by-your-leave.

It was tedious, tiring, backbreaking work, but after an hour of this, I had successfully ploughed a small tract. I'm sure Thai farmers do what I did in ten minutes or less, but nonetheless, I felt proud of my achievement.

The next step was to get down on my hands and knees in the mud and sow rice seeds into my freshly plowed section. The farmers, thoroughly enjoying the entertainment I was providing in the fields, kept urging me to make my line of seeds straighter, and I checked and rechecked the alignment of every little seed I sowed until my eyes crossed over. Once I had a thirty-foot line of seeds planted in the ground, I came back to the start and placed another string right next to it. This went on for approximately three hours, and by the time I was done sowing my patch, I was sunburned to the point of resembling the Kool-Aid mascot, and tired enough to keel over and sleep for a week.

Finally, the farmers decided I'd had enough of a lesson for one day, and they hauled me off to a small hut five minutes away from the paddy fields, washed me up, and gave me a Chang beer from a refrigerator.

I honestly cannot remember a time in my life when the sight of beer has been more welcome. The ice-cold beverage trickled down my parched throat, and I felt the life force slowly return to my body. A wonderful feeling of well-being began to replace my tiredness, and as I drank more, I felt I could forgive the buffaloes for their constant bowel movements, the plow for its dead weight, and the farmers for laughing at my predicament. I even felt a prick of sadness that I wouldn't be there to harvest the patch I had just ploughed and sowed.

A few hours of working the fields, and already I was feeling a proud sense of ownership in my paddy; small surprise, then, that the Thais have such a soul connection with the rice they endure such hardships to grow.

When I returned to Bangkok that evening and ordered fried rice for dinner, this thought bounced around in my mind, making the dish seem extra special to me. As usual, I was careful not to waste a single grain or drop any on the floor. But this time, it was not in reverence to any Thai traditions. This time, it was because of me. Now I too was a rice farmer, and by the grace of Goddess Mae Posop, nobody was going to disrespect a single morsel of the rice I had toiled, sweated, and waded through buffalo dung for.

### Baan Kwai

Located on Suphanburi-Chai Nat Road in Amphoe Si Prachan in Suphanburi Province, the village is well connected by trains, buses, and taxis from Bangkok. The distance, depending on which route you take, is at least 110 kilometers. If you're traveling with a group, your tour operator can arrange a rice-farming experience for you. If you're an independent traveler, just make your way to the village and ask around.

### Eating sticky rice

Eating starch laden, glutinous rice can be a sticky affair, unless you know how to go about it. This staple from northern Thailand is served in fist-sized balls that refuse to come apart when prodded with a spoon. The right way to tackle sticky rice is with your hands. Break off a bit from the ball, and roll it into a smaller ball between your thumb and forefinger. Then dip it into sauce or curry, and enjoy!

### Sweet treats

*Khao neow ma muang* is Thailand's most popular dessert, consisting of sticky rice and sliced mango topped with rich coconut cream. Thais also love this dessert with durian instead of mango. In the spirit of adventure, try it at least once with this pungent fruit.

## CHIANG MAI

### Deborah Annan is grateful for bao–bao massages in Chiang Mai

After my first massage in Bangkok, I came to an extremely painful conclusion: people who claim to love Thai massage are just plain liars.

For one interminable hour, I had endured a Thai massage during which my muscles were subjected to merciless pressure by the massage woman, who pushed down on them with all her fingers, hands, and feet. Not satisfied, she had twisted my leg at awkward angles, stood on my back, and pinched at my arteries till they throbbed. She almost broke my dear old bones in the name of this two-thousand-year-old massage technique.

Instead of crying out or stopping the treatment, I had simply lain there and taken the abuse. And when the hour was up and I could finally drag my aching body out of the massage room, I had two bruises the size of a quarter—one on my right thigh, one on my left arm—in some sort of diabolical symmetry.

"Okay. I don't get it," I huffed at my friend Celeste as we left the massage parlor. "What exactly is the fun part?"

"What, you didn't like it?" Celeste asked, incredulous.

"Are you kidding? Does a traitor enjoy torture?" I answered rhetorically, showing her my two battle scars.

"Why didn't you tell her to go lighter?" a horror-struck Celeste exclaimed, as she stared at the purple circles of truth marking my limbs.

Well, because I was too busy telling myself to take the pain and pretend it was okay until the session got over. Besides, the woman spoke no English. How would I ask her to ease up on the pressure, or even stop her for that matter, without gesturing in a way that seemed rude?

In any event, it was clear that I wasn't a good candidate for Thai massage. My muscles lacked forbearance and my pain threshold was low. I swore never to lie down on a Thai massage mat ever again.

But Celeste was having none of it. In Chiang Mai, she dragged me to Lek Chaiya, her favorite massage parlor in the city, which she believed would convert me into a raving Thai massage enthusiast.

She just needed to give me the magic word that would effect this transformation: *bao-bao*.

So there I was, back on the mat again, wearing the customary Thai massage pajamas and trying not to panic. When the massage woman arrived, I timidly repeated the magic word to her. "*Bao-bao*."

"Ah. *Bao-bao*?"

"Yes. *Bao-bao*."

What happened after that, I can only describe as a Zen-like transformation of my general state of mind and body. I could feel the knots of tension inside me uncoil, stretch, and dissipate, leaving a mellow, all-pervasive sense of well-being in their wake. The woman's fingers palpated and worked my body with such terrific *bao-bao* that I didn't even realize when she was finished.

I felt her tap on my legs, then my arms, then my legs again. The tapping got a little harder, and it still felt great. I sensed her circling around me as the taps got more urgent. Finally, I managed to open my eyes just a little bit to see her face hovering very close to mine. She was, intently and nervously, checking for my vital signs.

It was only then I realized that she probably thought I had passed out on the mat. It also dawned on me what the tap-tapping that had been going on for a good five minutes, while I lay perfectly still, was all about. She was trying to make me get up and get a move on.

She didn't know how to say it in a way I would understand, and I—silly

me!—didn't understand what tap-tap meant in her massage language.

I hurriedly got dressed, trying not to laugh out loud. I felt so fantastic. Revitalized, energetic, and peaceful all at the same time. It was so much more than just a full-body massage. It was as if the woman had reached inside me and massaged fresh life into my soul.

And all thanks to *bao-bao*.

By the time we left, I had already signed up for a two-hour massage the next day. I was in Chiang Mai for four more days, and *bao-bao* massage was going to be a daily event, like brushing my teeth.

I was a raving Thai massage enthusiast now, just as Celeste had said I would be. I couldn't get enough of this amazing passive yoga therapy of the Thais, as long as it was *bao-bao*.

*Bao-bao* ... as in "gentle." That is all the word means in Thai. One common word that had the power to change my whole perspective on Thai massage.

Remember it, if you too happen to be somewhat delicate like me. And if you're in pain or discomfort during a massage in Thailand, don't hesitate to use it.

*Lek Chaiya Nerve Touch Massage*
79/1 Ratchadamnoen Road
(near Thapae Gate)
Chiang Mai
(053) 278 325
www.nervetouch.com

NORTHERN THAILAND

# CHIANG RAI

## Eric Petersen gets hammered in Chiang Rai

Being a tour group leader means always going first. It means walking into less-than-pleasant situations sometimes, burdened with an "open mind," to find interesting things for travelers to do while they are holidaying in a foreign country. So it was with the "Hammer Massage."

I was in Chiang Rai, following a lead to a most unusual massage treatment that involved getting beaten with a hammer. Apparently, it was a northern Thailand specialty, and after my body had been tenderized like a filet of beef, I was told I would emerge from the session feeling like a whole new man.

From several spas around Chiang Rai that offered Hammer Massage, I chose one called Arisara Thai Massage. Arisara was affiliated to the Rajabhat University's School of Traditional and Alternative Medicine, and I figured it was safer to go under the hammer in a place where the pulverizing at least had some basis in research and science.

When I got to Arisara in time for my noon appointment, I found the spa looked reassuringly peaceful and tranquil from the outside. Instead of the sterile, antiseptic building I had envisioned, inside which nervous customers were ruthlessly beaten by masked practitioners under the glare of cheap, fluorescent tube lights, Arisara was charmingly decorated like an ornate Buddhist temple.

Buoyed by this pleasant discovery, I took a deep breath and stepped inside. A bevy of friendly female staff met me at the reception desk. Without much ceremony, they led me into a large hall where separate massage nooks had been created by hanging curtains on all sides.

I changed into the baggy massage gear I was given and followed instructions to lie down on the table. Arisara did not stint on the air-conditioning, and I lay there for a few minutes by myself, gratefully soaking in the blessed coolness. As I listened to the piped music floating through the hall, the traditional Thai sound of it gave me an encouraging idea. Maybe, the Hammer Massage was going to be no worse than a plate of red-hot pork-and-basil stir-fry: a frightening prospect to begin with, but a delicious and authentically Thai experience in the end.

My massage lady arrived with her massage tools, and the first few minutes of the treatment that followed thereafter left me thinking just one thing: *I had been lied to.* You see, there were no hammers. The word was slang, if you will, for an herbal compress, as big and round as a grapefruit. Whoever had come up with the hammer analogy to describe the way the compress was applied to the body had done this massage treatment a great disservice.

The compress was a benign, muslin cloth wrap inside which were six ounces of ten healing herbs. My masseuse first steam-heated the compress to activate the herbs, and then she hold the "hammer" in both hands and rolled it over my body from side to side.

No high-impact pressure, just a firm rolling motion of the compress that filled my nostrils with the pleasant herby scents of tea, lemongrass, mangosteen, *moke* blossoms, coconut, and French lavender, with a hint of some athletic pain ointment like Tiger Balm.

A second "hammer" came into use midway through the session. I eyed it nervously, but this one too turned out to be quite innocent. The masseuse kneaded the new hammer like bread dough all over my body, and the sensation was exquisite. Somehow the heat and elasticity of the compress sent strong vibrations of well-being through my body, until I could visualize my nerve ends almost quivering with renewed energy.

The hour passed too soon. The masseuse tapped gently on my back to indicate that the session was over, and I opened my heavy-lidded eyes a crack to see her bob a courtesy and depart, taking those amazing compresses with her. Reluctantly, I got up, dressed, and went to pay at the reception counter. I left a nice tip for the masseuse and stepped out into the bright afternoon sunshine feeling, if not like a whole new man, then certainly a very happy one who had taken a leap of faith and come out on top.

In the end, my Hammer Massage experience went off pretty well. The practitioner manipulated the hammer compress instead of my body directly, and what I enjoyed was a kind of ripple effect from that manipulation. If anyone got hammered, it was the compress and not I.

Would I recommend this Hammer treatment to customers who want to try a unique massage in Chiang Rai? Yes, most certainly, especially to people who find the normal Thai deep-tissue massage too vigorous and painful. I suffered no negative

NORTHERN THAILAND

after-effects such as soreness or de-hydration from the massage the next day, and the feeling of well-being lasted a very long time.

So, would I reveal the secret of the hammer not really being hammer?

Perhaps not. Let others find out about that the way I did. No point coming to Thailand, if you're not going to take your chances, live a little dangerously, and stop to taste the red-hot pork-and-basil stir-fry.

### Arisara Thai Massage

125/1 Moo 12, Robwiang
(Opposite the PTT gas station in Prasobsuk Square)
Muang District, Chiang Rai
(053) 719 3556
arun_een@hotmail.com

### Arisara around Bangkok

The Bangkok outpost of Arisara is called Sumalai Thai Massage.

159/14 Sukhumvit 55 Thonglor 7-9
Opposite Thonglor 8
Wattana, Bangkok
(66) 2392 1663
http://sumalaimassage.com

### If I had a hammer

Visitors to Arisara can purchase compress hammers or just the individual herbs that go inside them. The staff will show you how to heat them up and use them at home.

### Kristianne Huntsberger is bloody steamed in Chiang Rai

I had come to the Akha Hill House in the Chiang Rai mountains to try a very unusual hill tribe spa treatment: the blood vine sauna, a process that would marinate my body in the herbal steam of a mysterious plant that oozed "blood."

I spotted the sauna as soon as we pulled into the grounds of the Akha Hill House resort. It was just an ordinary hut, a papaya-colored clay structure on stilts similar in construction to the buildings in which the hill tribe people lived. A sign outside the hut proclaimed "Sauna From Blood Vine." People passed back and forth in front of the sauna, but nobody entered.

This was nothing like the other spas I had encountered in Thailand. There was no hint of any spa luxury: no tranquil Zen gardens, no soothing ambient music or whiffs of scented oils wafting in the air. This was un-apologetically rustic, a kind of place that focused only on the treatment as practiced over generations by hill tribe people.

I scheduled my session to begin right after breakfast the next day, before the rising temperature combined with the swelter of the sauna and made simple things like breathing unbearable. A man arrived to escort me to the sauna hut. Once there, he showed me where he had stoked a wood fire under a big blackened pot.

Steeping in hot water inside the pot were large chunks of the fabled vine, oozing a thick, syrupy, blood-colored sap. The steam rising from the concoction went through a bamboo pipe and poured into the hut. As I stepped inside, I was conscious of the strong, earthy aroma of the warm steam enveloping me in the darkness. I tried to get my bearings in the small amount of light that spilled in through the crack under the door and a couple of tiny chinks in the thatched roof. I could make out the sauna's skeleton, constructed of woven bamboo strips, which gave me the impression of being inside a big cylindrical basket. There were three plastic chairs, and I settled down to relax and drink water for the next two hours, while the blood vine steam did its magic.

There was an unearthly quietness inside, and I caught myself listening intently to the sound of my own breath and the creaking of the walls swelling and settling in the rising steam. Even though I was alone in the hut, it did not feel spacious, but I had enough room to maneuver the plastic chairs into a makeshift platform on which I could stretch out.

As time passed, the stress seeped slowly out of my mind and body, leaving me almost lightheaded in its wake. It can be surprisingly difficult to travel, especially for those of us with limited budgets who must cobble together transportation, lodging,

and reasonably priced food as we go. I had no idea there was so much stress dammed up inside me until the blood vine steam carried it all away. Lying on the hard, uneven surface of those plastic chairs, I felt this was true relaxation. I did not miss the mood lighting or the aromatherapy oils and scented candles that spas normally use to create a pampering atmosphere. After a while, I sat down on the mud-packed floor, and the effect was amazingly grounding. I breathed deeply in and out and let the blood vine steam fill my lungs.

When I finally emerged from the hut two hours later, I felt alive and invigorated. To finish the experience, I went looking for more information about this amazing blood vine. A kitchen was adjacent to the sauna, and I asked a woman there to show me a piece. She brought out frozen slices of the vine, which were wrapped in plastic and resembled cuts of fresh raw meat. The woman did not have a lot of information to share, but I did understand that this peculiar vine grew in the jungles in this region. She suggested I take a guided trek to see the plant for myself.

Though nearly twenty guests came and went during my three-day stay at the Akha Hill House, I was the only one who tried the blood vine sauna. Everyone was curious, but few could overcome their hesitation about the mysterious vine. Instead, they perused the catalog of trekking options and set out for elephant camps or a tour of the nearby hot springs. The jungles tours from here included interesting activities like building a shelter from banana leaves and cooking in the open air with handmade bamboo tools. But I was content without excursions.

The slow pace of my days at the Akha Hill House was quite addictive, and I postponed all scheduling decisions for the time being. My plan had been to stay two nights here, as I told a woman from England while we sat around the evening bonfire, but I had already been here for three. She knew exactly how I felt; she was going to stay for two as well, but was now on her fifth. "It's pretty hard to leave this place, isn't it?" she remarked companionably.

I didn't answer. One of the tour guides had just picked up an old guitar and started to sing a hauntingly beautiful folk song that rose up to serenade the distant stars.

### Akha Hill House

97/7 Doihang Muang
Chiang Rai
(053) 918 442
www.akhahill.com

## Eric Petersen dances the night away in Chiang Rai

Chiang Rai's Saturday night market is the only one I've found in Thailand that hardly has any foreign tourists. It's the locals who come here after the sun goes down, to meet friends, eat, shop, and enjoy outdoor entertainment shows. If, like me, you also happen to be strolling aimlessly among the street stalls on that day, you're just as likely to be invited to hang out with them.

On the Saturday I chose to visit, there were no other Westerners in sight. The night market was crowded with Chiang Rai residents bargaining over clothes, small trinkets, and household goods. About two blocks into the market, I ran into an impromptu limbo show and took a few photographs before walking past food vendors tempting me with northern-style fried snacks that they assured were "not spicy."

The sound of loud music was emanating from somewhere inside the bazaar, and I let my ears lead me to its source. In the midst of the busy marketplace, I was amazed to find a large field with an open stage, on which a middle-aged man was belting out popular folk songs. Thais love going on stage, and the man was performing with an eagerness that perhaps exceeded his talent, but the families that had gathered around didn't seem to care. They stopped chatting every now and then to cheer him on, and I had to admit that the music created a nice background sound for all the eating, drinking, and gossiping that was going on around me.

I meandered through the crowd until I found an empty chair. As I sat down to watch the locals enjoying their big Saturday night out, I realized that my presence here hadn't gone unnoticed. People were nudging each other and looking at me curiously until a group of seven Thai men took the initiative and invited me over to their table for proper introductions.

Of them, two could speak a little English, but they needed no language to welcome me into their circle of close friends. I understood that they gathered here every Saturday, and were pleased to share their evening with a visitor to their town. After the introductions were over, the conversation resumed, and I smiled and nodded at everything I couldn't follow. Whenever there was a lull in the conversation, I was amused to see the men fill small glasses with rice wine and toast each other. The rice wine flowed, as did the lighthearted bantering and jokes that went around the table. The evening was passing so pleasantly, it was hard to believe we had only just met.

Our attention was drawn back to the stage when the music changed suddenly to let people know that dancing was about to begin. A tall pole was set up in front of the stage with colorful streamers flowing out in every direction. A dozen or so Thai women wearing white blouses over royal blue skirts started dancing in a circle around the pole with streamers in their hands. It was much like the Maypole dance of Western Europe, where young farm girls come out in their prettiest dresses to dance around a pole hung with ribbons. Though the women in the Chiang Rai version of this Anglo-Saxon spring ritual were well into their forties and

fifties, they were physically fit and the show they put up was choreographed well.

After their performance, the crowd was given a cue to participate in the dance, and I was coaxed by four of my new friends to take part in the fun. The dance was easy. Everybody walked counterclockwise around the pole. About three steps forward and then one back. On the back step, I had to twist my body a little bit. I wasn't too concerned about how well I did, because ability was irrelevant. Appearances, too. It was Saturday night, and everybody was joining in for the pleasure of letting it all hang out.

As I danced, I remember thinking how well the moniker "Land of 10,000 Smiles" suited the country; I caught heaps of grins from the locals that night. Every Thai I made eye contact with had a smile for me. The shyness that had held them back earlier dissipated in the excitement of the dance floor, and people started approaching me in ones and twos to ask all sorts of friendly questions.

The dancing and drinking went on until late into the night. When our party finally broke up, my seven friends gave me their mobile numbers, and instructed me to contact them when I returned to Chiang Rai. Especially if it was a Saturday night. I took photographs of the group, and have the reprints ready to give them when we meet again.

For meet we definitely will. The rapport I established with my "cronies" in just one evening is reason enough to return—on the same day, at the same time, at this very dance party in the market of Chiang Rai.

### Saturday night live

The Saturday night market is located on Thanalai Road, which runs east-west through the center of Chiang Rai. Dancing is held at the minipark near the east end of the road, facing south.

### Photo tip

Eric adds: I find that I make friends very easily in Thailand when I am roaming around with a camera. The locals simply love to look at themselves in the viewfinder. Most of them don't possess cameras, and the few that do had to save up for it. They are grateful if you take the trouble to give them a copy, so I hand out reprints all the time—affordable and easy.

## NORTHERN THAILAND

*Kristianne Huntsberger celebrates Christmas fourfold in northern Thailand*

Because I was traveling alone in Thailand during December, I assumed I would go without Christmas.

Back in the States stores would be decked out in shiny red and green, blaring various versions of "Deck the Halls" and offering free gift wrapping. My mother would be baking sheets of cookies, and my sister's children would be peeking at gift tags under a plastic tree. But I was in a predominately Buddhist country, so I imagined the whole holiday might pass me by. The more I thought about it, I had no doubt about it—I would go without a Christmas celebration.

Instead, I had four.

The morning I planned to leave Sukhothai for Lampang, I went to Mae Sot on the Thai-Myanmar border instead, three hours west by bus. The road to Mae Sot was a climb, full of belching trucks. Trying to catch some fresh air through the window while avoiding the hot glare of direct sunlight, I arched my body awkwardly in the narrow space allotted me, my bags stacked on my lap, someone else's baggage piled at my feet.

I was seated in the back behind John, a man originally from Myanmar whom I had just met at the bus station. "What are you going to do in Mae Sot?" he asked, assuming I was either one of the town's many NGO workers or a traveler who needed to make a border crossing to renew a visa. I was neither, I told him.

John had lived in Mae Sot for years while running an education program for immigrant children from Myanmar, though now he was back in Bangkok with his family. He provided me with a few sightseeing suggestions: a drive to nearby waterfalls, a visit to the sauna at the temple, a day trip into Myanmar. Or, he added, I could join him in creating two Christmas parties, one for an unofficial school that had sprouted up near the town dump and another for some of the street kids he used to work with.

For two days, I helped John play Santa Claus to more than one hundred migrant children. I went with him to the market, where he greeted people in Thai or Burmese, asked about bulk prices for oranges and figs, and purchased a big sack of individually wrapped preserved fruit, which he explained is a favorite treat in Myanmar. We bought little coconut milk pancakes called *khanom krok* and plastic trays full of a Burmese custard called *shwe gi*, made with sticky rice and sugar.

In the open dirt courtyard at the community school by the dump and at John's guest house in town the next day, we helped children pour juice into paper cups and play ring toss games. We gave each of their families a small plastic bag filled with basic supplies like shampoo, bars of soap, toothpaste, and a toothbrush or two. We blew up balloons, handed out pencils, and raffled off donations that John had gathered in Bangkok: small notebooks, piggy banks with company logos emblazoned on their bellies, stuffed animals, a handful of herringbone throw blankets, throw pillows printed with smiling faces of cartoon characters, decorative magnet clips, pens with bobble-headed clowns and cartoon bears, and other little stocking stuffers. The children laughed and used me to practice English phrases they had learned.

In the evening, John told me that not all the children he worked with were Christian. Some of the families were Hindu, and many were Muslim—but that hardly mattered, he thought. Wasn't Christmas, he asked, a time to support people in need?

In my first two holiday celebrations, there were no Christmas decorations, no Christmas songs or kitschy snowmen and reindeer. The lack of familiar commercial items of the season was made up for in my third Christmas, which had all the trimmings. This celebration was in the town of Lampang, where I stopped for a few days to ride a bike along the meandering river path and visit temples.

The central area around the clock tower had been blocked to traffic and was filled with booths of food, handicrafts, and addictively good orange juice. There was a huge illuminated tree and a stage where Christmas standards, sung waveringly in English, were broadcast across the square and the adjoining park. Packs of red-nosed clowns made balloon sculptures, and several Santas, dressed in red suits and false white beards, posed with kids for picture-taking parents. A parade of marching bands and schoolchildren opened up a path through the celebration. Everyone was costumed in Santa hats, reindeer antlers, angel wings, and, a little more inexplicably, in cowboy hats and chaps or giant-headed manga character costumes. Rumors were flying that someone was bringing in a snow-making machine.

Despite the tinsel on the trees and the clanging of "Silver Bells" through the streets, I was sweating in my light, sleeveless shirt, so the thought of snow seemed antithetical. I walked to the edge of the scene and sat in a streetside noodle shop near a middle-aged Thai couple who told me the pageantry in town grew larger every year. When they were children, Christmas was a blink. "But we like to celebrate things here," the woman said.

My final Christmas celebration was in Chiang Mai on Christmas Day. The young Thai owners of the guesthouse where I stayed had arranged a gathering on the rooftop deck that looked over the old city. Though there was no tree, glowing plastic snowmen, or reindeer, several of the guests had helped with blowing up balloons and putting together a gift exchange.

Like my other three parties, this was mostly a chance to step back from the everyday and celebrate. Ten of us gathered together, ate, had a few beers, and practiced our creaky Thai language skills.

As the night got longer, the guests grew nostalgic. There were definite things that were missing, according to two German girls, like the special pudding that a favorite aunt made and a walk in the snow. A young man who was cultivating new dreadlocks argued that he traveled during this season specifically to miss the holiday mess of family quarrels, mindless shopping, and all the waste. Other

people on the deck, in their hammocks and folding chairs, bantered and poured themselves more drinks. A few excused themselves and went downstairs to talk on computers to their families, who were all somewhere else, just beginning or maybe ending the holiday.

It was late when one of the young Thai men, who had been lounging with us on the deck and talking about colored shirts and holiday snacks, went downstairs and came back with a large paper lantern. He lit the wick, and as the flame heated the air inside, the pale paper ballooned and then lifted into the night. We stood together and watched the lantern rise and grow slowly smaller until it was just one tiny point of light amid many in the sky.

## KHON KAEN

*Danielle Koffler
has an "eary" feeling
in Khon Kaen*

When I moved to Khon Kaen in northeastern Thailand, my apartment was close to Khon Kaen University campus and across from Bung Nong Waeng, a small manmade lake. Every weekday around dusk, I heard music playing from the other side of the water. When I went out to investigate, I found the quiet, usually deserted park surrounding it had transformed into a busy venue full of people from the neighborhood who were enjoying their evening hours there.

A small shop had been set up where couples and families were painting statues and canvases for a small fee. Others were walking or jogging, while some were using the blue exercise equipment that had been placed at regular intervals around the lake. I had never seen anyone in this park in the daytime, but at nightfall it was obviously the place to be.

Intrigued by the discovery, I kept walking until I came to the source of the music. A flamboyant Thai man was leading a large group of ladies in dance aerobics. At the back of the group were about ten grandmas signing people in and collecting the 5-baht fee. I wasn't dressed appropriately for dance aerobics, so I came back the next night, ready to try something very different from the gyms and dance studios back home.

I was the only foreigner who had come to take the class. The old women collecting money handed me a pen and asked me to sign the attendance sheet. My Thai language skills were marginal at this stage, but I wrote my name in English in a column that looked appropriate and scribbled a few illegible words in the other columns to make them look filled up. I put 5 baht in the collection bowl and found a spot at the back of the class where I wouldn't make too much of a fool out of myself.

Because I couldn't understand the teacher's instructions given in Thai, I had to closely watch what the other people were doing. I spent the first part of the class following the girl in front of me, who had her own interpretation of the dance moves, which looked significantly different from the rest of the class. Several times, I bumped into my neighbors because I didn't see they had switched moves, but they were very kind to the only foreigner in their midst, knowing full well that I had no clue what was going on.

The old ladies who had been collecting the money came to join the dance aerobics and took positions at the back with me. They did the moves a little bit slower than everybody else, but I have to say that their endurance was incredible. I could barely get through the hour-long class, which I blame on my bum knees and heat exhaustion, while these women who were forty years older than me were still dancing the night away and not breaking a sweat!

I was probably the worst dancer in the group that day, but I'm sure I was also the one who had the most fun.

There are similar workouts taking place in public parks all over Thailand— Bangkok's Lumpini Park being the most famous, where hundreds of locals come to exercise in the open air with friends and strangers. But this little park by the lakeside in Khon Kaen somehow seemed more special because I was exercising with my Thai neighbors and there weren't any foreigners in sight. Plus, I had found the place all by myself, and that made the pleasure even greater.

### Aerobics in Khon Kaen

To find Danielle's dance aerobics class in Khon Kaen, ask a *tuk-tuk* driver to take you to Bung Nong Waeng—not to be confused with Wat Nong Waeng, which is a beautiful temple next to a different lake in the city. The class usually begins at sundown.

### Mass workouts in Bangkok

Lumpini Park is a rare and precious green space in central Bangkok, where people come at dawn and dusk to take part in group exercise activities like aerobics, yoga, and tai chi. The classes are usually free, or at the most you'll be charged a very small amount to participate. A lot of tourists join these classes for the experience as well as the exercise.

## KOH PHI PHI

### Charles Benimoff challenges a friend in Koh Phi Phi

Having heard countless Muay Thai fight tales from other travelers, Jeff and I were really hoping to watch one before our Thailand adventure ended. We shadow-kicked at each other with great enthusiasm whenever the subject came up, but somehow we never made it to a match.

The traveler's wheel of fortune, however, turns in unpredictable ways, and what did happen is that we stumbled upon a chance to get into the ring and do some Muay Thai fighting ourselves. Although we didn't take it, this essay will lead you to the place where you can roll up your sleeves and finish this unfinished piece of business for us.

We were in Koh Phi Phi, and it was our first night on the island. We were checking out the nightlife when we stumbled upon an establishment called the Reggae Bar. The place stayed open late and offered drinks, dancing, and a golden opportunity to beat up the most irritating member in your travel group. What's more, if you dared to step into the ring, you got a free Bucket, compliments of the Reggae Bar. The infamous Thai Bucket is an assortment of hard alcohol, soda, and Red Bull, which you mix in a plastic pail to make a strong punch. Not a quality drink by any standard, but popular nonetheless on these tourist islands because they get you drunk cheap and fast.

Adjacent to the Reggae Bar was a hand-scribbled sign with an interesting proposition: "Beat your friend up in the ring and get free Bucket and European fight good entre!" Jeff and I pondered the last bit about "European fight good entre." Maybe we weren't European, but we were young and cool and could do a nice American-style "entre," whatever that was. So we decided to go inside.

In the main hall, a huge fight ring was set up in the middle and the place was packed. Two professional locals were going through the Muay Thai moves, flexing hard muscles, kicking out with grand flourish, and generally setting the standard that all Westerners in the room would be held to. The crowd was lapping it up, ooh-ing and aah-ing every time a fighter took a nasty hit and collapsed in a graceful heap on the floor. It was a beautifully choreographed performance, and the fighters were pushing all the right buttons to encourage drunk customers to enter the ring.

After they were done, a massively overweight (and hardly sober) Caucasian guy was the first to rush in, waving at his friend to come join him. The friend arrived in short order, and what transpired after that was positively cringe-inducing. The Muay Thai music, an essential accompaniment to Muay Thai fights, broke into drum rolls each time one of them raised a heavy leg a few inches off the ground to attempt a kick at the other. The crowd hooted in delight. Technically, one of the guys won at the end of it, but I'd say it was pretty embarrassing for both parties.

I pestered Jeff to fight me, challenged him for the sake of the silly story it would make to tell our friends later, but Jeff wouldn't budge. I told him he had an edge over me, as thanks to the backpacker diet I weighed sixty-one kilos to his sixty-four, making me officially skinnier

than him for the first time in recorded history. I told him we'd never have a chance to try Muay Thai again; maybe this would be even better than watching a real fight; we'd get to wear shin pads, gloves, and shiny shorts; we could time our kicks to the beat of the Muay Thai music—but he still said no. The overweight European guy had undone all the enthusiasm the professionals had generated in Jeff's heart, and he wasn't allowing me to help him make a public fool of himself. So we drank some more and left. As we walked out, the "European fight good entre" sign outside mocked at our departing backs. Apparently, Thai kick-boxing experts believe Europeans make better Muay Thai fighters than Americans, and Jeff and I had just proved it. We had let our side down. When I think back, I still feel bad that we didn't get to show the proprietors of the Reggae Bar that Americans are as good at "entre" as any European ... if only to shame them into taking that sign down.

### Reggae Bar

Located in central Tonsai on Koh Phi Phi, this bar encourages customers to try Muay Thai for themselves in an authentic setting. It even provides shorts, gloves, and other Muay Thai accessories. Fights are held every day of the week, and women too can fight for glory and a free Bucket—even though female boxers, known as Nak Muay Ying, are a recent phenomenon in Thailand. Purists will

# Paying it Forward

*Suggestions for giving back while you're on the road*

L et me begin here by telling you a story about the generosity of spirit that inspires a lot of tourists to give something back to the Thai people they get to know and care for during their travels. My friend Dipa and her family had just arrived in Bangkok after a long tour of Far East Asia, and her mother declared she couldn't go another day without homemade Indian food. This was many years ago, when Indian restaurants were not common in Thailand, so they went to a small, family-run Thai food stall where Dipa's mother taught the cook how to make a basic boiled egg curry with whatever ingredients were available in the kitchen. The next day, when they went to eat there again, the cook dragged Dipa's mother away to see the restaurant's peeling, old signboard. Below the small menu of Thai dishes painted on it, the cook had proudly added a new one: "Indian boiled egg curry."

Dipa's mother was so overwhelmed by the gesture, she startled everyone by bursting into tears. Now, you could well argue that it was she who had unwittingly helped the cook by teaching him a new dish. But isn't that the beauty of paying it forward? You end up feeling grateful for the opportunity to be able to make a small difference in somebody else's life.

In Thailand, unexpected opportunities to help like this are everywhere. You just have to look beyond the warm, ever-ready smiles of the local people and find a need that you can fulfill.

Writer Dà wèi once told me about a Thai family he made an unusual deal with: he would spend a night in their house to see what their typical evening was like, and in return, they could come and stay at his hotel. So they all spent an evening together watching a small TV at the Thai family's modest little home, enjoyed Dà wèi's special treat of pizza from Pizza Hut, and slept on the floor, six people in a small room on a mat. The next night, they all packed up and moved into Dà wèi's luxurious two-bedroom hotel suite with a separate living room. The Thai

As for the dogs, as I was keeping to my new regime of "vegetarianism-almost," I avoided my own specialty food on that day. Instead, I chowed down on a couple of Mr. Donut nutty chocolate doughnuts and a six-pack or two of Oreos, to give me plenty of energy to keep up with the delightful children who I hope had as memorable a Halloween as I did.

## CCF Foundation

Through this organization, you can donate to the welfare of local children or even sponsor an individual child. The foundation's goal is to improve the quality of life of marginalized and needy children in Thailand through educational and other developmental programs.

www.ccfthai.or.th/ccfeng/history.php

# PATTAYA

XXXXXXXXXXXXXXXXXXXXXXXXXXXXXXXXXX
○○○○○○○○○○○○○○○○○○○○○○○○○○○○○○○○○○○○

## Lisa Koenig puts her best foot forward in Pattaya

My dad and stepmom took me with them to the Baan Jing Jai Orphanage in Pattaya to serve lunch to the kids. They figured we would spend an hour or two at the orphanage and then move on with our lives. But after meeting the orphans, who in spite of their age had the maturity to accept misfortune and deprivation as a fact of life, I found I simply couldn't walk away. Where was the justice in my having everything— a bed, nice clothes, a nice school, a family, a future—when these kids couldn't even have a proper childhood?

As soon as we returned to the United States, I began taking apart my closet, looking for things to send back to the orphans. What I found was a lot of shoes. Mostly running shoes from my track and cross-country years. I knew my other running friends would have just as many shoes, so I asked them to save those up for me. Word spread, and more and more kids came forward to help. Before I knew it, I was advertising the donation drive at my school, William Fremd High School in Palatine, Illinois.

That is how I started the Thai Your Shoes Foundation in 2008. As soon as I was done with my schoolwork, I would run around picking up donations and printing signs to put up in my school and around my community. I started a website, talked to businesses about sponsorships, and organized fundraisers.

I discovered that the people in my area were very willing to hear about the Baan Jing Jai Orphanage in faraway Thailand. They came forward with their spare shoes, and I gratefully accepted everything. When a shipment of donations was large enough, a team of people from a company called Corporate Graphics paid to help me send it via UPS to the orphanage. And then I continued my planning of new fundraising events to get even more.

An interesting issue that came up during the shoe drive was size. Thai children have a much smaller foot size compared to the average American's, and I was always glad to get real tiny shoes because I knew they would be useful to a larger number of kids. Besides shoes, I also started collection drives for clothes, toys, school supplies, and other items that the children needed.

Being able to help remotely like this is a great joy for me, but those times when I can actually go to Thailand and be at the orphanage give me fresh inspiration and a renewed sense of purpose. It's like I'm going home to derive strength from my large, loving family of now seventy-four children.

These kids are hilarious. One of my favorite stories was when my dad decided to treat them to a little bit of America. He ordered Happy Meals for everybody from McDonald's—just your standard hamburger and fries, thinking it would be a nice change from their usual dinner of soup and rice or a little bit of fish. But the children went crazy at the prospect of actually eating a McDonald's burger. Of course they had heard about McDonald's and knew the big, yellow M sign, but they'd all assumed that the opportunity to actually eat this precious bit of pop culture themselves was never going to happen. The

packets of ketchup definitely puzzled them. Some kids just tore them open and squeezed the sauce directly into their mouths, while others squirted it into a giant glop over the top of their hamburger buns.

It's amazing how enthralled they are with small, everyday things that you and I take for granted. Like ketchup. Or Post-its—I mean, when was the last time you got excited by these little squares of colored sticky notepaper? But you should have seen the kids when they first received Post-its in their school supply packs. One minute, everyone was sitting calmly and examining their new belongings, and the next thing I knew, the Post-it notes were everywhere— most notably on the children's faces and backs.

It's hard when the time comes to part from these children, but I know I'll be with them in spirit as I work to raise awareness about the Baan Jing Jai Orphanage in America. In their own way, they are always helping me too: how easily I could have been another college-going American kid, living in an insular world that revolved around parties and boys, had they not come along to give a more meaningful direction to my life.

My dream is to build a school at the Baan Jing Jai Orphanage, one that will offer education to children in nearby orphanages as well. That dream is still far away. I will have to collect a lot of money before I can undertake such a project. But my seventy-four kids are waiting, looking at the Thai Your Shoes Foundation to

# RESOURCES FOR THE ROAD

*Practical advice to help you prepare for your travels*

As *To Thailand With Love* draws to a close, it is time to look at the practical side of planning your trip. To supplement all the tantalizing travel possibilities our authors have filled your head with, this final chapter offers a variety of essays and lists that have been carefully chosen to help you prepare for the journey.

For visitors who like to read, Janet Brown has put together a marvelous selection of her favorite books on Thailand. Since Janet is too dismissive of her own title—*Tone Deaf in Bangkok*—to include it in her list, it is up to me to tell you that there probably isn't a better book written about Bangkok from an expat's perspective. In my opinion, at least. The lively collection of essays that make up *Tone Deaf* is so funny, so honest, so very, very Janet, you'll gladly want to follow this feisty American woman through all her triumphs and travails, as she tries to make a home in the capital.

*Very Thai*, an illustrated book on Thai pop culture, comes highly recommended by Caroline Fournier, who enjoyed using it like a manual to negotiate her way through the country's many delightful "eccentricities." And to cover your language needs, we have an essay by Alice Driver, who recommends a language school that offers quick crash courses in Thai. After a five-, ten-, or fifteen-hour lesson package here, you may not be able to translate the finest nuances of your mind's inner workings in lucid Thai, but you should certainly be able to speak with locals at a very basic level and communicate to them your most pressing needs. For those who don't have a ear for languages, Hugh Leong describes his portable "talking dictionary," a nifty computer program that does all the translating for him.

Other resources for the road include websites our authors have used to connect with other travelers and expats, to find restaurants that serve vegetarians/vegans, for example, and to learn about the latest modus operandi that scamsters are adopting to cheat foreigners in Bangkok and other tourist

MOVIES

a vengeful female ghost. But that stereotype has thankfully been broken, and over the last decade or so, the genre has truly come of age. If like me you're a fan of scary films, I recommend that you buy English-subtitled DVDs of some of these great "Asian horror" movies produced by Thailand.

### Alone

In this film, Pim decides to separate her body from Ploy, her conjoint twin, as she has fallen in love with a man and wants to lead her own life. Though they are separating their bodies, Pim and Ploy make promises to each other about never parting in spirit. But Ploy dies in surgery, and her angry spirit returns to haunt the live twin, who has married and consigned this tragedy to the past. Besides the promised scares and thrills, *Alone* offers an interesting take on the delight and despair inherent in the universal bond of sisterhood.

### The Dorm

The young male protagonist of this movie, Chatree, joins a boarding school in the middle of the term and has trouble adjusting to his new environment. He is constantly picked on by students who try to scare him with stories about their school being haunted. As the film progresses, an increasingly uncomfortable Chatree begins to suspect that these ghost stories may not be lies. The "scare" element in the film is restrained, and you might want to watch it even if you're not a horror film buff.

### Shutter

The plot of this film revolves around spirit photography. A photographer and his girlfriend kill a woman in a road accident, and then run away from the scene. Soon afterward, the spirit of the victim starts to appear as strange, inexplicable "inclusions" in his photographs (see page 63 for a description of such an experience). The plot gets more complicated from there on, as we learn that the victim was no stranger to the photographer after all. *Shutter* was a massive hit at the box office, and a Hollywood version of the film was released in 2008. But Asian horror fans still swear by the original.

### Nang Nak

*Nang Nak* is Thailand's favorite ghost story. In this visually stunning remake of the classic tale, a woman returns from the dead to live with her husband and child, and then turns vengeful when she is thwarted in her efforts to lead a happy, "human" family life. *Nang Nak* is a rare romance-horror film that is sensitively told and makes an emotional connection with the viewer. Keep in mind that *Nang Nak* has been directed by Nonzee Nimibutr, so that you don't accidentally purchase a different version of this same story.

### Buying DVDs in Thailand

Bootleg DVDs are sold everywhere in Thailand, but we recommend supporting filmmakers and heading for any of the country's big music or bookstores, where you can buy legal copies. All of the movies recommended in this essay are easily available with English subtitles.

# LANGUAGE LEARNING

*Alice Driver immerses herself in an intensive language course*

When my husband, Isaac, and I enrolled in Pink Chilli, a language school that offers classes individually tailored to suit a student's needs, the founders of the school told us, "We offer very short courses for tourists and busy expats—five, ten, and fifteen hours—which concentrate on spoken Thai in everyday situations." We thought this sounded like an excellent opportunity for travelers to pick up some Thai on the run.

Although many people told us that a week was not enough time to learn any Thai, our experience proved otherwise. With only seven days' worth of language learning, we were able to greet people, ask about prices, count to twenty, and make small talk. These skills were invaluable in rural areas where Isaac was carrying out a research project on indigenous boat-building and most people did not speak English.

Pink Chilli used to hold classes on Silom Road in Bangkok, but now it is an online school, which makes it extremely convenient for people traveling outside the capital. Even if you can spare only a few hours for lessons, you can learn enough practical language skills to navigate through Thailand using some Thai.

In our opinion, the practical approach of this school is what made the lessons so successful for us. The founders believe that if you don't use what you learn, you end up forgetting it quickly. They only teach language that they know students will use immediately, a vocabulary based on basic situations and simple daily interactions.

The shortest session involves just five classes lasting thirty to forty-five minutes each, during which Apple, the cofounder of Pink Chilli, teaches you all the basic sentences you're likely to need. The key to committing these foreign terms to memory is to practice them shamelessly with everyone you meet.

A week of intensive language training here helped Isaac and me in a hundred different ways during our two months in Thailand. We perused local markets, chatted with bus drivers, forged relationships with boat-builders, and arranged to go spear fishing with the Moken sea gypsies on the Surin Islands. Even when our Thai was at its worst and we mangled words or said something nonsensical, locals were gracious and helpful. People were charmed by our efforts to speak their language, and our repertoire of pidgin Thai

LANGUAGE LEARNING

paved the way for meaningful friendships with local Thai people.

## Pink Chilli
www.pinkchilli.co.th

## Hugh Leong depends on a talking Thai dictionary

I know a little about dictionaries. I have seven Thai-English volumes at home, and I use at least three online versions as well. But ever since the PC-based *Thai-English English-Thai Talking Dictionary* has resided on my desktop, I've become a loyal fan, since I don't have to leaf through thousands of dictionary pages or be connected to the Internet to use it.

Two years in the making, this "talking dictionary" is full of the stuff that I have long had on my wish list of features. Ajarn Benjawan's linguistic expertise, along with the computer genius of her collaborator Chris Pirazzi, have created what I feel is a must-have addition to my Thai studies library.

The special features packed into this software are what make it really fun to use. Each word, for instance, is accompanied by a high-quality sound recording of Ajarn Benjawan's voice, giving you the correct pronunciation. Besides the two obvious English-to-Thai and Thai-to-English options, you get a third one: Sound-to-Thai. Enter an approximation

of a Thai word's sound, and this dictionary will guess which word you might be looking for. It usually gets it right!

While putting this dictionary through its paces, I found that all I needed was to type a few letters, in either English or Thai, and the word I was looking for would be displayed, in the same way words are "guessed" at by various search engines. Another feature I find very useful is the ability to copy Thai words from the Internet and paste them in the search box for an immediate translation.

My advice would be to play around with the free trial version and see what you think of this software dictionary. If you are serious about learning Thai, you will probably put this it to good use—especially if, like me, you spend a large part of your day on the computer.

## Thai-English English-Thai Talking Dictionary
Created by Ajarn Benjawan Poomsan Becker and Chris Pirazzi, this dictionary is downloadable. You can even download a trial version for free. By the time this book goes to press, an iPhone version should also be available. Currently, all purchasers are allowed free upgrades for life.

www.word-in-the-hand.com

## COOKING CLASSES

*Nabanita Dutt cooks up a list of top culinary classes*

Much as I love eating Thai food, the low-heat, glass-top stove in my kitchen makes it highly unlikely that I'm going to become an inspired Thai chef any-time soon. I did take a cooking class at the Mandarin Oriental Bangkok hotel, though. I learned a wonderful jungle curry that I made continuously, until I ran out of the fresh ingredients I had bought in Bangkok, and my family ran out of their enthusiasm for the dish and started to complain bitterly about hav-ing to eat the same thing day after day.

Given the inadequacies of my own Thai cooking experience, I felt I should consult some seasoned Thai food chefs and find out where they ac-quired their skills. I polled the authors of this book, too, and was surprised to discover how many of them had taken a cooking course in Thailand. As a result, these recommendations are from people who have firsthand experience of some great classes in different parts of the country, and who understand the rudiments of Thai cooking much better than I.

### BANGKOK

**Bussaracum Royal Thai Cuisine**

Bussaracum restaurant is considered *the* temple of Royal Thai cuisine. If you have dined there and enjoyed the food, you can eat like a king at home by joining a cooking class and learning the intricacies of Royal Thai cuisine from the master chef himself. All recipes remain true to Thailand's culinary heritage, and some are even based on documented preparations from the late nineteenth century. Most Thai cooking schools teach basic fruit carving, but the food pre sentation techniques demonstrated here are definitely a cut above.

912/6 Sukhumvit 55 Road
Klongton Nua, Wattana
(02) 714 7801
www.bussaracum.com

### KRABI

**Time for Lime**

Honeymooners and young couples are especially susceptible to the romantic setting of these classes, held on a picturesque beach on Lanta Island. The accent is on experimen-tal Thai-style food rather than the traditional fare, so if you like being adventurous in the kitchen, this one is certainly for you. In addition, the *entire* fee you pay goes to the Lanta Animal Welfare Donation Fund—yet another good reason to enroll here.

72/2 Mo 3. Klong Dao Beach
Saladan, Koh Lanta
(075) 684 590
www.timeforlime.net
www.lantaanimalwelfare.com

## KOH SAMUI
### Samui Institute of Thai Culinary Arts
This institute offers a balance of dishes (for example: stir-fry *and* curry) for holidaymakers short on time, as well as serious learners who are willing to devote several days to intensive training. There is a different menu for each day of the week, so visit the website before booking and select a day that demonstrates the dishes you're most likely to cook at home. A nice feature here is the "gift" class: you can purchase a cooking class to present as a gift to a friend.

46/6 Moo 3, Chaweng Beach
(077) 413 172
www.sitca.net

## PHUKET
### Pat's Home
Chef Pat Teinthong offers one of the few—if not the only—home cooking options in Phuket. She holds regular morning classes at her house in the city, and also offers something really special: private lessons in the evening at her sumptuous Balinese-style home on top of a hill with a spectacular view of the Andaman Sea. Pat also runs a bed-and-breakfast at this hilltop property, but space is limited, so you have to make your reservations well ahead of time.

28/4 Moo 3 T. Vichit, Chaofa Road
(081) 538 8276
thaicookingclass@hotmail.com

## CHIANG MAI
### A Lot of Thai
The warm hospitality of the husband-wife duo Kwan and Yui has a lot to do with the success of the cozy classes they offer at their home. Foreign visitors, especially, are enchanted by Yui's ability to simplify the complexities of Thai cooking for Westerners, as well as the couple's facility with the English language, which makes time spent with them a valuable opportunity for cultural interaction.

165 Soi 9 Chiang Mai-Lampoon Road
T. Nonghoi Muang
(053) 800724
www.alotofthai.com

*Recipe for success*

Many cooking schools in Thailand include a tour of a produce market. Take full advantage of this opportunity to gain a better understanding of Thai ingredients. And make sure to ask your guide to explain unfamiliar herbs, vegetables, fruit, fish, and seafood that you may come across.

During class, you will probably be taught to make a basic curry paste from scratch, but the process is time-consuming and even restaurants often don't bother to make their own. Shop-bought pastes are perfectly adequate, so don't feel guilty if you never pound and roast another batch of that pungent paste in your life again once your class is over.

After the cooking part of the class is through, the food you have just prepared will be served for lunch or dinner. Some schools will even give you a certificate and small mementoes, such as an apron inscribed with the logo of the school, a recipe book, or a chef's hat.

# TIPPING

*Dà wèi*
*offers tips on rewarding*
*a job well done*

The Thais are shy when it comes to talking about tips. And although I could never really get a straight answer about what I should tip in specific situations, I was determined to crack the code.

Tipping, after all, is a fine art. While I didn't want to arrogantly flaunt money, I didn't want to shortchange people who work very hard for very little either. By finding the right balance, I could make a meaningful difference and get great service too. So I asked questions, did some math, and came up with what I feel is the correct tipping amount wherever I go.

## Tipping while traveling upcountry

Recently, I had the opportunity to stay at The River Kwai Jungle Rafts hotel in Kanchanaburi. It was a wonderful experience to just drift on bamboo raft rooms on the historic Kwai River and use wick lamps instead of electric lights at night.

We were staying for a while at this eco-hotel, and I am one who always likes to talk with people to see how things work behind the scenes. In one such conversation, the topic turned to tipping the staff. I was curious about how much of an impact tips had on the lives of these people who worked on the raft-hotel. Predictably, the conversation tapered off at that stage, and the staff would only say, "Up to you." Not a lot of help.

So I changed tack and asked how much the hotel paid them. That was a fair question, and for once, I got a straight answer. The hotel staff mostly got a salary of 60 baht a day, but if they spoke English it could be 80 baht or even up to 120 baht. That surprised me, because I knew that the Thailand minimum wage was 206 baht a day. Ah, but the staff was allowed to sleep at the hotel and was fed, so their 60-baht pay came after deductions for food and lodging. That's $1.80 a day for us Americans, by the way.

Now, you can probably do the math as well as I can: a 20-baht tip is a third of a day's wages. That's a *lot* of money and certainly makes a difference. This calculation, based on a 60-baht-a-day wage, was for upcountry workers near Burma. I am sure the salaries are much higher in Bangkok.

## Tipping at a massage parlor

There is a little massage place in Bangkok that I like to call Foot Joy, just into Soi 8 off Sukhumvit. It has a great staff and gives an honest massage.

The parlor charges 250 baht for a leg massage, out of which the masseuse gets between 60 and 80 baht. On a typical day a masseuse will do one or maybe two massages. Three massages in one day is the exception. So the massage girls are living on about 100 to 200 baht a day. That's a lot of hard work for not much money.

Having observed the situation, I have seen that a good customer will tip between 60 and 100 baht per hour for a well-done massage. This means that the tips are half of a masseuse's daily income. It also means that somebody working in a busy massage parlor is living on about $5 to $7 per day.

While you never want to come across as a "rich foreigner" (which is viewed poorly and can be insulting), don't forget how very important a 60- or 100-baht tip is when you get a massage that lasts an hour. And when— unlike the hotel staff in the previous example—your tip is probably the only one the masseuse will get that day.

## Tipping at a city hotel

The hotel that I often stay at in Bangkok has a guard posted by the elevators on the lobby level. One day, I handed him a 20-baht tip, just to see what would happen. He did a sort of double-take and acted as if I was the first person ever to tip him.

The second day, I again gave him a 20-baht bill, just to see if the same reaction happened again. This time I got a grin.

On the third day, he had the door open and waiting for me, and when I entered the elevator, the button was already pressed for my floor. He had remembered me and had noted the floor I got off at from the day before.

It is this sort of thing that feels really great when you're on vacation— a sort of "I have your back, and you cover mine" feeling. Now I know that if I am ever in trouble, this elevator guard will recognize me and help me. And it is nice to enjoy the special treatment of him holding the elevator door open when I get in and having the button already pressed.

Once another guest asked me what floor I wanted and I said, "The guard already pressed it." He asked how the guard knew, and I said that he remembered me from the previous day, when I gave him a 20-baht tip. It was a lot of fun when I bumped into the same guest later on at the elevators—and the beaming guard had pressed *both* of our buttons. The guest simply said, "You sure don't get service like that back at home."

Indeed.

When you're staying at a hotel in Thailand, find somebody that you routinely interact with—your housekeeping maid or doorman or counter staff — and casually give them 20 baht while saying "thank you." After doing this a couple times, the service you receive will improve in subtle but clear ways. The Thais like to be appreciated and like to treat others with respect as much as you do. Best of all, it adds an element of fun to your trip!

## The River Kwai Jungle Rafts
Go to page 128.

## Taxi tipping
Unlike in the West, taxi drivers in Thailand don't expect tips—especially if they suspect you know that they deliberately took the longer, scenic route to add extra miles to the trip and extra baht to the taxi meter. To reward an honest taxi driver, though, you may want to give him a little something. A driver who picks you up and drops you off without a fuss, and who doesn't go through the charade of not knowing the address you give him, deserves special recognition as a rare breed—especially in Bangkok.

# TELEPHONES

## David Kovanen phones in tips on telecommunications

### GSM phones

One of the first concerns international travelers always have is how to stay in touch with people back home as conveniently as possible. In Bangkok, the answer is ridiculously simple and cheap. Bring with you an unlocked GSM telephone. They cost about $30 on eBay. And if you don't have one, don't worry—they cost about $20 in Bangkok.

Simply go to the fourth floor of the MBK Center. There, you will see what mere description cannot convincingly describe: literally hundreds of small booths selling phones. All kinds of phones—new and used, smart and dumb.

If you will be in Thailand for a month or less, I suggest you buy any "AIS 12 Call" SIM card, which will cost you between 100 and 300 baht. Have the store activate the SIM card for you, and presto—you have a phone number in Thailand and can make cheap calls. The phone number will start with a *0* for calls placed within Thailand. In order for people

TELEPHONES

to call you from outside Thailand, drop the leading *0* and replace it with the country code *66*. For example, 0812345678 would become 66-812345678.

To make cheap calls back to the United States or other countries, dial 00500 and then the country code. The secret trick is to dial 00500 and not just 005. This is something that is only printed in Thai so the locals know about it but the tourists do not. The 00500 prefix will halve the price of your call—about 3.5 baht per minute to the United States. It's also good to know that incoming calls are free, so your friends can call you using VOIP services and it costs you nothing. Keep in mind, though, that as of the time of this writing, Skype is a rip-off in Thailand, as it charges 17 cents a minute, while the typical rate should be about 2-3 cents.

To see how much credit you have, dial *121# and a text will pop up telling you your balance. And when you need more money on your calling card, go to any 7-Eleven convenience store and ask for a "12 Call Top-Up 100 Baht." The clerk will print a slip of paper for you. Dial *120* plus the 16-digit code on the paper; then dial # and press "send": *120*xxxxxxxxxxxxxxxx#. This will add the amount to your phone and will show you the new balance and expiration date. Note that Thai dates are in DD/MM/YYYY format, unlike in the United States.

## iPhones

Another option is to use your iPhone in Thailand. In the United States, iPhones are locked to certain carriers, but many iPhones can be unlocked so that you can use them in Thailand and elsewhere. This can be done by most of the little phone shops at the MBK Center mentioned above. The typical price for this service is 200 baht (about $6); the people at these shops are geniuses in making an iPhone work. It will take about half an hour, and the process can be easily undone when you return home by "restoring" your Apple firmware—though I have found no reason for undoing it. Make sure to bring your email passwords with you, as you may need to reenter them. And ask to have your notes, photos, and apps backed up, just in case they're erased in the process.

If you have a smart phone such as an iPhone, remember that you will be billed a terrible rate for data—on an iPhone, it will typically cost about $12 a day. Ouch! But there is an easy way around this when using an AIS 12 Call SIM card. Dial one of these codes to purchase a data plan:

- 138*34# for about 7 days of service (350 baht).
- 138*37# for about 14 days of service (500 baht).
- 138*65# for unlimited use for 30 days (650 baht).
- 139*3# to check your remaining time.

This will allow you to use data to send and receive emails and surf the web. Note that the APN and UserID and password fields should be blank. And also note that the service is for GPRS, which means it isn't especially fast, and people calling you will get a busy signal when your phone is in data mode.

Despite these inconveniences, I find it wonderful that I can snap a photo on my iPhone and immediately email it back to friends at home. It makes my trip very interactive.

### Repair services

Do you have an iPhone with a cracked screen? Or perhaps a Black Berry with a broken keyboard?

I have seen no place on earth with the level of telephone electronics mastery that equals the shops found on the fourth floor of the MBK Center. It is worth witnessing even if you don't have a phone in need of repairs. There are hundreds of young men at the booths who appear to be no older than seventeen, all looking through magnifying glasses and soldering chips on the circuit boards of cell phones. Apple probably just tosses the boards and never replaces the individual chips. But the wizards at MBK will pull chips on and off the boards and do true microsurgery on your phone. Repairing a broken screen or case is no problem. Putting in a fresh battery is entry-level work for them.

Overall, I am fascinated by the cell phone–fixing capabilities of the people of Thailand. For tourists, it is one thing to see the Thai people serving a wonderful traditional cuisine and giving great traditional massages. But it is quite another to

discover seventeen-year-old kids working with electronics at a level of expertise that may no longer exist in America. That, in my opinion, is a real cultural eye opener!

### MBK Center

Not just for tourists, MBK Center is where Bangkok locals go to buy or fix their cell phones, MP3 players, and other electronic goods. Some booths on the fourth floor will also let you trade your old items in for new ones.

444 Phayathai Road
Patumwan, Bangkok
www.mbk-center.co.th
Skytrain: National Stadium

## TIPS FOR PARENTS

### Katrina Wilton weighs in on massages for moms-to-be

When I was six months pregnant, my husband and I went to Phuket for our "babymoon"—our last relaxing hoorah as a childless couple before the baby would come and change our lives, and indeed the way we holiday, forever.

One of the joys of Thailand for us is the sensational massages, available

our experience of Thailand, as he seemed to make us more accessible to the locals.

I can almost hear the protective gasps from all the Western moms out there who are reading this, but believe me, the Thai people are extremely nurturing and quite infatuated with babies. Once I got over my initial qualms about handing over Nathan, I discovered something that's an incredible treat in Mommy World: two free hands, with which I could shop, eat, and do whatever I liked.

Before arriving in Thailand, I was plagued with worries about how I would survive such a long stay with a baby in tow. I read many guidebooks, spent hours doing online research, but found very little practical information for new mothers like me. Left to my own devices, I coped with all the baby-related issues that came up as best as I could, and I'm happy to share a few of them here, with the hope of helping other moms prepare for their own trips abroad.

**Bring a baby carrier**
Baby carriers are a must-have in Thailand, especially Bangkok, where the congested roads are not conducive for strollers. In eight weeks, I made only one excursion with our stroller, and had a horrid time trying to push Nathan over the uneven sidewalks. It felt so much better to go out with Nathan safely nestled in his carrier, safe from the high-speed cars that whizzed past us on the narrow *sois*.

**Don't fry your appliances**
If you use breast-pumps or baby monitors, this is very important. The American 120-volt plugs are *not* compatible with Thai 220-volt outlets. You will need a transformer *and* an adapter if you want to use your American appliances here. Hopefully, this will save you from repeating our costly mistake of accidentally plugging in (and destroying!) our expensive baby monitor.

**Feel free to nurse in public**
One of my greatest uncertainties in Thailand was how Nathan and I would go on tours, given that he was breastfeeding at the time. In the United States, I am comfortable nursing discreetly in public, but I wasn't sure about doing that in Thailand for fear of offending the more modest locals. While I personally opted to pump at night and carry breast milk–filled bottles when we traveled, I was assured by both Thai and expat women that the locals are quite accepting of foreigners nursing modestly in public.

**Enjoy exceptional pediatric care**
When are babies most likely to get the "funk"? You guessed it! On vacation. Whether it's because of the time zone shift or airplane germs, access to medical care is a necessity when traveling with a baby. Thankfully, Bangkok is equipped with state-of-the-art hospitals, such as Samitivej Hospital, which we used. Our highly respected U.S. pediatrician paled in comparison to the child-centered care we received there. We were

greeted by English-speaking pediatri-
cians and nurses and were able to
obtain appointments on the same day
we called in for them. We were even
given paperwork to file with insurance, though I recommend inquiring
about international coverage before
your trip. I was so pleased that I sent
pictures of Nathan in the cartoon-
covered lobby to assure his con
cerned grandparents back home that
he was in perfectly safe hands.

### Be prepared
The good news is that baby supplies
are plentiful in Bangkok I could even
replace a broken component in my
U.S.-bought breast-pump without any
problem. The bad news is they are
expensive. So if you're on a budget,
bring as many diapers and other baby
care products as you can from home.
An added bonus: as they get used
up, you'll find more space in your
luggage to fill with goodies to take
back home.

### Samitivej Hospital
www.samitivejhospitals.com

### Buying baby supplies
Before you hit the department
stores, check out the big hypermarkets such as Big C or Tesco
Lotus first. They have branches all
over Thailand, and their prices are
more reasonable in comparison.

## HEALTHCARE

### David Kovanen treats himself to superb medical care

I have a superb medical insurance
plan in the United States. It pretty
much covers anything, anywhere. Do
you find it surprising, then, that I save
up all of my medical needs for my
trips to Thailand?

When most people consider medical tourism, they think about saving
money at cut-rate facilities in far-off
places like India and Mexico. But I go
to Thailand because of the country's
top-quality medical services. Saving
money is my last reason for using
Thai doctors and hospitals—instead,
it was my own personal experience
that made me a devoted fan.

One day, I woke up with a pretty
bad eye infection. My eye was red
and sore and needed attention.
So I decided to go to Bumrungrad
International Hospital, a world-class
facility in Bangkok.

I headed for the eye care clinic
and got in queue to see a doctor.
After about five minutes, a nurse
came to me with an apology: they
were very busy that day, and the wait
might be twenty or even thirty min-

MEDICAL CARE

utes. They were sorry. I was given a coupon to go down to the McDonald's or Starbucks counters and have a treat on them. Now when was the last time your U.S. care provider apologized for a half-hour wait and then rewarded you for your patience?

When my turn came, the doctor introduced himself and sat me in the ophthalmologist's chair. He peered into the problem eye and took some photos, which he then displayed to me on a forty-four-inch LCD flat screen mounted on the wall of his office. He pointed out the blood veins and said he thought the problem was possibly more general, not only my eyes, and he recommended that I see an internal medicine doctor.

I walked over to internal medicine, and when I got there I found they were expecting me and I already had a place in the queue. Five minutes later, the internal medicine doctor explained that I had either a bacterial or a viral infection that was showing up in my eye. He recommended a blood test. They took a blood sample and told me to come back in forty to sixty minutes. I did, and it turned out to be a viral infection. I was told to go to the cashier's desk. I paid my bill, and they handed me a prescription for Tamiflu.

By then, I was starting to feel absolutely miserable: hot, cold, sneezy, achy. I just wanted to crawl into bed. I went home, swallowed the Tamiflu, and woke up six hours later feeling like new.

Let me explain that in the United States it could have taken a few days to get to even see the doctor. If they ordered a blood test, the results wouldn't be available for another one to two days. By then, it would have been too late for treatment, because Tamiflu must be taken within the first forty-eight hours.

See the difference here?

Another time that I was dumbfounded by the quality of medical service at the Bumrungrad was when my friend was diagnosed with the early stages of cervical cancer.

Her doctor in Japan had recommended the usual invasive procedure. I suggested a second opinion from Bumrungrad in Bangkok. So we went. Bumrungrad confirmed the diagnosis. But the twist was that they recommended treating the cancer with medicine for three months.

I had visions of my friend's hair falling out, sickness, and all the other difficulties that often attend cancer treatments. So when the hospital explained that the type of cancer she had progressed relatively slowly, and that they'd had a very good success rate with just medication, we agreed to go with it.

Imagine my shock when the medicine turned out to be a special type of nonsour, time-release vitamin C and a large daily dose of folic acid! In Thailand, doctors believe that some cancers are caused by viruses, and that the viruses, if caught early enough, can be treated with simple treatments like vitamin C. In my friend's case, the cancer was caught early.

My friend followed her prescription for the medicine exactly and precisely. Four months later, we returned to the hospital, where the doctors declared that the virus had left her body. Her early-stage cancer was gone, and she was now in perfect health.

I asked why nobody I had talked to in the United States had ever heard of such a treatment. The doctor calmly answered, "Who is going to pay for a million-dollar clinical study to sell vitamin C as cancer medicine? In Thailand, we are concerned with treating people, not with protecting cancer research."

The results seemed too good to be true. So my friend returned home to Japan, where her stunned doctor confirmed that the cancer was simply gone. A miracle!

Periodical follow-ups have confirmed that the cancer has not returned. I asked the doctor what percentage of patients respond as she did. The answer: at an early stage like hers, much higher than 90 percent.

I have been to Bumrungrad many times over the years. I go there because of the quality of treatment, and not because the cost is so minimal. The level of care and attention equals that of a five-star hotel. They also have equipment that U.S. hospitals simply cannot get access to because of the costly and lengthy FDA approval process.

Best of all, most insurance plans will pay for medical treatment at Bumrungrad, as the hospital is a Blue Shield member. In addition, most of the doctors are U.S. trained and many are U.S. Medical Board certified.

So if you are thinking of visiting Thailand as a medical tourist, know that you won't just be saving a whole lot of money. There is a very good reason why Bumrungrad is filled with rich people from all around the world—sheiks, millionaires, government leaders, and people like me who can afford medical care at any facility in the world. For we know that we'll get a better quality of care than we could ever dream possible in our home countries.

*Bumrungrad International Hospital*

33 Sukhumvit 3, Soi Nana Nua
Wattana, Bangkok
(02) 667 1000
(02) 667 2525 (emergency)
(02) 667 1555 (outpatient appointments)
www.bumrungrad.com

# Epilogue

*One writer attempts to go home again ... and again ... and again*

## JANET BROWN ATTEMPTS TO GO HOME AGAIN ...
### AND AGAIN ... AND AGAIN

I should have remembered Thomas Wolfe when I was planning my visit to Bangkok. "You'd be bored stiff," I explained to friends who claimed to wish they were going with me, "I'm going to my other home for two weeks; it won't be exciting. I'm going to stay in the apartment building that I used to live in; I'm going to eat in my old neighborhood; I'm going to see friends. I'm just going to do what I did when I lived there."

I didn't pack for this trip by trying to stuff my life into two suitcases, the way I always used to do when returning to Thailand to live and work after time spent in the States. I had never gone back with a shopping list before, and I went to the airport with a weird little cluster of tension in my neck rather than with my customary wild jubilation over leaving the old country for the home I had chosen. I'd been gone for a record absence of four years, and I was only going to be in Bangkok for a little while.

I got on the plane feeling as though a meeting with an old boyfriend were looming in my future, with that strange mixture of anticipation and dread. Somewhere in the back of my mind was the fear that once I got to Thailand, I might abandon the life that I had so carefully reconstructed in the States.

What I didn't expect was that during my four years in the USA I had turned back into an American.

I had worked so hard to become a resident of Thailand, the kind of foreigner who learned to accept, if not love, every aspect of my new surroundings, and who blended in as well as my oversized nose would allow. I'd learned to walk at a snail's pace, to use toothpicks behind a shielding hand after every meal, to look at diseased dogs without visible disgust, and to do my damnedest to behave like a well-mannered, reserved

Thai life riding them. Now, as an American visitor, I took taxis and the Skytrain and the subway. I took the time to ride the bus twice and each time I felt very out of place.

I was out of place in my old neighborhood also, although people were too polite to make me feel that way. Instead they asked me where my family was, why my sons weren't traveling with me, and why I didn't come with friends. Old ladies lavished me with kindly attention that made me twitch, assuring me every day that my clothes were beautiful and asking me where I was going and what I would do when there. Vacationers don't usually come to that part of Bangkok, and the strain of having one in their midst was a huge responsibility, even when it was a vacationer with a familiar face. After the day that one of the friendly noodle-stall owners tried to set me up with a teaching job, I began to leave quite early in the morning and to return after dark to avoid running the gauntlet of concerned curiosity.

There are so many things I miss about Bangkok, and I've been planning my next trip ever since I got back to the States after this last visit. Next time I'll know enough to know that I'm traveling, not stepping back into an old life. I'll stay in a hotel; I'll travel outside of the city; I'll have an itinerary that I just might stick to. But still, I'll do all of that with the knowledge of how it felt, a few years ago, to ride behind a motorcycle driver, watching the late afternoon sun sparkle on the lake at Beung Khum where men sit beneath the trees, smoking and fishing for their suppers.

*Night Fishing - Nakhon Phanom*

# CONTRIBUTOR BIOGRAPHIES, CREDITS, AND INDEX

## Deborah Annan
(page 17, 218)
www.etsy.com

Deborah lives in Seattle. By day she edits a Microsoft website; by night she writes her book or designs jewelry. She pushes pages for wages so that she can support her extensive travel and jewelry-making habits. She is dying to return to Thailand soon so she can buy more hill tribe silver and get more *bao-bao* massages. To view her jewelry, visit Ginger Gems, her online shop.

## Douglas Paul Baird
(page 250)
www.jadeisus.com

Born in Liverpool, England, Douglas got his first job as a food porter at the John Lewis department store in town. It started as holiday work because he desperately wanted a motorbike—a Yamaha 50 chicken chaser. Today he lives in Thailand and sells quality jade jewelry through his website.

## Laura Bartlett Jurica
(page 65, 95, 168)
www.creativeartdesigns.bravehost.com

Laura and her husband Cory Jurica are inspired by their travels. They create one-of-a-kind artwork based on the countries that they visit. Their artwork can be found on their website.

## Martyn Bartlett
(page 179)
www.thaisabai.org

Martyn is a fifty-plus-year-old pharmaceutical worker living in the UK, and his dream for a long time has been to retire in Thailand. He's getting there, but not quickly enough. Martyn's full-time link to the Land of Smiles is through his blog *Beyond the Mango Juice*.

## Ananya Basu
(page 161)

As an Odissi dance exponent, Ananya frequently finds herself on the road, taking her performances all over Asia and Europe. After her marriage to a German software engineer, Ananya is now based in Pune, India, and concentrating on researching her first book on Indian *ragas*.

## Jenny Beattie
(page 53, 57, 275)
http://tea-stains.blogspot.com

Jenny was born in Kent in the UK. She has had a variety of mostly unfulfilling jobs, while continuing to search the "Situations Vacant" columns. In 2005, she and her family moved to Bangkok, where she finally applied herself to writing her first novel, *Polite Lies*. Her writing can be found on her blog.

## Charles Benimoff
(page 230, 234)

Charles is a recently graduated film student who was initially drawn to moviemaking because of its ability to impact people in sweeping ways. But after doing some volunteer work in a Nepalese orphanage, he discovered that he'd rather have an impact in education, doing what he can to make sure local youth are as lucky as he was growing up.

**Adam Bray**
(page 149)
www.fisheggtree.com
Adam is a full-time travel writer, journalist, photographer, and fixer based in Mui Ne, Vietnam, since 2003. He has contributed to seventeen guidebooks on Southeast Asia, including the *AA Thailand Keyguide*. He also writes regularly for CNN. Follow his archaeological and jungle adventures on Twitter (fisheggtree) or on his website.

**Elizabeth Briel**
(page 125)
http://EBriel.com
Elizabeth is an artist who explores Asia with her camera, notebook, and paintbrushes. She prints nineteenth-century Cyanotype photos of disappearing places, paints pictures of sharp-witted women in different languages, and writes about the arts of Asia. In Cambodia, she taught photography to street children, and in Hong Kong she founded a community gallery. Find out more at her website.

**Janet Brown**
(page 269, 297)
Janet is a writer and editor who bounces between the Pacific Northwest of the United States and Bangkok, where she has lived off and on since 1995. She is hopelessly in love with Southeast Asia, especially the northeastern corner of Thailand, where she always encounters the most interesting food and the most delightful people in the Kingdom.

**Miranda Bruce-Mitford**
(page 137)
Miranda is an academic and writer specializing in Southeast Asian art. After spending time in Africa and the Middle East, she studied Burmese Language and Literature and, later, Oriental Philosophy at The School of Oriental and African Studies. Tutor and lecturer for the British Museum and SOAS Asian Arts Course, she has escorted many tours to Southeast Asia. The author of *The Illustrated Book of Signs and Symbols* and *Signs and Symbols: An Illustrated Guide to their Origins and Meanings*, she has contributed to various books on Asian Art and has recently finished a novel set in Southeast Asia.

**Robert Carmack**
(page 70)
www.asianfoodtours.com
www.globetrottinggourmet.com
Robert is the author of several books on Asian cooking, and writes widely on food and travel for international publications. His career as a television food stylist divides his time between Australia, Thailand, and the United States. He is also director of Globetrotting Gourmet food tours to Southeast Asia and edits the *tgtgNewsletter*. He and partner Morrison Polkinghorne are founding lights of the Isaan Food & Wine master class, held in Khao Yai.

## Elizabeth Cassidy
(page 138, 146, 196)

Elizabeth loves to travel so much that she does it for a living, working as a flight attendant for United Airlines. When she's not working, she's planning her next adventure. Her travel style is more off the beaten path—looking for the hidden gems, staying in guesthouses over high-rises, and adventuring with a backpack. Presently, Elizabeth lives in Chicago, Illinois.

## Karen Coates
(Pg. 84)
www.ramblingspoon.com

Karen is an author, journalist, and media trainer who has spent many years in Asia. She was a 2010–11 Ted Scripps Fellow in Environmental Journalism at the University of Colorado, where she created the online forum AppetiteEARTH, examining the future of food. She writes the food blog *Rambling Spoon*.

## Rob Costello
(page 257)

Rob is an elementary school teacher who has spent the past five years volunteering at the Soi Dog Foundation in Phuket, where he bathes dogs and gives them treats and lots of affection. He is a proud parent to three *soi* dogs that he met while volunteering at the organization and brought back with him to San Francisco.

## Tom Crowley
(page 213)

Since 1966, Tom has worked in almost every country in Asia. This included service with the U.S. Army, the U.S. state department, and the General Electric company. He is currently a volunteer with an NGO assisting street children in Bangkok. His recently published book is *Bangkok Pool Blues*.

## Dà wèi
(page 209, 285)

Dà wèi travels to Thailand and throughout Asia, but lives in America. He says life should be simple; beauty comes from small things. He walks so he can hear neighborhoods, he rides the subway in rush hour so he can smell the people in a new city, and he opens menus to random pages and feels obligated to order something from where they open.

## Amiya Dasgupta
(page 261)

A travel agent by profession, Amiya has designed hundreds of tours and set up scores of film shoots all over Nepal, India, Thailand, and China. His innate charm and intimate knowledge of Asia has won him accolades in the tourism industry, but he brushes all that aside and talks only of his current passion: working with impoverished school kids and launching a special tourism package he has designed for people interested in an intensely spiritual experience of Nepal. write2dg@gmail.com

**Alice Driver**
(page 201, 281)

Alice's freelance writing has appeared in *To Vietnam With Love* and the magazines *Transitions Abroad, Abroad View, Cultural Survival,* and *South American Explorer.* In 2011, her article "Of the Flesh: Graphic Images of Femicide in Ciudad Juárez" appeared in the book *Restructuring Violence in the Spanish Speaking World.*

**Scott Earle**
(page 103)
www.scottearle.com

Scott is a British expat who has lived in Thailand since the beginning of 2004. His interests include computers and traveling, as well as studying Thai language and culture, and enjoying Thai food. Scott keeps an irregularly updated blog.

**Oliver Fennell**
(page 14, 19, 55)

Oliver swapped rainy Wales for sunny Thailand in 2008 to work for the *Bangkok Post,* the kingdom's biggest English-language newspaper. In visiting more than fifty countries to date, Oliver has honed an appetite for the unusual and an aversion to the tourist trail. Covering news, travel, sport, the arts, and food and drink, he has been published by newspapers and magazines in the UK, USA, Thailand, and Hong Kong.

**Geena Fife**
(page 47, 117)

Born in New Zealand, Geena moved with her husband to Sydney, Australia, when they were both in their midtwenties. The plan was to work and live for six months and then head on to England, but they got stuck in Sydney, falling in love with the city. Still keen to travel and explore other cultures, however, they finally plucked up the courage to quit their jobs and head off to backpack around Southeast Asia, Sri Lanka, and Nepal for a few months.

**Caroline Fournier**
(page 60, 271)

Daughter. Sister. Friend. Leo. French Canadian. Independent. Right-brained. Clumsy. Easily amused. Strong-willed. Grateful. Open-minded. Curious. Dreamer. Accountant. Weekend cook. Amateur photographer. Solo traveler. Blogger. Accidental writer. That is Caroline in fifty words or less ...

**Andrew C. Godlewski**
(page 186, 215)
www.mytb.org/skimango

Andrew has spent the past two years traveling around the world, writing about his experiences from wherever he goes. If you would like to read more about his travels and blunders through Thailand, Europe, and Asia, please check out his blog.

## Monisha Gupta
(page 278, 279)

Monisha helps run a medical institution in Kolkata. At a moment's notice, she has her small overnighter packed and is ready to travel wherever anybody is willing to take her. She loves to talk about yoga, and religiously follows a daily yoga routine. She relaxes with Hindi/Bengali soaps on TV; playing with her granddaughters Chiki, Chia, and Chika; and knitting tiny cardigans for all the gods displayed on her altar.

## John Henderson
(page 39, 141, 272)
http://hipbelt.blogspot.com

John's full-time occupation in Bangkok is husband. To pay the rent, he also has a day job at a branch of the U.S. Embassy. Read all of his travel tales at his blog.

## Will Heron
(page 244)

Will has lived in Bangkok for most of the past decade. He is a director at DTC Travel and works as the volunteer project coordinator for the Gift of Happiness Foundation. Born and raised in Montreal, Canada, he has worked in magazine publishing, advertising, politics, and labor in the United States.

## Colin Hinshelwood
(page 120)
www.cpamedia.com

Colin first came to Thailand in 1987 and has since written numerous articles on the region. He has also written several guidebooks, including Frommer's *Day-by-Day* guide to Bangkok 2009. He is a partner at CPA Media in Chiang Mai. You can read more of his work at the CPA website.

## Jennifer Hughes
(page 21)

Two weeks after graduating from the University of Oregon School of Journalism, Jennifer hit the road—on her bike. She rode 1,900 miles from Vancouver, B.C., to San Diego, California. Along the way, she discovered an urge to travel and booked a plane ticket to Thailand. After five weeks in beautiful Thailand she returned home to Eugene, Oregon, where she spends her time running, writing, and planning her next trip abroad.

## Ryan Humphreys
(page 62, 198)
www.bangkokbooks.com

Ryan lived in Bangkok for five years and wrote *Bangkok Exit*, a biographical account of his time teaching and traveling in Thailand. Most recently, he spent two years teaching in Guatemala. At the moment, he is back home in Vancouver, Canada, where he teaches Spanish part-time, writes because he can't help it, and dreams of returning to Asia. His new book—tentatively titled *The Flirtations of Dan Harris*—is a fictional story set in Thailand. Look for it soon from Bangkok Books.

**CONTRIBUTORS' PROFILES**

**Kristianne Huntsberger**
(page 222, 226)
http://spectatorspots.blogspot.com
kristianneh@gmail.com

Kristianne is a writer and performer from Seattle, among other places. Specializing in folklore and DIY community expression, her work focuses on the creative techniques people use to define physical and personal space.

**Steven King**
(page 41)

Steven is a dedicated beer enthusiast who has worked and traveled across Asia as a consultant in a range of editorial, executive, and management positions in publishing, advertising, television, creative, and production industries.

**Lisa Koenig**
(page 248)

Lisa is a freshman at Vanderbilt University, studying Human and Organizational Development. She grew up in suburban Illinois with the most amazing mother in the world. Her father moved to Thailand after her parents divorced, and she has subsequently had the great privilege of spending many summers with him, her stepmom, and the children of Baan Jing Jai Orphanage in Pattaya.

**Danielle Koffler**
(page 24, 33, 228)
www.wakeupanddance.wordpress.com

After graduating from the University of Colorado with a degree in Environmental Studies, Danielle packed her bags and went to teach English in Khon Kaen, Thailand. She has traveled extensively around Southeast Asia in the past three years. Stories and pictures from Danielle's travels can be found at her blog.

**David Kovanen**
(page 29, 130, 176, 287, 293)

David is a consummate observer of details and nuance. Everybody notices the big statue. David notices that water pipes in Thailand are all blue and that Thai spirit houses never have shadows cast upon them by the house they are protecting. He wants to believe in reincarnation, so he can come back as an Asian.

**Matthias Lehmann**
(page 256)

The last ten years of Matthias's life have been spent between London and East Asia. He lives in Mae Sai, Thailand, and works for DEPDC/GMS and Baan Doi, Home and Healing Center for Children. He is especially interested in working toward antitrafficking measures that are guided by sensible analysis of accurate information.

**Hugh Leong**
(page 31, 282)
http://ebooksinthailand.com
retire2thailand.com
http://ebooksinthailand.com

Hugh first came to Thailand in 1969 as a U.S. Peace Corps volunteer and is now retired in Chiang Mai. He authors the website Retire2Thailand and an accompanying blog, and writes the retirement column for *Chiang Mai City Life* magazine. His latest book, *Retired Life in Thailand* is available at *eBooks in Thailand*.

## Stu Lloyd
(page 76, 86, 184)
www.worldsmith360.com

Rhodesian-born Stu has spent fifteen years in Southeast Asia and now calls Bangkok home. He has been called "the perfect storyteller" by *The Telegraph* UK for his seven books, including the best-selling *Hardship Posting* in his Expat Misadventure in Asia series. He has also been named one of the World's 100 Favorite Travel Writers by TripBase.com.

## Natalie Magann
(page 212)

Although a secretary by trade, Natalie excels in travel. In fact, she lives for it. When all is said and done, memories are all you have, and she is making great ones with unusual activities and cultural experiences—though to do it for a living would be the ultimate dream.

## Asha Mallya
(page 164)

Asha is a Pune-based scientist working with hepatitis vaccines. When she is not in the lab, she is furiously making plans for her next long road journey with friends and son Aniruddha. Wherever she goes, Asha is passionate about tasting all the local delicacies, which is odd because she usually disapproves of most of them.

## Tim Matsui
(page 252)
www.timmatsui.com

Tim is a multimedia journalist and producer focusing on human trafficking, alternative energy, and the environment. He has worked with one of the world's leading multimedia production companies, MediaStorm in New York City, and is a past Blue Earth Alliance Project photographer. He is the founder of a nonprofit using documentary multimedia to create dialogue about the lasting effects of sexual violence and is a cofounder of the Travel and Outdoor Photographer's Alliance.

## Steven McCall
(page 232)

Steven was born on an army base outside of Indianapolis, Indiana. He traveled the world as a small child and doesn't remember a thing about it. Now he's building new memories, but writing them down this time. When not on the road he's in a small office above his kitchen overlooking a lake near downtown Orlando, Florida.

## Ian McNamara
(page 27, 143)
www.iamkohchang.com

Ian made Koh Chang his home in 2003 with the idea of doing as little as possible while enjoying the island lifestyle. He now runs Baan Rim Nam guesthouse—a renovated fisherman's house on Klong Prao beach—and writes at his website, which provides visitors with a slice of the real Koh Chang.

### Adam Mico
(page 63)

Adam spends his weekdays as a professional public servant. When he is not working, he looks to strengthen his mental and physical health by cherishing time with his family, exercising, preparing for the next vacation, and contributing anonymously as a reviewer of music and products on various blogs and websites.

### Chris Mitchell
(page 200)
http://Divehappy.com
http://Travelhappy.info

Chris is a British scuba diving journalist based in Bangkok. He runs the Asian scuba diving website Dive Happy and the Thailand travel site Travel Happy. He is also coauthor of *Thailand's Underwater World*.

### Jamie Monk
(page 25, 193)
www.jamiesphuket.com

Jamie has been living in Phuket, Thailand, since 1999. After many years traveling in Latin America, Africa, and Europe, Thailand persuaded Jamie to stop moving. Now married with two children, Jamie writes a website about Phuket and is also manager of a scuba diving center.

### Adrianne Myers
(page 35)

Adrianne lives and works in London, Ontario, with her husband and one small, angry cat. She works in finance to support her passion for travel, food, and writing. She went to Thailand in 2009 and fell in love with the culture and the country.

### Chang Noi
(page 110)
www.changnoi1.blogspot.com

An amateur writer, travel photographer, and freelance travel consultant, Chang is a native from the Netherlands who started to travel to Southeast Asia in 1985. Since 2000, he has found his roots in Thailand. His blog was created to promote traveling "behind the highlights" in Southeast Asia—focusing on the small things, in other words, that make traveling so worth doing it.

### Monsuda Kay Nopakun
(page 126)

Monsuda Kay was born and raised in Bangkok, where she took great interest in music. She holds a degree in Computer Science and currently works in the family business. During her free time, she likes to write, travel, and spoil her Thai Bangkaew dog, Ice.

### Brendan O'Reilly
(page 134, 191)

Brendan is from Seattle, but he has spent much of his adult life living in China and India. He has worked as a grill cook, street musician, and English teacher. He is the author of *The Transcendent Harmony*, an innovative study of world religions available from Apple's iTunes store.

## Eric Petersen
(page 166, 220, 224, 241, 254)
www.travelpod.com/members/eric
Eric lives and works in Southeast Asia as a tour guide. He has led over fifty groups of Westerners through Vietnam, Cambodia, Laos, and Thailand. Two of his passions are responsible travel and cultural exchange. To read more about Eric's journeys, please visit the following website.

## Emily Pevsner
(page 291)
Traveling with a baby put a kind of maternal spin to Emily's whole Thailand experience. For instance, she loved to watch women manage food stalls with their babies sleeping on the counters beside them and was appalled at the sight of nursing infants being taken out on the streets to beg with their mothers. Little Nathan's presence made Emily more observant about Thai family life and how women played out their roles as mothers and breadwinners in a tradition-dictated society.

## Jan Polatschek
(page 99, 128, 247)
http://travelwithjan.com
Jan loves Thailand. What's not to love? Flavorsome food, subtropical climate, good-hearted people, the Thai smile. The sea, the mountains, the BTS Skytrain. From his home in Bangkok, he travels throughout the region and beyond. His journals and photographs appear on his website.

## Laurie Rhoads
(page 106)
Laurie was born and raised in Hershey, Pennsylvania, and developed the travel bug early thanks to her parents. Most recently, she spent nine months in Southeast Asia, teaching in Ban Phe and Chonburi, Thailand, and traveling through other parts of Thailand, Laos, Cambodia, and Vietnam before returning home to Boulder, Colorado, where she teaches preschool.

## Michael Roberts
(page 93, 159)
A fashion photographer by trade, this New Yorker likes to live life on his own terms—run five miles a day, sleep behind the sofa in the living room, and raid the refrigerator at three in the morning. He travels to distant countries whenever the mood seizes him and takes great interest in local cuisines.

## Mike Rose
(page 68, 113, 115, 236)
Born in Mansfield, UK, Mike joined the British Army from school and served in Cyprus, Germany, and Northern Ireland as an intelligence officer. Later he worked as a police officer before becoming a teacher at a large community college. A keen blogger, birder, cyclist, and photographer, he has always indulged his passion for travel whenever possible. Mike now lives in retirement in central Thailand, where he spends his days with his Thai partner pursuing his hobbies and traveling around the country.

**Linda Saleh**
(page 245)

From Albany, New York, Linda is a trained nurse who traveled the world with her Lebanese husband, Ali. After the sudden passing of her husband, Linda moved to Florida and keeps herself busy with her music, needle arts, and listening to Michael Savage's radio talk show.

**Raaj Sanghvi**
(page 81, 276)

Raaj is a student of McGill University in Montreal who's always looking for an opportunity to sneak off to Mumbai to hang out with friends and eat at the Thai Pavilion, his favorite restaurant in the world. If he's not to be found in Montreal or Mumbai, he is certain to be in Bangkok, holidaying with his dad and taking a connoisseur's interest in the food and shopping available there. Nobody has a better T-shirt collection than Raaj, who has a secret supplier somewhere around Siam Square in Bangkok.

**Lot Schuringa**
(page 207)

Lot, or Charlotte Hélène, traveled for nine months in Southeast Asia. In Bangkok, she landed a job as a bicycle tour guide and got to know the city like the back of her hand. She now studies in the Netherlands at University College in Maastricht and hopes to return to Southeast Asia for her master's in International Relations.

**Keya Sen**
(page 278)

Keya is a student of Rabindranath Tagore's famous educational institution in Shantiniketan (West Bengal, India), and like many other graduates of her alma mater, she excels in the creative field. Her exquisite embroidery and sitar-playing talents keep her company when she is not indulging in her third great passion: traveling.

**Oindrila Sen**
(page 156)

A sales executive in the United States, Oindrila is a hardcore liberal who cheered the loudest in her life when Barack Obama was voted into the White House. She loves to cook, and along with women's rights issues, her favorite topic of discussion is usually food. She wins every episode of *Jeopardy* from her living room, constantly listens to NPR, and is willing to bring any abused animal home.

**Joe Shakarchi**
(page 97, 100)
www.joeshakarchi.com

Joe is a poet and memoir writer who lives in Bangkok and San Francisco, where he teaches writing. His book of poems, *Sunrise in the West*, includes a poetry/music CD featuring Doors drummer John Densmore and other musicians. Visit his website for poems, MP3 samples, and more information.

## Helene Shapiro
(page 157, 277)

Helene, from New York City, has worked all her life for the same hospital she was born in. Postretirement, her plans include lots of beach holidays, building up her frog collection, and keeping Mimi, her ancient cat, alive. She is also working on a stand-up comedy routine she hopes to perform someday soon.

## Dee Shapland
(page 43, 189)

A commercial balloon pilot by profession, Dee has spent the last fourteen years flying and traveling around Southeast Asia, enjoying hot air, hot food, hot weather, and the warmth of the local people. He has always endeavored to have fun and continually practices at it, hoping he'll do a better job of it next week.

## Mick Shippen
(page 72, 78)
www.mickshippen.com

Mick is a freelance writer and photographer based in Thailand since 1997. He is the author of *The Traditional Ceramics of South East Asia*, a book documenting the life of craftsmen in the region.

## Roberta Sotonoff
(page 144)
www.robertasotonoff.com

A Chicago-area-based travel junkie, Roberta writes to support her habit. She leads a bipolar life. When not traveling to incredible destinations, she is chained to her computer. Her work has appeared in dozens of international and domestic publications.

## Timothy Talen Bull
(page 44, 259)
http://ThailandLandofSmiles.com

Born and raised in America, Timothy discovered Thailand in 2006. He moved there in the summer of 2010 and now calls the Land of Smiles his home. He writes daily about Thailand, the Thai culture, and his adventures in the Kingdom on his blog.

## Robert Tilley
(page 108, 131)

Robert is a veteran Fleet Street (London) journalist, who came to Thailand in 2000 on a three-month contract and stayed. He still writes for various publications from his Chiang Mai base and runs the city's media gaff, The Writers Club and Wine Bar. He has written a memoir and two slim books rooted in his experiences in Thailand.

## Nicholas Towers
(page 13, 74, 181)
http://21thailand.blogspot.com

After falling in love with the country during an exchange semester at the University of Singapore, Nick took a year out between finishing university and practicing as a barrister to live and work in Thailand, where he sought adventure and experience. More about his time in Thailand can be found at his blog diary.

**Kristina Wegscheider**
(page 175)
www.diwyy.com

Kristina is a world traveler from San Jose, California. She has visited all seven continents and over forty-five countries. Her favorite travel destinations have been Antarctica and the Galapagos Islands. Kristina is the cofounder of *Do It While You're Young*, a travel website encouraging young women to travel.

**Don Willcox**
(page 264)

Don has lived and worked as a volunteer in Nepal and Thailand for the past twenty-eight years. He is the founder and coordinator of the Foundation To Encourage The Potential Of Disabled Persons in Chiang Mai, Thailand, and the founder of the Hands In Outreach program in Nepal. He is also the author of *Getting It Right—A Volunteer Handbook*, which is available for free online.

**Katrina Wilton**
(page 289)
www.katrinawilton.com

Katrina is a happily married mother who got married on the beach in Koh Samui. Her passion for Thailand continues, and she enjoys regular visits to the Land of Smiles with her family. An entrepreneur and property investor, Katrina favors a lifestyle of freedom over the constraints of employment.

## CREDITS

"Chang Noi shifts his resident spirits to a new house in Khorat" reprinted in an edited and updated form from "Our New Spirit Houses," originally published at *Thailand Stories* (www.thailandstories.com). Reprinted by permission of the author. Copyright © 2009 Chang Noi.

"Jamie Monk recons in a Bang Rong mangrove forest" reprinted in an edited and updated form from "Kayaks In The Mangrove," originally published at *Jamie's Phuket* (http://jamie-monk.blogspot.com). Reprinted by permission of the author. Copyright © 2009 Jamie Monk.

"Jamie Monk searches out Phuket's well-kept gastronomic secret" reprinted in an edited and updated form from "Restaurant Tip: Lakeside," originally published at *Jamie's Phuket* (http://jamie-monk.blogspot.com). Reprinted by permission of the author. Copyright © 2009 Jamie Monk.

"Janet Brown attempts to go home again ... and again ... and again" reprinted from "Going Home Again," originally published in *Tone Deaf in Bangkok*. Reprinted by permission of the author. Copyright © 2008 Janet Brown.

"Kristianne Huntsberger celebrates Christmas fourfold in northern Thailand" reprinted in an edited and updated form from "Christmas, take four," originally published at *Spectator Spots* (http://spectatorspots.blogspot.com). Reprinted by permission of the author. Copyright © 2009 Kristianne Huntsberger.

"Martyn Bartlett tells tiger tales from Kanchanaburi" reprinted in an edited and updated form from "Kanchanaburi Revisited—The Tiger Temple," originally published at *Beyond The Mango Juice* (www.thaisabai.org). Reprinted by permission of the author. Copyright © 2009 Martyn Bartlett.

"Scott Earle marvels at the power of tattoos in Nakhon Pathom" reprinted in an edited and updated form from "Wat Bang Phra Tattoo Festival," originally published at www.scottearle.com. Reprinted by permission of the author. Copyright © 2010 Scott Earle.

"Tim Matsui applauds the prevention of STDs in Chiang Mai" reprinted in an edited and updated form from "MPlus, A Community for gay, transgender and male sex workers in Chiang Mai, Thailand," originally published at *Tim Matsui, Multimedia Storytelling* (www.timmatsui.com). Reprinted by permission of the author. Copyright © 2010 Tim Matsui.

## INDEX

## Nabanita Dutt

## Marc Schultz

A journalist by accident, Nabanita Dutt started her career with a news magazine in order to finance her obsession with clothes. The excitement of running a business desk, however, soon took the edge off her fascination with fashion, and she surprised both herself and her employers by displaying a talent for the job She went on to edit the weekend feature magazine for one of India's largest-selling newspapers, and her career in journalism continued. Almost every month, she finds herself in a different country, and she uses these trips to explore ethnic cuisines and culture, while also writing travel features for publications in the UK and Asia.

Marc Schultz is a Bangkok-based, fine-art travel photographer who is passionate about capturing scenes from behind the lens of customary Thai life. He has traveled extensively throughout Asia and Thailand, with cameras in hand, and he spent more than five years capturing the imagery in this book. Accredited as an official press photographer by the Thailand Ministry of Foreign Affairs, his exquisite images detail simple, everyday Thai life, its religious aspects, basic trades, and the rich culture and traditions of the people from both the old and the new Siam. In September 2002, Marc received recognition in the field of visual arts from England's prestigious Royal Photographic Society. More of his Thailand travel photography can be seen at his website.

www.photographythailand.com

## To Vietnam With Love
*A Travel Guide for the Connoisseur*
Edited & with contributions by Kim Fay
Photographs by Julie Fay Ashborn

## To Thailand With Love
*A Travel Guide for the Connoisseur*
Edited & with contributions by Nabanita Dutt
Photographs by Marc Schultz

## To Cambodia With Love
*A Travel Guide for the Connoisseur*
Edited & with contributions by Andy Brouwer
Photographs by Tewfic El-Sawy

## To Myanmar With Love
*A Travel Guide for the Connoisseur*
Edited & with contributions by Morgan Edwardson
Photographs by Steve Goodman

## To North India With Love
*A Travel Guide for the Connoisseur*
Edited & with contributions by Nabanita Dutt
Photographs by Nana Chen

## To Japan With Love
*A Travel Guide for the Connoisseur*
Edited & with contributions by Celeste Heiter
Photographs by Robert George

## To Nepal With Love
*A Travel Guide for the Connoisseur*
Edited by Cristi Hegranes and Kim Fay
Photographs by Kraig Lieb

For more information, visit www.toasiawithlove.com

# ThingsAsian Press

*Experience Asia Through the Eyes of Travelers*

*"To know the road ahead, ask those coming back."*
CHINESE PROVERB

Whether you're a frequent flyer or an armchair traveler, whether you are 5 or 105, whether you want fact, fiction, or photography, ThingsAsian Press has a book for you.

*To Asia With Love* is a series that has provided a new benchmark for travel guidebooks; for children, Asia comes alive with the vivid illustrations and bilingual text of the *Alphabetical World* picture books; cookbooks provide adventurous gourmets with food for thought. Asia's great cities are revealed through the unique viewpoints of their residents in the photographic series, *Lost and Found*. And for readers who just want a good story, ThingsAsian Press offers page-turners—both novels and travel narratives—from China, Vietnam, Thailand, India, and beyond.

With books written by people who know about Asia for people who want to know about Asia, ThingsAsian Press brings the world closer together, one book at a time.

**www.thingsasianpress.com**

# NOTES

# Notes

# NOTES

# Notes

# Notes